———— VESTAL VIRGINS, SIBYLS, AND MATRONS ————

VESTAL VIRGINS, SIBYLS, AND MATRONS:

Women in Roman Religion

BY SAROLTA A. TAKÁCS

UNIVERSITY OF TEXAS PRESS

Austin

Requests for permission to reproduce material
from this work should be sent to:
Permissions
University of Texas Press
P.O. Box 7819
Austin, TX 78713-7819
www.utexas.edu/utpress/about/bpermission.html

⊗ The paper used in this book meets the minimum requirements of
ANSI/NISO Z39.48-1992 (R1997) (Permanence of Paper).

Library of Congress Cataloging-in-Publication Data

Takács, Sarolta A.
  Vestal virgins, sibyls, and matrons : women in roman religion / by
Sarolta A. Takács. — 1st ed.
    p.   cm.
  Includes bibliographical references and index.
    ISBN 978-0-292-71693-3 (cl. : alk. paper) — ISBN 978-0-292-71694-0
(pbk. : alk. paper)
    1. Women and religion—Rome.   2. Women—Religious life—
Rome.   3. Rome—Religion.   4. Rome—Religious life and customs.
5. Women—Rome.   6. Rome—Social life and customs.   I. Title.
  BL815.W6T35   2008
  292.07082—dc22
                                                  2007024432

To My Family and to MDK

CONTENTS

LIST OF ABBREVIATIONS

MODERN SOURCES

AE	= *L'Année Épigraphique*
AJA	= *American Journal of Archaeology*
AJAH	= *American Journal of Ancient History*
AJPh	= *American Journal of Philology*
BullCom	= *Bulletino della Commissione Archeologica Comunale de Roma*
Calderini	= A. Calderini, *Aquileia romana, ricerche di storia e di epigrafia* (Milan, 1930)
CIE	= *Corpus Inscriptionum Etruscarum*
CIL	= *Corpus Inscriptionum Latinarum*
CQ	= *Classical Quarterly*
EE	= *Ephemeris Epigraphica*
HSCP	= *Harvard Studies in Classical Philology*
IGR	= *Inscriptiones Graecae ad res Romanas pertinentes*
ILS	= *Inscriptiones Latinae selectae*
Inscr. Ital.	= *Inscriptiones Italiae*
Inscriptions de Glanum	= H. Rolland, *Inscriptions de Glanum (Saint-Rémy-de-Provence), Révision et complement du Corpus Inscriptionum Latinarum,* in: *Gallia* 2 (1944), 167–223

IRCPacen	= J. D'Encarnação, *Inscrições Romanas do Conventus Pacensis* (Coimbra, 1984)
JRS	= *Journal of Roman Studies*
LTUR	= *Lexicon topographicum urbis Romae*
MDAIR	= *Mitteilungen des deutschen Archäologischen Instituts in Rom*
MEFRA	= *Mélanges de l'École Française de Rome*
NS	= *Notizie degli Scavi di Antichità*
OCD	= *Oxford Classical Dictionary,* 3rd revised edition, eds. S. Hornblower and A. Spawforth (Oxford, 2003)
OLD	= *Oxford Latin Dictionary,* ed. P.G.W. Glare (Oxford, 1982)
OGIS	= *Orientis Graeci Inscriptiones Selectae*
PapOxy	= *The Oxyrhynchus Papyri*
PCPS	= *Proceedings of the Cambridge Philological Society*
PHI	= *Packard Humanities Institute*
PIR	= *Prosopographia imperii Romani*
RE	= *Realencyclopädie der classischen Altertumswissenschaft*
REL	= *Revue des Études Latines*
RhM	= *Rheinisches Museum*
RVV	= *Religionsgeschichtliche Versuche und Vorarbeiten*
SIG	= *Sylloge inscriptionum Graecarum*
TAPA	= *Transactions of the American Philological Association*
Viri Illustres	= *Viri Romae illustres a Romulo ad Augustum*
ZPE	= *Zeitschrift für Papyrologie und Epigraphik*

ANCIENT SOURCES

Ael.	Aelianus
NA	*De natura animalium*
App.	Appian
B. Civ.	*Bella civilia*
Hann.	Ἀννιβδïκή
Apul.	Apuleius
Apol.	*Apologia*
Arist.	Aristotle
Pol.	*Politica*
Aug.	Augustine
De civ. D.	*De civitate Dei*
Cato	Cato
Agr.	*De agricultura*
Orig.	*De re rustica Origines*
Cic.	Cicero
Att.	*Epistulae ad Atticum*
Cael.	*Pro Caelio*
De or.	*De oratore*
Dom.	*De domo sua*
Fam.	*Epistulae ad Familiares*
Font.	*Pro Fonteio*
Har. resp.	*De haruspicum responso*
Mil.	*Pro Milone*
Mur.	*Pro Murena*

Nat.D.	*De Natura Deorum*
Q. Fr.	*Epistulae ad Quintum Fratrem*
Dio Cass.	Dio Cassius
Dion. Hal.	Dionysius Halicarnassensis
Ant. Rom.	*Antiquitates Romanae*
Festus	Festus
Frontin.	Frontinus
Gai.	Gaius
Inst.	*Institutiones*
Gellius	Aulus Gellius
Noctes Atticae	
Geopon.	Geoponica
Hor.	Horace
Epist.	*Epistulae*
Hdt.	Herodotus
Isoc.	Isocrates
Nicocles	*Nicocles*
Jos.	Josephus
AJ	*Antiquitates Judaicae*
BJ	*Bellum Judaicum*
Jul.	Julianus *imperator*
Or.	*Orationes*
Juv.	Juvenal
Lact.	Lactantius
Div. Inst.	*Diviniae Institutiones*
Liv. Andron.	Livius Andronicus
Od.	*Odyssia*

Livy	Livy
Ab urbe condita	
Lucr.	Lucretius
Lycoph.	Lycophron
Mart.	Martial
Macrob.	Macrobius
Sat.	*Saturnalia*
Obsequens	
Oros.	Orosius
Ov.	Ovid
Am.	*Amores*
Ars am.	*Ars amatoria*
Fast.	*Fasti*
Met.	*Metamorphoses*
Polyb.	Polybius
Plin.	Pliny (the Elder)
HN	*Naturalis historia*
Plut.	Plutarch
GG.	*Gaius Gracchus*
Caes.	*Caesar*
Cic.	*Cicero*
De fort. Rom.	*De fortuna Romanorum*
De Is. et Os.	*De Iside et Osiride*
Marc.	*Marcellus*
Mor.	*Moralia*
Num.	*Numa*
Quaest. Rom.	*Quaestiones Romanae*

Rom.	*Romulus*
Prop.	Propertius
Prudent.	Prudentius
Quint.	Quintilian
Inst.	*Institutio oratoria*
Sall.	Sallust
Cat.	*Bellum Catilinae* or *De Catilinae coniuratione*
Sen.	Seneca
Ep.	*Epistulae*
Solin.	Solinus
Strabo	Strabo
Suet.	Suetonius
Aug.	*Divus Augustus*
Caes.	*De vita Caesarum*
Tib.	*Tiberius*
Tac.	Tacitus
Ann.	*Annales*
Tert.	Tertullian
Ad nat.	*Ad nationes*
De spect.	*De spectaculis*
Tib.	Tibullus
Val. Max.	Valerius Maximus
Varro	Varro
Ling.	*De lingua Latina*
Rust.	*De re rustica*

Vell. Pat.	Velleius Paterculus
Verg.	Virgil
Aen.	*Aeneid*
Ecl.	*Eclogues*
Vitr.	Vitruvius

ACKNOWLEDGMENTS

This book grew out of a discussion with Peg Fulton at an American Philological Association Meeting many years ago. At one point, as it happens with many projects, it took a different turn. Instead of becoming a general book on Roman women, it became an inquiry into Roman religion and women's roles in it. I would like to thank my students at Harvard and Rutgers University, who attended my courses on Roman women, women in antiquity, Greco-Roman religion, and Roman civilization. Their questions and comments made me rethink more than one explanation. The generosity of the Alexander von Humboldt Stiftung and the welcome atmosphere of the Seminar für Alte Geschichte Heidelberg gave me the opportunity to start working on this book. I continued it at the Center for Hellenic Studies in Washington, D.C., and finished it at my present academic home, Rutgers University. My heartfelt thanks go to Professor Jack Cargill, who read the finished manuscript carefully and made me think anew, Professor Dr. Dr. h.c. mult. Géza Alföldy, Professor Dr. Jens-Uwe Krause, Dr. Eftychia Stavrianopoulou, Professor Dr. Christian Witschel, Professor Gregory Nagy, and the Center for Hellenic Studies' dedicated library staff for all their assistance. Harvard University supported my endeavor with a Harvard Junior Faculty Grant and the Harvard AIDE program. My Harvard research assistants Dr. Mary DiLucia, Mr. Walton Green, and Ms. Deborah Sternlight, and especially my Rutgers University "knight in shining armor," Mr. Andriy Fomin, and Mr. David Danbeck deserve my gratitude for their unceasing help as do the anonymous readers and the copyeditor, Nancy Moore, and members of my family on this and the other side of the Atlantic. I dedicate this book to all of them.

Rutgers, The State University of New Jersey
New Brunswick, NJ
Summer 2006

INTRODUCTION

The purpose of this book is to elucidate Roman women's role and function in Roman religion and, by extension, its history and culture through literary and epigraphic sources. The Roman state was an agricultural, patriarchal, militaristic, and imperialistic society. While men acquired territory and controlled Rome's Empire, women functioned as the guarantors of the continuance of the state. Social spheres were strictly defined: a man's world was the public sphere; a woman's, her home. In other words, politics of the state were pursuits of men; child rearing and caring for family members were duties of a Roman matron. Roman writers, ever ready to point out moral or immoral behavior of their protagonists, have lots to say about women who moved outside their assigned sphere. Most of these women were troublemakers, disruptors of the social order, and thus examples of immoral or un-Roman behavior.

Only women who entered the political sphere to act on behalf of the state so that it could maintain or return to its customary sociopolitical status quo were rewarded with approval and thought to be examples of proper behavior. Although religious ceremonies did bring Roman women into the public sphere, these rites were carried out on behalf of Rome and, by extension, its Empire. In these sanctioned roles, women strengthened the established order. The underlying elements of a woman's sphere, the domestic, were procreation and nurture. Projected onto the public sphere through religious ceremonies carried out by women, the same fundamentals come to the foreground. Placed within an agricultural cycle, these rituals stressed fecundity and continuation of life.

Roman women, heroines or villains, drive historical narratives. In this epistemological formation, what writers adopted as their rhetoric or discourse, the quiet and silent women were the morally upright ones, whereas the unprincipled ones acted loudly and noisily. A good example of this discourse can be found in the historian Livy's work, *From the Founda-*

tion of the City (Ab urbe condita), which serves, despite its prejudice toward women, as an invaluable source for early Roman history. In his narrative, a man's heroic action surpasses that of a woman every time, and the narrative space given to any of his heroines to speak is very limited. Direct speech is reserved for Rome's heroes. Livy tells us wonderful, even fantastic, stories of Rome's early period. Although fictitious accounts (the Greeks called them myths), these stories became essential parts of Rome's history. They contained an underlying discourse to explain and perpetuate Rome and Romanness within a moralistic framework.

In contrast to Livy, the poet Ovid's lens in his *Fasti,* the poem presenting us with information about religious festivals for the first six months of the year, is altogether different, as he suspends the opposing structure of morally good and bad behavior and moves the focus from men to women's actions as primary agents of Rome's formation. Roman literature then gives us insights into the workings of Roman society and its culture. We need, however, to be attentive to each author's focus, as, for example, we can see with Livy and Ovid. We also have to bear in mind the overarching discourse that shaped the way Rome's history was understood.

In addition to literature, inscriptions will be included in the discussion dealing with religious activities in the provinces. While epigraphic evidence affords us insights in to workings of Roman society and its culture away from the political center, inscriptions convey this information, albeit in a formulaic way, without the constraints of a literary genre and an author's particular perspective embedded in the perpetuated discourse. But, whatever way literary narratives may have subdued women's actions, the reality was that women were involved in the making and upkeeping of Rome.

Proper religious performance was crucial in maintaining the state; and, as we will see, women were executors of important religious cults in and outside Rome. Although Roman religion tended to preserve traditional cultic actions, adjustments that reflected new social and political realities could be, and others were, made. The emergence of Rome as an imperialistic Republic and then as an Empire changed women's roles, in particular, those of imperial and elite women. This evolution introduced changes to the existing cultic form, that is, the way a ritual was enacted, as well as new cults that accommodated these changes. The imperial cult, a cult that emerged with the Principate, is a good example of such an alteration. Elite provincial women, the *flaminicae,* and their male counterpart, the provincial *flamen,* performed religious rites on behalf of the state and the imperial household, the *domus Augusta.* Powerful women were involved, and, especially, women of highest social standing, such as the empress Livia, the wife of Augustus, were instrumental in stimulating interest and advancing deities as well as cults.

Although Roman religion was conservative, it had a flexibility that allowed for modifications of old and the integration of new cults. Thus, the priesthood of the Vestals, believed to go back to Rome's beginnings, was altered, with the most decisive modifications possibly occurring during Augustus' Principate. In terms of Roman culture and religion, decisive changes occurred at the time of Rome's contact with the Greeks of southern Italy; Rome's struggle with Carthage in the third century BCE; Augustus' Principate, and, lastly, the emergence of Christianity as the Empire's defining religion. Existing cultic actions could be changed, if these alterations were necessitated by circumstances that were understood as divinely ordained. The single most important necessity was the preservation of the *pax deorum—pax hominum* (the peace among gods—peace among humans), the reciprocal relationship between the divine and human sphere. The Roman success in acquiring and maintaining Empire was linked to appropriate religious behavior; Empire was the proof that the gods were favorably disposed toward the Romans because they carried out religious rituals properly and in a timely fashion, thus keeping this very relationship intact.

The political sphere was off limits for women, but women were instrumental in the maintenance of social stability. It is Roman religion that provides us a unique opportunity to understand better women's societal importance. Whenever Rome encountered political or social problems, there were also portents that expressed the gods' displeasure. The highest-ranking pontiffs (*pontifices maximi*) recorded these unusual occurrences, and the Pontifical Books (*libri pontificales*), which documented them, became the basis for annalistic history writing. Romans sought the cause for any social discord or political failing that had the potential to destabilize Rome by looking in the religious sphere; the same was true of the remedy. In short, cause and corrective were always a religious act. At its most extreme, a human life was required to restore order and a healthy state of affairs. The human scapegoat, in the most dramatic circumstances a Vestal, carried the guilt and failings of all others and in death expiated the whole society.

The book's first chapter will explore the way Roman authors fashioned Roman women and their roles in Roman society. Literary sources are still the privileged means of creating explanatory models because they are perceived to be the least fragmented and treated as the most insightful of all surviving material from Rome's past. Augustus' Rome, its history, culture, and religion that were fashioned by, with, and through the first emperor, will serve as the book's central and final point of reference.

The second chapter focuses on the Roman calendar and festivals carried out by and for women. The aim here is to explain through the lens of religion why women continued to hold crucial religious positions in this highly militaristic and patriarchal society, how, in effect, they helped perpetuate the system. This chapter begins with a cursory analysis of how time was reckoned and how a calendar anchored time in a tangible structure of reference points. The discussion of women's cultic activities throughout the calendar year will reveal that most rites took place in the first half of the year, closely following the agricultural cycle. In addition, women's actions never occurred in isolation, for every important ritual carried out by women there followed one by men. The Roman ritual calendar was in this way holistic. Roman women were "the second sex" and legally, without question, subordinate to men; it was a select group of women, the Vestals, however, whose religious activities functioned as guarantors of Rome's continued well-being. Their actions on behalf of the Roman people occurred at crucial moments in the agricultural year.

The subsequent chapters focus on some of Rome's female deities and entities that helped forge Rome, and also, in contrast, on women that were accused of putting the state at risk. The Sibylline Books, utterances of inspired women, the Sibyls, served as the basis for determining what was needed to reconstitute the relationship between the Roman people and its gods. The Sibylline utterances were also instrumental in the formation of Rome, since they had ordered the Romans to bring Mater Magna (the Great Mother) to the capital. Female deities, like the Mater Magna from the Troad and Egyptian Isis, were conduits through which Rome adopted and integrated Greek culture into its mythic history, its artistic expressions, and its religion. In contrast to these constructive forces, the Bacchantes, female worshipers of the god Bacchus or Dionysus, jeopardized Rome's existence in 186 BCE, and a Vestal, disregarding her vow of chastity during the Bona Dea festival of 62 BCE, did the same. Through such examples we will see that political issues, that is to say problems that had arisen in the male sphere, were translated into religious problems. Since women had the potential to destroy the very world men had built, men had to control women and curtail their movements and actions to use this female potency for their own means.

The book's final chapter explores the provincial female flaminate and the original Celtic triad of the Matres/Matronae. The flaminate of the emperor, initiated by Augustus, was implemented in the provinces as a means to single out, and thus honor, exceptional provincial leaders. In areas where women could, unlike in Rome and Italy, be in the public eye and recognized for their benefactions, or simply for their privileged position among the provincials, the female flaminate served as a way of publicly acknowledging and honoring a woman who, or more generally whose family, had done something outstanding for the community. Essentially, the provincial flaminate presented Rome with the provinces' best, including women. While this flaminate originated in Rome and was adopted in the provinces, the Matres/Matronae were ancestral tribal gods who were carried by individuals, in their case soldiers, beyond their original location. This dissemination resulted in a broadening of the worshiper pool. The female flaminate and the Matres/Matronae exemplify religious dynamics that shaped societal cohesiveness and reciprocally bound the center, Rome, to its periphery, the provinces.

The coming together of communities in ritual celebration not only created a bond among the participants but much more importantly brought them into line and enabled them to work toward one and the same goal: the survival of their communities, Rome at large, and the perpetuation of a ritualistic belief structure that was the key to success. Men made all decisions that had an impact on the political sphere, but women had important roles in maintaining what Roman men had reaped in success: Empire. The adopted discourse or rhetoric of the ancients most often obscures women's importance by reducing their actions to moral examples, but the lens of religion provides us with the opportunity to explore beyond a narrative's paradigmatic character and come to a better understanding of women's importance in Rome's cultural formation. In this book, I hope to provide information and insights to assist those interested in exploring women's role in Roman religion and thus come to gain knowledge of an ancient culture that, in turn, shaped our own.

NOTE: The translations are mine, unless otherwise noted.

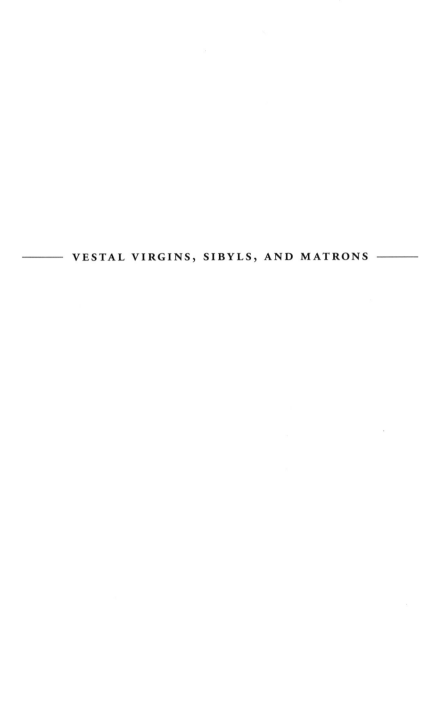

VESTAL VIRGINS, SIBYLS, AND MATRONS

ONE

THE SILENT ONES SPEAK

Women have their uses for historians. They offer relief from warfare, legislation, and the history of ideas; and they enrich the central theme of social history. . . . Ladies of rank . . . are a seductive topic.

—RONALD SYME, *THE AUGUSTAN ARISTOCRACY*

Literature, a cross-section of genres, provides us with paragons and opposites of Roman womanhood. It is here that we encounter makers and destroyers of Rome, where we see women move outside the private, domestic sphere and enter the public arena. Some were harshly judged for their abandonment of family; others were not. All the judges were men, for it is their records we have, employ, and analyze. Literary examples make clear the distinctions between a respectable and disreputable Roman woman. The emphasis is on moral behavior, understood as the single most important factor for the proper functioning of society. Roman historical writing, in particular, demanded moralization and much hinges on the private/public category.

The most revealing literary evidence in regard to women and their actions taken for the benefit or detriment of Roman society often surfaces in accounts linked to transitional periods of Roman history. While Rome's political structure remained that of a city, which was simply projected onto an expanding empire, the social and economic fabric changed rapidly. Romans and their gods formed a single community. Politics and religion were intertwined. Ancient societies were culturally more integrated than modern ones. Thus, unlike their modern counterparts, who try to step outside societal boundaries, ancient writers and artists were involved in representing and perpetuating their society and its norms. It is no surprise then that Latin writers relate a person's or group's moral failing or a religious ritual not properly executed as the single most important cause for social or political problems, regardless of how complex they might actually have been. One can make a case that this type of reductionism to simple sequences of cause and effect remained intact until the Enlightenment.

Moreover, Latin literature was very much a product of Rome's self-definition vis-à-vis the much cherished Greek intellectual accomplishments. Decisive in the emergence of Latin literature was Rome's success over Carthage, in particular, the Second Punic War (218–201 BCE), which resulted in Rome's hegemony over the Mediterranean World. Another such watershed moment for Latin literature was the Age of Augustus (31 BCE), part of the so-called Golden Age of Latin literature (ca. 75 BCE–14 CE). Scholars have established and accepted it as the highpoint of literary achievement and the ultimate measure for anything literary before and after.[1] But even more, Augustus' reforms touched every aspect of Roman life. His marriage laws and religious innovations, for example, are at times interpreted as a reactionary attempt to return to true Republican values, which had been lost through the continued civil war period. Looking at the evidence, however, one can argue that Augustus' attempt was a turning back to a fictitious past, a fiction that ultimately became a defining reality. Texts, which form the core of the study of Roman history, provide the potential of remembrance and temporal continuity. But the coherent whole, construed from various literary sources, is in fact inconsistent. It is the task of the modern historian to analyze these reporting and reflective, diverse, creative sources, as well as the material evidence, to discover a more complete picture and generate a better understanding of Rome.

BEGINNINGS

Rome's beginnings are shrouded in myths. It is only with the fourth and third centuries BCE that historical information can be confirmed. The late Republican antiquarian Varro (116–127 BCE), writing the *Antiquities Human and Divine,* established the city's founding date as April 21, 753 BCE.[2] The most detailed account of the founding, however, we find in the first book of Livy's historical narrative *From the Foundation of the City.* It so happened that for a time without any tangible literary data, writers produced highly detailed narratives. Artistic creativity found in myths, for example, material that was refashioned to form a cohesive historical narrative. Mythic and historical times that were fused together shaped, and still shape, our understanding of regal and early Republican Rome.

The twins Romulus and Remus were descendants of the kings of Alba Longa (Figures 1.1a, 1.1b). Ascanius Iulus is thought to have founded this city south of Rome. The connection between Troy, Alba Longa, and Rome became popular in the third century BCE. The myth of Aeneas was already known in Etruria in the sixth century BCE.[3] In terms of historiography, it was the explanation recorded by the late fourth- and early third-century BCE historian Timaeus of Taoromena that placed the ever expanding central Italian power, Rome, into a Greek frame of reference; Rome's foundation was connected to the most mythological and recognizable war of all history—up to that point—the Trojan War.[4] Rome was linked to the world of Greek gods and heroes. Thus, the Greeks of Southern Italy and Sicily, versed in mythologies and stories of old, were able to explain away the unsettling fact that another group exerted control over them. In one swoop, with one good story, the Greeks eliminated the basic cultural differences between the conquerors and the conquered. Even better, the Roman elite integrated a Trojan hero into their earliest history, where, in fact, there had been no history at all. With this mythological connection, Rome's cultural heritage was simultaneously Greek and not Greek in origin.

Aeneas, who was a minor figure in the Homeric epic cycle, escaped the burning Troy with his father Anchises perched on his shoulder. Aeneas also had with him his small son, Ascanius Iulus,[5] and Troy's household gods, the *penates*.[6] Aeneas, son of the goddess Venus, displayed, under the trying circumstances of flight, profound *pietas* (piety) and *virtus* (virtue) toward his family and the state. Composing the epic around Aeneas and the foundation of Rome during the time of the first emperor, Augustus, Vergil focused on these and other ancestral customs, which are called the *mos maiorum*. These ancestral customs form an ethical framework, which Aeneas embodied. Crucial to Rome's foundation myth is that Aeneas had to give up his personal wishes and desires for Rome to come about. Sometimes, the consequences of living or having to live in accordance with these *mos maiorum* strike us as heartless, yet setting aside the personal for the good of the state is a theme that will be encountered many times over in Roman history. It was a core principle that could, however, also be abused. Generals of the late Republic, Pompey or Caesar, for example, jockeying for power illustrate such breaches. Personal ambitions were cloaked as needs or remedies for a failing political system.

In Rome's foundation women played an important, albeit tragic, role. While the family fled burning Troy, Creusa, Aeneas' Trojan wife, fell behind. She eventually disappeared in the commotion that followed the fall

FIGURE I.IA.
Roma depicted on Roman Republican denarius *(obverse). Special Collections
and University Archives, Rutgers University Libraries, Sydenham 461
(a) = Crawford 235/1a.*

of the citadel. Aeneas touchingly spoke of his wife when he related his story
to his host, the queen of Carthage, Dido. Aeneas also told the queen of his
encounter with the shade of Creusa, who foretold long travels and the es-
tablishment of a new home on the Tiber.

> What use is it to indulge so much in frenzied sorrow, o sweet husband?
> Without the gods' influence (*numen*) these things do not come about;
> nor is it divine law (*fas*) that you carry Creusa as your companion (*comes*)
> from here, since the ruler of high Olympus himself lets it be so. There is
> a long exile for you and plowing (*arandum*) through the vast expanse of
> the sea, and you will come to a western land, where Lydian Tiber flows
> in a gentle stream through rich fields of men. There will be apportioned
> for you things full of joy, kingship, and a royal spouse; stop crying for
> beloved Creusa. I will not gaze upon the proud home of the Myrmidones
> or of the Dolopians, nor will I enter into servitude to Grecian mothers, I

4

FIGURE I.IB.
Wolf, Romulus, Remus with shepherd, depicted on Roman Republican denarius *(reverse).*
Special Collections and University Archives, Rutgers University Libraries, Sydenham
461 (a) = Crawford 235/1a.

a Dardan and daughter-in-law of divine Venus; but the great mother of
the gods (*magna deum genetrix*) holds me back on these shores, but now
farewell and protect the love of our common son.[7]

Vergil's word choice here is significant. As *comes* (companion) connotes a
superior (Aeneas) over an inferior-ranked person (Creusa) and infers a male-
gendered context, *coniunx* (spouse, from *con-iungere* to join, yoke together)
points to a more equal partnership. It is the partnership with Lavinia, the
regia coniunx, through which Aeneas will receive *regnum* (kingship). Whatever has been, is, and will happen is ordained by divine law (*fas*). Aeneas
will make it to Italy from the shores of Troy (*Troiae . . . ab oris Italium . . .
venit, Aen.* I.I–I.2), while the *magna deum genetrix* (the Great Mother of the
Gods = Mater Magna of the Troad) kept Creusa from leaving the shores of
Troy (*his detinet oris*). In addition to this internal connection, there is an external one that recalls Lucretius' *Venus genetrix* in *On the Nature of Things*

5

(*De rerum Natura*) and Catullus' *mater creatrix* and *genetrix* of poem 63. Aeneas, the founder of the Roman people, is to plow (*arandum* from *arare*) through the sea; his descendants, the Romans, will be proud to be, first and foremost, farmers.

Aeneas was both anchored in the past (his duty: *pietas*) and bound to the future (his son and the kingdom to come). His personal wishes and desires were inconsequential. He was fated to become the founder of the Roman people. Although Aeneas loved the queen of Carthage, Dido, he had to leave her on the gods' behest. Dido, abandoned by her lover and thus vulnerable to a world filled with former suitors, committed suicide. Shortly before dying, Vergil's Dido uttered a curse and foreshadowed the turbulent relationship between Carthage and Rome, which, historically, were the three Carthaginian (or Punic) Wars.[8] Once in Italy, the Trojan newcomers fought until Aeneas killed Turnus, a leader of an indigenous tribe, the Rutulians. Aeneas then founded a new city, Lavinium, named after his Latin wife, Lavinia. There the Trojan *penates* found a new home. Turnus' killing, which forms the ending of Vergil's epic, is disturbing but also signals to the reader that Rome was born in blood and that it came about and was defined by aggression and war.

Three women played crucial roles in Aeneas' journey from Troy to Lavinium: Creusa, Dido, and Lavinia. Of the three, Dido was the most developed literary character and was portrayed as the most active. As a founder of a city, she not only was the equal of Aeneas but was also shown to be capable of negotiating politics and power, which were traditionally the sphere of men. While Dido outlined the area of a refuge for her and her followers, locals and envoys from surrounding cities urged the foundation of what was to become Carthage.[9] In the Roman world of understanding, the act of founding a new city and delineating boundaries was a man's business, and founders throughout Greco-Roman history were men of heroic stature. Leading magistrates were in charge of the religious ritual that marked the area where the new city was to stand. The furrow cut by a plow along the lines delineated by the *augures* (interpreters of auspices) was a religious line, the *pomerium,* within which the city had to be built.[10] Only in this manner could a place be considered legally and religiously a Roman city. There is no record that Alba Longa, and subsequently Lavinium, was founded in this way, nor, in fact, Rome. Tradition, however, which came to determine Roman understanding of its history, emphasized that Rome was founded by augury and auspices.[11] Rome's success depended on its obligation to keep reciprocity between the world of humankind and that of the gods intact. The peace or harmony between these two worlds (the *pax hominum* and the *pax deorum*) was nourished by proper execution of religious rituals.[12] Thus, Romans, whom the orator and statesman Cicero called the most religious of all people, would understand its political success in this context. As long as Romans worshiped their gods properly, Rome would be successful.

ROMULUS' FOUNDATION

Rome's beginnings were humble. Its legendary founders were twin boys, Romulus and Remus, born to a Vestal Virgin, Rhea Silvia, also known as Ilia. Her uncle Amulius usurped his brother Numitor and forced Ilia to become a priestess of Vesta.[13] Ilia was fetching water from a spring in the sacred grove of Mars, where she was raped.[14] Afterwards the rapist, a divine-looking man, revealed himself as Mars and prophesied that the twin boys she would bear would surpass all men. When Amulius discovered the reason the pregnant Ilia was unable to perform her official duties, he decreed that the unchaste Vestal Virgin and her sons be put to death. An old law advised that a Vestal who had transgressed was to be buried alive[15] or thrown from the Tarpeian Rock, located at the southeastern part of the Capitoline hill.[16] Ilia's cousin, Antho, made a plea on her behalf, and the sentence was changed to solitary imprisonment. The twins were put in a wicker basket that was placed in the floodwaters of the Tiber River, which flowed down toward what was to become Rome.

As the floodwaters receded, the basket became wedged near to a fig tree. A she-wolf found the two babes and nourished them until a shepherd discovered them. Romulus and Remus grew up, became shepherds, and founded settlements on the Palatine and Aventine hills. The location, about fifteen miles up the Tiber from the sea in a volcanic area, provided many natural advantages, among them an excellent defensive position and access to fertile land and trade routes. Romulus, who slew his brother for scoffing at his city wall by jumping over it, became Rome's first king.

To increase the population of his foundation, Romulus allowed outlaws to settle and, because there were no women, kidnapped Sabine women during the harvest festival of the Consualia. Titus Tatius led the Sabines in retaliation against Rome. He captured the Capitol thanks to the treachery of a certain Tarpeia, who was more interested in material goods than in the well-being of her country. When the Sabines asked her what she wanted as a reward for her information (the location of a secret passage way to the Capitoline), she answered: "What you wear on your left arms." Tarpeia had her eye on the golden bracelets the Sabine wore, but the Sabines heaped their shields, which they held with their left hands, upon her. According to tradition, the location where Tarpeia was crushed by the enemies' shields received her name, the Tarpeian rock.

Sources claim that Tarpeia was either the daughter of the garrison commander (Livy) or a Vestal Virgin (Prop. 4.4). The story is a patchwork myth, for Rome did not have any women until the "rape of the Sabine women." Moreover, the idea that Tarpeia was a Vestal introduces an explanatory circularity. The place named after Tarpeia, supposedly the first deviant Vestal Virgin, was where traditionally Vestals and criminals were put to death by being thrown off the rock. This action seems closely related to the ritual of the scapegoat, which was the purification rite a polluted city or country performed to regain lost fertility or success. The expulsion or sacrifice of a person who took on the pollution of the whole community cleansed that community of its guilt.[17]

In antithesis to the treacherous Tarpeia stood the Sabine women, who had become loyal Roman wives and mothers. They ended the battle between their original Sabine and their new Roman families by holding up their children and appealing both to their fathers and husbands.[18] Thus, Romans and Sabines became one people. The poet Ovid, however, offers a different story of the consequence of the rape.

> Newly wed bride, what do you expect? Neither powerful herbs, nor prayer, nor a magic formula will make you a mother.
>
> for there was that day, when by a harsh lot the wives gave their husbands hardly any children.
> Romulus exclaimed: "What advantage was there to me to have snatched the Sabine women,
> if my injustice brought not strength but war?"
>
> and the goddess (Juno) spoke wondrous words in her own grove,
> she said: "Let the sacred he-goat go into Italian mothers."[19]

The Romans were shocked at the suggestion of sexual intercourse between a goat and a woman. An Etruscan augur, however, solved the puzzle. He killed a he-goat and cut straps from its hide. The women's backs were beaten with these hide straps. Ten months later, Roman men became fathers. Once more, women held the key to Rome's success and future; they became prominent either as facilitators between warring parties or as rejectors of wifely duties, only to become or be forced to be dutiful wives.

EXAMPLES FROM ROME'S EARLY HISTORY

Livy's history is filled with moral lessons from which the Roman reader learned about behavior that should be either imitated or avoided. There are four examples that demonstrate proper and improper female behavior that deserve a closer look. They involve the Roman women Horatia and Lucretia, and the Etruscan women Tanaquil and Tullia. When the Romans fought the Albans, two pairs of brothers, the Roman Horatii and the Alban Curatii, were pitched against each other. They encapsulated a war between two cities that were mythologically linked. The only survivor from this encounter was a Horatius who brought home the spoils of the Curatii. As he entered Rome, he encountered his sister, Horatia, who had been engaged to one of the Curatii. Horatia recognized the military cloak she had woven for her fiancé and began to mourn him. Horatius, enraged that his victory and Rome's triumph over its neighbor was marred by lamentation, ran his sword through Horatia, exclaiming: "Begone to your fiancé with your untimely love, you forgot your brothers dead and alive, you forgot your country. Thus shall perish every Roman woman who will mourn an enemy!"[20] Horatius was tried for her murder but acquitted. His father pleaded successfully that if the death penalty were invoked, he would be childless and Rome would be without its liberator and bringer of imperial power. The community, however, had to be cleansed of the blood guilt incurred by Horatius' killing of his sister. He was ordered to cover his head and pass under a beam, which was to signify a yoke. Thus, Horatius was symbolically subjugated. Horatia's murder was expiated, and a civic lesson was reinforced: Roman warriors do not kill kinfolk in anger, and Roman women only support their men and their country.

The Etruscan aristocrat Tanaquil, who had married a Greek immigrant's son, Lucumo, could not endure that her husband, because of his origins, was unable to advance politically. Tanaquil did not feel any obligations toward her native country because it did not recognize her husband's abilities. Hence, the two set out for Rome, a city that promised rewards for able bodied, energetic men. Tanaquil, also a master in the art of augury, supported her husband wholeheartedly, and after years of hard work, including diligent networking, Lucius Tarquinius, the former immigrant Lucumo from Tarquinia, was chosen king.[21]

Tanaquil also chose her husband's successor, Servius Tullius, whom divine signs had marked worthy of kingship. Livy pinpoints Tullius' daughter, Tullia, as the source of Rome's crisis.[22] In Livy's narrative, Tullia, emulating her grandmother, had her father and her husband murdered. She even "usurped the rights of men by literally invading their territory, in a brutally open fashion"[23] when she drove a chariot over Servius Tullius' corpse, which lay abandoned in the street. Tullia's second husband, Tarquin the Proud, subsequently became king, but with such beginnings, no good would come of this. Immoral actions triggered punishment, and, for Tarquin the Proud, this meant loss of kingship.

Tarquinia's downfall began very innocently. A war Rome was fighting reached a stalemate. Rome's leading men, who had nothing to do, decided to ride home. Everywhere they went, they found wives being merry and enjoying themselves. The exception was Lucretia, Lucius Tarquinius Collatinus' wife, who was spinning industriously together with slaves by lamplight.[24] Livy expertly juxtaposes the merry-making wives' behavior with what is projected as the perfect behavior of a Roman matron: working the spindle and the loom in the dead of night. When he saw Lucretia, Sextus, the Etruscan king's son, fell madly in love with this paragon of a matron. He returned the following evening and, having been greeted as a guest-friend, violated every aspect of it; he raped Lucretia. The victim, whose innocence and helplessness was recognized, nevertheless was polluted, and when she decided to kill herself, neither her husband nor anyone of her family held her back. Lucretia, the victim of the crime, turned herself voluntarily into the scapegoat necessary for the communal cleansing; she even became her own executioner. Her dead body then served as the visible pledge that the Etruscan ruler, Tarquin, had to be expelled.

Transgression was answered with aggression unleashed on an internal foe, which had earlier been directed at an external enemy but had produced a stalemate, boredom, and, ultimately, rape instead of victory. Lucretia's body was also a warning that aggression within a group led to societal disintegration and, in the end, to Rome's downfall. The violated female body featured prominently in Rome's early history, maybe because the fear of disintegration, even obliteration, was so real.

Archaeological data confirm written source material that violent changes occurred in the late sixth century and early fifth century BCE, a time linked to Rome's last king, the Etruscan Tarquin the Proud.[25] His ascension to power came after his wife murdered her father, and his reign extended into the initial period of the early Republic. Literary tradition turned a domestic dispute among the Tarquin family into a struggle between a tyrannical Etruscan overlord and Romans, who were ready to govern themselves. More likely, though, the Etruscan warlord Lars Porsenna of Clusium ousted Tarquin. The Romans, in turn, defeated Porsenna at

Aricia in 504 BCE, and subsequently, Rome came in conflict with its Latin neighbors.[26]

EARLY REPUBLICAN ROME

Embedded within the narratives of early Republican Rome, which deal primarily with aggression and war, are stories of women. The first account features a heroine, Cloelia, whose act of courage saved young Roman men. The second is about Coriolanus' mother and wife who pled against internal division and civil war for Rome's unity. The final story features the killing of a young woman, Verginia, which in turn spawned political reform.

Mucius and Cloelia

Livy highlights two heroic deeds in connection with Lars Porsenna's occupation. One is Gaius Mucius Scaevola's demonstration of manliness (*virtus*), and the other is a woman's, Cloelia's, leadership in rescuing a band of female Roman hostages.[27] Although Cloelia was far more successful in her endeavor than Mucius, Livy recounts her action in much less detail than that of the heroic Mucius. In fact, Livy makes Cloelia's action dependent on Mucius' deed. His undercover action had to fascinate the historian much more, mainly because men's military exploits, not women's, fashioned Roman history. Yet Cloelia's heroism was so extraordinary that even Livy's narrative structure cannot obscure it. Since Cloelia's endeavor is set against Mucius', a quick sketch of the latter's feat is warranted.

Mucius crossed the river Tiber and entered the enemy's camp in an attempt to kill Porsenna. Unfortunately, Mucius mistook Porsenna's scribe for the warlord and killed him. Porsenna's bodyguard seized Mucius and brought him before the man he intended to kill. In turn, Porsenna ordered Mucius killed (thrown into a fire) unless he divulged the Roman plot to kill him. Mucius put his right hand into the fire. As it burned, he explained how little Roman men thought their bodies were worth compared to the glory (*gloria*) that comes with killing an enemy. An impressed Porsenna freed Mucius. Upon his release, Mucius told Porsenna that there were three hundred other young Romans who were willing to risk their lives as he had done. Livy's Porsenna is disturbed by Mucius' blunder (*error*) in not recognizing that his life had been spared. Nevertheless, Porsenna and Rome reached, at least in this traditional story, a peace agreement. The Etruscans then left the area with Roman hostages as peace guarantors, among them the future heroine Cloelia.

In the Mucius narrative, Livy's use of the words *fortuna* (fate), *ignoro* (to be ignorant of), *error, gloria,* and *virtus* deserves a closer look. The concept of *fortuna,* or in Greek, *tuchē,* is one that features predominantly in Polybius' work as the dynamic force that drives human action; that is historical events, which when recorded, become history. *Tuchē* also connotes a degree of randomness—fate is blind—as well as the linear, that is, the sequential ordering of cause and effect. Cause and effect can be interrupted, and the true hero or heroine is the one who adapts most adroitly to a new, unforeseen situation. Livy's Mucius refrained from asking Porsenna's identity "lest his ignorance of the king would reveal who he was (*ne ignorando regem semet ipse aperiret quis esset*)." Hence, Mucius, without crucial information, had no choice but to follow (blind) fate after he was captured; he assumed the king's scribe to be Porsenna. We might wonder about such a haphazard undertaking and ask how the Roman elders (the *patres*) could have supported such an ill-planned action as sending Mucius alone into the enemy camp. Under such conditions, the chance of success was small, and *error,* the most likely consequence. On the other hand, such extreme risk taking makes Mucius a warrior par excellence. He demonstrated physical courage, endurance, strength, and skill and displayed honor. These *are* the values that make a warrior.[28] The Latin word *virtus* (manliness) embodied these qualities of courage, endurance, strength, and skill; honor is the reward the individual could enjoy. *Gloria* (glory) is honor memorialized from which not only the individual but also his family could reap future benefits.

Unlike the deeds of the Scaevolae, who furnished the Roman state with prominent politicians during the late Republican period, Cloelia's heroic deed did not produce *gloria.* Livy introduces her action as inspired (*exitatae*) by Mucius' virtue. She showed physical courage and endurance, and under Cloelia's leadership, the Roman women who were held hostage (she was one of them) eluded armed Etruscan guards by swimming across the Tiber. From beginning to end, Cloelia exhibited strength and skill. Livy marks Cloelia as a warrior type when he labels her *dux agminis virginum* (a military leader of a military column composed of girls of marriageable age). Lars Porsenna declared Cloelia's action greater than that of Mucius because she succeeded and also praised Cloelia's virtue (*virtus*). Here Livy's voice comes through in the guise of the Etruscan leader's voice. As such it is safe and does not take away from Mucius' heroism. Lars Porsenna was the other, the Etruscan enemy, who was free to say anything, in this case, that a woman was virtuous and more successful than a man. Whatever Livy made Porsenna say in no way diminished what Roman tradition had established; virtue was a manly trait.

Cloelia's successful flight, however, infuriated Porsenna, who demanded her return and promised that he would give her back. Porsenna and the Romans agreed; after all, war and negotiations were men's business. Once in control again over actions, the Etruscan king and the Romans were able to work out an agreement. Porsenna, who was allowed to save face, in turn, gave Cloelia the choice of taking half of the Roman hostages, which were in the Etruscan camp, home with her. The Roman heroine chose boys below the age of puberty (*impubes*), the group most vulnerable to (personal) injury (*eam aetatem potissimum liberari ab hoste quae maxime opportuna iniuriae esset*), thereby demonstrating a strong sense of civic responsibility. Livy's Cloelia understood that a loss of future warriors was harmful to the state and that these young men, if not freed, would be exposed to an Etruscan rather than a Roman life during their most formative years.

The Romans commemorated Cloelia's virtue with a new kind of honor (*novo genere honoris*), an equestrian statue with a *virgo* (*un*married woman). Traditionally, equestrian statues were reserved solely for men. This unusual statue was placed at the top of the *Sacra via*. Servius stated in his commentary on Vergil's *Aeneid* (8.646) that the statue was still standing in his time, the fourth/fifth century CE. The historian Dionysius of Halicarnassus, writing during the last decades of the Republic, however, mentioned that the statue no longer existed (5.35.2). Pliny the Elder, in his writing about bronze statues, mentions the equestrian statue of Cloelia as something "over the top" (*HN* 34.13), as it were. Was it not enough that she wore a toga (*ceu parum esset toga eam cingi*); why should Cloelia be portrayed in a statue when Lucretia and Brutus had not been, he asks.

Coriolanus, Veturia, and Volumnia

The period following the Etruscan ousting from Roman territory was marked by internal and external instability. There were tribal migrations and different ethnic groups continuously forced each other out of their acquired territories. All the while, leading Romans jostled for political power within Rome. This was the beginning of the struggle of the orders, the assertion of the *plebs* (the common people) that they too ought to have political rights vis-à-vis the patricians, the descendants of the elders, the *patres,* who had been present at Romulus' founding of Rome.[29] Tradition, part of mythic history, puts in this time the story of the patrician Gnaeus Marcius Coriolanus. This successful warrior was so distraught by the advancement of the plebs that he left Rome, only to return to Rome at the head of a Volscian army. The Volsci, an Umbrian-speaking people, controlled the southern part of Latium.

With Rome now internally divided, the Senate saw no alternative to war. The plebs, however, abhorred war (the fickle mass lacked *virtus*), sent Coriolanus' mother, Veturia, and his wife, Volumnia, as well as his children to plead with him. Veturia's speech convinced Coriolanus to halt his advancing troops. The key, in Livy's rendering (2.40.7), is a series of questions that moved from Rome as a country to Coriolanus' family and his household gods, still located in Rome. "Are you capable of devastating this land, which gave you birth and nourished you? (*potuisti populari hanc terram, quae te genuit atque aluit?*)" and "are not within these walls my house, my household gods, my mother, my wife, my children? (*intra illa moenia domus ac penates mei sunt, mater coniunx liberique?*)" As a result of this intercession, Coriolanus chose exile over the potential destruction of his native home. A mother, a wife, and children had stopped a fight of "brothers." In Livy's recounting and reshaping of early Roman history, we find that men tend toward aggression to resolve conflict, while women find resolution through compromise and discussion.[30]

Verginia

Another episode from the early Republic that plays on this theme of male aggression in contrast to female resolution through compromise was the appropriation of a person who legally belonged to someone else. Appius Claudius, one of ten men appointed to codify the law around 450 BCE, desired Verginia after seeing her walking on the street. Verginia's father was away on campaign at this time, and her fiancé was unable to stop Appius, thereby leaving her unprotected. Appius found a man who claimed that Verginia was a slave and, thus, Appius could simply take legal possession of Verginia. Since Verginia's father was powerless against a magistrate who socially and politically outranked him, the only option left to him to reclaim his daughter was to kill her. This he did, exclaiming: "There is only one way, my child, to make you free."[31] As in the Lucretia story, the injustice resulted in an uprising and a readjustment of political power. The monarchy gave way to the Republic. Again, we see a private affair projected into, and resolved in, the public sphere. One man's aggression against another's asset resulted in Verginia's vindication, which provoked political reform, in this case, the reestablishment of the Republic.

REPUBLICAN ROME

Unlike the early period of Roman history, the time of continued internal struggle between patricians and plebeians and Roman territorial expansion beyond central Italy does not provide stories of individual women. The only instances in which women are mentioned are during the time of the Gallic invasion (390 or 387/6 BCE). This attack, which has to be considered a spontaneous incursion of a mercenary band,[32] left a deep anxiety within the Roman psyche. The Romans were taken by surprise, their city was sacked, and only after a large payment of gold was made did the attackers leave. Had it not been for the married women (*matronae*) of Rome and their generosity in giving jewelry willingly, the state would have had to dip into temple treasures (*sacrum aureum*) to pay off the attackers. As a gesture of thanks for the women's selflessness in a time of crisis, the Senate voted that the *matronae* had the right to receive eulogies at their funerals. In a society driven by the *mos maiorum* (the ancestral custom that guided behavior), praise in private or in public of a noble character and action was considered morally constructive as well as an honor. Even in a rigid agnatic society, eulogies for cognate and maternal relations were used to edify the society as a whole.[33]

There is very little information about the importance of Roman women during Rome's encounter with Carthage. Livy provides the only account (34.1–34.8.3) when he relates that there was an attempt to repeal the Oppian Law of 215 BCE in 195 BCE. The original law stated that

> no woman should possess more than a half ounce of gold, nor should she wear garment of changing sheen, nor should she ride in a carriage to the city or a town, nor should she be closer to it (a city or town) than a mile (1.45 km), except for public holidays.[34]

The historian devoted, according to a modern commentator, "over an eighth of the whole book—to what might appear to be a comparatively minor question."[35] In times of war, however, if not all resources were needed, then at least those that were needed had to be mustered to have a chance at survival and, most positively, victory. The control of available resources seems hardly a minor question then, nor is retaining control over all groups comprising a society a negligible detail. The latter seems to have been, in my opinion, the more important objective. Any subgroup would have needed to be controlled to guarantee a common communal goal, in this case, the warding off of all outsiders.

Under the Oppian Law the bulk of liquid assets (precious metals or jewelry) was to be in the hands of men, the warriors and protectors; women were allowed neither to stand out and display themselves nor to be mobile. Women were, in fact, forced to stay within their group and, ultimately, choose their mates within a circumscribed pool.[36] It could be argued that the larger Rome's acquired territory grew, the more attempt there was to control and define the sphere in which Roman women were allowed to move. While it is possible to see such restrictions in movement as the protective, caring action by men, the stronger group, in favor of women, perceived as weaker and in need of protection, it can also be perceived as an action to prevent the broadening of a selection pool of potential mates for the women. One can speak of the Oppian Law of 215 BCE as being a clear defensive act during war, but the same cannot be true when looking at the same behavior practiced in time of peace, in 195 BCE. Whatever the conditions (war or peace) a group finds itself in, its first instinct might be its self-preservation and regeneration from within. A woman who stepped outside her traditionally assigned sphere had therefore the potential to upset the established order, in which men were assured a superior position.

After Rome's victory over Carthage, the Oppian Law was no longer sensible. Some politicians advocated its repeal in 195 BCE, but Cato argued for its retention. Livy's Cato voiced it in the following way: "So if you will let them . . . be raised level with men, do you think that they will be tolerable? As soon as they begin to be our equals, they will be our masters. . . ."[37] Cato expressed a fear that women had the potential of becoming masters over men, but he may have had also an economic reason in mind. One example should suffice to make his position clear. Property left to a married woman passed out of her birth family and into her husband's family, ensuring that sons were privileged over daughters.[38] Thus, laws were devised to keep property within the originating family and here again, Cato has a few words to say on the issue of dowry that could not be entrusted to the husband. For him, the issue was not so much the law as the fact that letting the property pass to the woman's birth family was another sign of a woman's control.[39] One could easily argue, though, that it was the woman's family, that is, the head of her family, its *pater familias* (her oldest living male relative), who kept power over most of the dowry. No family would give up easily any economic advantage, and daughters had the potential to upset this balance. Women needed to be controlled in order to guarantee socioeconomic and sociopolitical stability. Hence, women were urged to be dutiful wives, mothers, and daughters and to stay within social and cultural norms, making them more easily controlled. Importantly, it is these women who observed these ideals that served as models of the good and proper Roman woman.

Aemilia and Cornelia

The historian Polybius tells the story of his patron, Scipio Aemilianus, the sole heir to the fortune of his great aunt Aemilia, who unlike some of her male relatives, enlarged her inheritance many times over in successful business dealings. An "upper class" woman's economic survival, however, was not dependent on her working, because she had choices. Hers was a preference of *negotia* (work) over *otium* (leisure). Susan Treggiari noted that "in the upper classes profit-making ventures were viewed as an extension of domestic economy." [40] This view explains that Aemilia was not seen as forsaking her duties or to have been meddling in men's business. Although businesswomen had in fact left the private (domestic) domain to enter the public sphere, they were not perceived as having done so. Aemilia's actions in this were seen as an "extension of domestic economy." [41]

Scipio distributed a share of this inheritance from his great aunt to his impoverished mother, the divorced wife of the great Africanus, victor over Carthage, because divorced females often faced grave economic losses. Scipio, as well, paid off dowry balances still owed to the husbands of his sisters. Polybius writes that everybody admired "Scipio's goodness and generosity." [42] However generous Scipio was, his economic worth was not depleted from being so; Scipio did not have to fear the loss of the money given to his mother and his brother-in-laws. The law protected his assets, and the economic risk he took was minimal. Scipio retained indirect control over the money he distributed; he was the *pater familias.*

Scipio Aemilianus' mother-in-law, Cornelia, served as the paragon of Roman womanhood. [43] She was a highly educated woman, powerful and economically independent. There is no mention in the sources of a guardian who would have conducted legal business for her. As a respected Roman matron, widow, and mother, Cornelia could exercise control over her life and make her own decisions. Yet, to maintain the established mode of womanly behavior, Cornelia's independence needed to be counterbalanced: tradition primarily portrayed her as the dutiful daughter of Scipio Africanus and the caring, devoted mother of the Gracchi. The widowed Cornelia even refused a proposal of marriage from Ptolemy of Egypt, electing instead to devote herself to the education of her two sons. The focus of the myth/tradition/history had to be on her fulfillment of her duties as daughter, wife, and mother rather than on her as independent woman. By keeping this focus, the Roman ideal of a woman's social position was upheld and reinforced and the balance of power in favor of men maintained.

Independence and political acumen, however, did not necessarily always translate into a negative image. Cornelia possessed both and was still hailed a paragon of Roman womanhood. Her activities never threatened the boundaries that separated the private from the public domain. Cornelia, once widowed, managed her large household without consulting a male guardian. Legal regulations may have stressed *infirmitas sexus* (weakness of gender) of a woman and her *levitas animi* (fickleness of mind) and command her into the custody of a *pater familias* or a guardian. Because Cornelia did not threaten the status quo, however, there was nothing to criticize, and she was free to go her own way.

Claudia Quinta

This moving in and out of traditionally defined spheres can also be observed in the actions of the Vestal Claudia Quinta in 204 BCE. When the ship carrying the sacred stone representing Mater Magna (most likely the Great Mother of Mount Ida and not Cybele from Pessinus) ran aground in a shallow part of the Tiber and freeing the ship seemed impossible, Claudia Quinta came forward. Accused of immoral behavior, she asked Rome's newest addition to its pantheon to prove, in public, that she was innocent. Although it was Claudia, not the man designated by the state, who brought the powerful mother goddess to Rome, the narrative shifts the focus away from her act to the necessity of public proof of innocence and moral uprightness.[44] Ancient writers may have tried to convey that only men performed actions important for the state and noteworthy for generations to come, but reality interfered every so often with this imagined truth and warranted some kind of recognition. Claudia was recognized as innocent. She had not violated her status as a Vestal. At these moments of acknowledgment, we are offered a glimpse at the actual workings of Roman society.

Women and Order

We find every so often in the surviving literary sources accounts of misbehavior by Roman matrons and Vestal Virgins mentioned as the primary cause for disorder during Rome's formative history (from the time of the Struggle of the Orders to the end of the Second Punic War in 202 BCE). While a group of misbehaving matrons was usually needed to cause statewide troubles, a single Vestal Virgin could effect the same result if she did not uphold her vows of chastity and was subsequently found out. In the first case, the ability of the group to cause troubles arose from the reciprocal dependency of the private from the public sphere and the definition wrought by tradition of what moral behaviors constituted the basis for a well-functioning state. This is true as well of the Vestal Virgins, priestesses guarding the hearth of Rome, which symbolized the Roman people and Roman male procreative power,[45] except that the Vestals existed as an exclusive group in the public (male) sector.[46] In the first case, it was the action of a group that could put the state at risk, whereas in the latter case, it was a single Vestal Virgin.

Unlike fictional accounts, Roman matrons in real life, in a historically tangible period such as the late Republic, for example, voiced their opinions and their disagreements. A Roman woman could make money. As long as these business ventures were for the good of the family, there was no objection to them. Acceptable actions and transactions did not trigger comment; there was simply silence. When Cicero's daughter Tullia died shortly after giving birth in February 45 BCE, her father was distraught. His letters of this period to his friend Atticus show him attempting to find consolation in reading and writing. There is a discussion of building a shrine in honor of Tullia. "I shall naturally hallow her," writes Cicero, "with every kind of memorial which Greek and Latin genius can supply. Perhaps that will appease my wound."[47] In all the letters that touch on Tullia's death, we learn nothing substantial about Tullia. She was dutiful and simply there, silent, as all virtuous women were ideally to be. Cicero, mourning Tullia's death, portrays her as the ideal Roman woman, a type exclusively found in literature.

To be worthy of memory a Roman woman must have, above all, fulfilled her duties as a daughter, wife, and mother. Women who spoke out in public ran the risk of being ridiculed, especially if their cause was of a personal nature and did not serve a public good. A wonderful example of this is Cicero's defense of Marcus Caelius Rufus in 56 BCE. While some of Rome's inhabitants celebrated the first day of the *ludi Megalenses* (games in honor of Mater Magna, which featured theater plays), others watched a fascinating and entertaining spectacle in the lawcourts. He branded one of Claudius' infamous descendants, Clodia, Caelius' former lover and now turned accuser, a Medea of the Palatine (*Pro Caelio* 19) and a "woman of loose morals" who established herself in the public baths and bought the bath attendant with a "quarter."[48] Cicero not only argued, he performed, taking on the persona of the esteemed Appius Claudius Caecus as he defended Caelius against the charge of being involved in the murder of Alexandrian ambassadors who argued against Ptolemy XII Auletes' restoration.[49]

The rhetor Quintilian remarked over a century later that Caelius' nickname for Clodia had been *quadrantaria Clytaemnestra* (*Inst.* 8.6.53). Clytemnestra of Greek myth was the wife of Agamemnon, who, in contrast to Odysseus' wife Penelope, married another man, Aegistheus, during her husband's ten-year absence. When Agamemnon returned home, Clytemnestra killed him. The phrase *quadrantaria Clytaemnestra* turns Clodia into a disloyal, impious, cheaply bought, and thus utterly un-Roman, woman. Should this Clodia also have been the poet Catullus' lover, Lesbia, as was alleged in antiquity, modern commentators began to question only in the twentieth century.[50] We have to concede that this Roman woman hardly followed in Lucretia's and Verginia's heroic footsteps. Whether Clodia was as bad (irreverent of tradition) as surviving literature and subsequent explanatory models want us to believe is certainly open for discussion. One thing is clear, however, and the references to Medea and Clytemnestra reinforce this: Clodia meddled, or was *perceived* to have meddled, in politics, the sphere of men. Thus, her behavior was judged un-womanlike and un-Roman; her actions may have been for her brother's benefit, but they were perceived to be selfish. It cannot be discounted that these actions may in part be due to the fact that Clodia's brother was the infamous Clodius, whom Cicero deeply disliked.[51]

Cicero spoke and wrote with the assuredness that comes from being in the dominant (*vir*) position while debasing and deriding Clodia. Sallust did the same when he created the sketch of Sempronia, a supporter of Lucius Sergius Catilina (Catiline), who planned a coup d'état in 63 BCE, which Cicero, consul that year, uncovered and crushed. In Sallust's estimation, Sempronia had committed many misdeeds (*facinora*) often with manly audacity (*virilis audacia*). She was a woman well situated by birth and appearance (*genere atque forma*) and furthered by the status of her husband Decimus Iunius Brutus, consul of 77 BCE. Her son Brutus (Decimus Iunius Brutus Albinus) had a distinguished career under Caesar but, like the tyrannicide Marcus Iunius Brutus, he was also involved in the dictator's assassination. Sempronia was highly educated and possessed wit and grace (*multae facetiae multusque lepos*), but she meddled in politics; hence, even her positive attributes, which Sallust listed, worked against her.[52] Sempronia was a married woman (*mulier*), whose sole obligation and focus, ideally, was to be toward her husband, children, and family. Her manly audacity, already out of place for a woman, only intensified the negativity of her actions.[53]

AUGUSTUS' ASCENT

After Caesar's murder in 44 BCE, Rome again faced civil war. In 43 BCE, Marcus Antonius (Marc Antony), Marcus Aemilius Lepidus, and Augustus[54] formed a triumvirate to (re-)constitute the Republic (*tresviri rei publicae constituendae*).[55] Their first action was a proscription, which eliminated 130 senators and 2,000 *equites* (knights, Rome's second social order). The most prominent victim was Cicero, who had repeatedly spoken out against Marc Antony.[56] The proscription brought the triumvirs needed revenue, since the estates of those proscribed and killed went directly to these three men. The material gains from this political purging went to finance the war efforts against Caesar's assassins, Marcus Iunius Brutus[57] and Gaius Licinius Crassus. Taxes were also levied on the propertied classes in Italy, and a capital levy was instituted on rich women. The women, under the leadership of Hortensia, the daughter of one of the most prominent orators, rose in defiance.[58] First the rebellious women sought help from the female relatives of the triumvirs. Octavia, Augustus' sister, and Julia, Antony's mother, received them; Fulvia, Antony's wife, snubbed them.

Then the women led by Hortensia staged a demonstration in the *forum* (marketplace) and made their way to the tribunal (a platform on which magistrates' chairs were placed and from which pronouncements were issued). There, Hortensia addressed the triumvirs.[59] The women were eventually driven from the *forum,* but their protests reduced the number of women to be taxed from 1,000 to 400. Because women paid less and thus the lost revenue needed to be recouped from other sources, men in possession of more than 100,000 drachmas (read: sesterces) were taxed. It is interesting to note that Antony's mother, Julia, did not oppose the demonstrators, although her daughter-in-law, Fulvia, did.

The two women had worked together previously when, after the battle of Mutina (Modena) in 43 BCE, Marc Antony was declared a public enemy for besieging Brutus without the Roman Senate's approval.[60] The night before the matter was put to a vote, Julia and Fulvia clad themselves in mourning attire, in the manner of widows, and moved from one senator's house to the next, lamenting Marc Antony's fate in becoming a public enemy. Their act of fostering compassion was successful: the decree to make Marc Antony a public enemy failed. Roman women could sway political opinion, but outside their assigned sphere, in the realm of the public, they could easily become targets themselves.

Marc Antony's reputation, however, became suspect and vulnerable to attack when he joined himself to Cleopatra. Here was a woman, a foreign potentate, through whom, because there was a moralistic value system in place, a leading Roman general's character could be slandered and his very Romanness questioned. The sea battle at Actium in 31 BCE sealed Marc Antony's and Cleopatra's fate. Details of the battle are scanty.[61] We only know what Augustus, the victor, wants us to know: in his hands, Actium became the decisive moment of Rome's struggle against oriental potentates; Cleopatra and Marc Antony were transformed into the new Isis and her Dionysian lover.

In the *Aeneid,* Vergil depicts Cleopatra as a frenzied queen (*regina*) holding a rattle (*sistrum*).[62] The rattle is a trademark attribute of the goddess Isis, and so, without saying it, Vergil linked the Egyptian queen with the goddess. Since the expulsion of the last king (*rex*) from Rome and the formation of the Republic in 509 BCE, *rex,* the sources tell us, was a loathed term as monarchy was a reviled form of government. The feminine form of *rex* is *regina.* Using *regina* in this passage, Vergil, without any need for elaboration, suggests deep aversion. This new Isis opposed the Roman gods, especially Apollo, whom Augustus chose as his guardian deity. In Vergil's passage, Dionysian fury opposes Apollonian rationality; or Marc Antony's excesses and un-Roman behavior stood in opposition to Augustus' temperance and behavior grounded in the *mos maiorum.*

Augustus and his third wife, Livia Drusilla, who belonged to one of Rome's noblest families,[63] made sure that their actions were perceived as moderate, traditional, and solely for the welfare of the Roman state. Livia was praised for her matronly and domestic virtues. She was a devoted wife, mother, friend, and patron. Suetonius recounts how the wife of Rome's first man, the *princeps,* and her sister-in-law, Octavia, provided Augustus with homespun and woven clothing (Suet. *Aug.* 73) and pleased the people with acts of generosity. Both women were given *sacrosanctitas* (sacrosanctity), the same inviolability a tribune of the people possessed,[64] and free control of their finances. Livia, for example, the major shareholder in tile factories in Italy, which included exports, was a generous patroness to her friends and to the Roman state. When Plancina, the wife of Gaius Calpurnius Piso, was implicated in the death of the heir-apparent Germanicus in 19 CE, Livia ensured through her son, the emperor Tiberius, that her friend was not charged. This case of political involvement shows the far-reaching power of Rome's first lady.[65]

It is exactly this power to which a historian such as Tacitus strongly objected, a woman manipulating the affairs of the state indirectly, in effect, making her son the *princeps* her tool. Livia meddled in politics, the sphere of a *vir,* demonstrating *virtus.* One could argue that Tiberius reacted like

Tacitus to his mother's political involvement: politics was men's business. While Livia and Augustus ran a most successful political partnership over many decades, her son had no interest in continuing, nor any need to continue, such an arrangement.[66]

Politically less charged than intervening on behalf of an accused friend was Livia's financing of buildings that enhanced her status as benefactor. In Rome, for example, Livia financed the construction of the *porticus Liviae* (the Portico of Livia) and the restoration of the temple of Fortuna Muliebris (Womanly Fortune). A small shrine to Concordia (Harmony) was situated within the *porticus*. "While Octavia's portico [celebrated] good mothers of history and mythology . . . Livia's building evidently celebrated good wives, and the virtue of marital harmony, which the moral legislation of Augustus encouraged."[67] The temple of Fortuna Muliebris was thought to have been built in recognition of Venturia's and Volumnia's action in keeping Coriolanus from attacking his native Rome.[68] Like her husband, Livia fashioned herself as the paragon of Roman virtues, linking herself with extraordinary women such as the early Republican Venturia and Volumnia, who after all had saved Rome. In this, Livia also set herself up in opposition to the Egyptian Cleopatra or for that matter to any woman who meddled in politics against what was perceived to be the well-being of the state and ultimately the illusion of keeping the Republican structure intact. Toward the end of her very long life, Livia was proclaimed the *mater patriae* (mother of her country);[69] as the high priestess of her late husband's cult, she, like the Vestals, had the right to a *lictor*.[70] Livia, the wife and the mother of an emperor, endowed with the rights of the Vestals was thus transformed into a guarantor of Rome's prosperity.

CONCLUSION

As in the time of Rome's mythic history, women came to the forefront in the late Republic and the Principate. Like their ancestors, they played important roles, as either positive or negative examples, in illustrating how a dutiful Roman woman helped shape a new political system. It was again Livia who was able to embody all womanly virtues while taking full advantage of the political changes. She established herself as a powerful patroness, an influential power broker behind the scenes, and a model for empresses to come. While any future politically astute empress could take full advantage of the powers Livia and other Julio-Claudian women had amassed and gradually introduced into the sphere of the politically acceptable, it was not until the time of the Severan women (the Severan dynasty ruled 193–235 CE) that Rome saw empresses actively and openly shaping politics. It was the juncture between Republic and Principate that opened the door for change, and Livia seized this opportunity first and most effectively. Ancient writers of history, however, continued to judge their female protagonists, as they had always done, through a moral lens. Rome's greatness was linked to traditionally determined proper behavior; religion, the correct and timely performance of religious rites, was part of that greatness.

TWO

LIFE CYCLES AND TIME STRUCTURES

Religious rituals that were carried out by women for the well-being and continuation of the Roman state are the focus of this chapter. Rome was an agricultural society, which its cultic cycle reinforced. Like the seasons, there was great religious activity in preparation for and during the growing season, while there was little of note after the harvest season. Rome was a militaristic society, governed by male warriors, and one might expect that women had very limited roles in cultic activities. With Rome's historical understanding of itself, however, women played an important role in the creation of the state, as we have seen. A closer look at the calendar reveals that for every cultic action performed by women there was a corresponding activity that involved men. This theme of interdependence between female and male actors played itself out throughout the Roman calendar. Importantly, these ritual actions were carried out in a defined space, in other words, a sacred landscape.

Our main literary sources for the Roman calendar are, in chronological order, Varro, Ovid, and Festus. All three ancient writers provide us with pertinent information about the festivals, but they also impose constraints and shape our view of the Roman calendar. Varro's *On Antiquities Human and Divine* is fragmentary and among lost Republican prose writings; it is "perhaps the one we most sorely miss."[1] In Ovid's poem on the Roman calendar, the *Fasti*, we find descriptions of religious festivals from January to June in the context of a poetic composition that features, for example, narrative "I" in discussions with gods. While Ovid's *Fasti* collects traditions related to religious festivals and rituals, at the same time, it criticizes the state of affairs in Rome under Augustus.[2] Festus, a second-century CE scholar, abridged the lexicon of Marcus Verrius Flaccus, *On the Meaning of Words*. Flaccus had been the teacher of Augustus' grandsons, Gaius and Lucius. The first half of Festus' work, ten books altogether, are lost. Paulus Diaconus summarized the remainder in the eighth century CE. Festus' composite work is a good example of the complexities of an ancient source that are employed in explanations of the past.

The surviving literary and material evidence for the Roman calendar is fragmented; nonetheless, while being aware of this particular shortcoming, we can glean an understanding of women's role in the ritual calendar of Rome. Women were involved and important in the upkeep of the integrated community of Rome, the Empire, its inhabitants, and its gods. While men acquired and controlled territory, women ensured through religious ceremonies, in particular those focusing on fertility and agriculture, that the Empire continued to prosper. Calendars, and the Roman one is no exception, were linked to an agricultural cycle. The earth's fertility cycle, its production of food items, sustains life and guarantees basic survival.

The rising and setting of the sun and the waxing and waning of the moon[3] are discernible, recurring phenomena that provide cyclical patterns. These patterns related to seasonal phenomena, cold and warm weather, for example, help organize human life. Time, for humankind, became tangible and explicable only when connected to the sun, the moon, and a seasonal cycle. The various systems of reckoning time (solar and lunar) coexisted and coincided, as they do today. Specific actions were linked to specific time periods; there was a time that was good for hunting deer and a time for gathering nuts or fruit. Some actions eventually became habit; if, for example, a ceremony was performed before the onset of hunting or gathering, which then seemingly produced a good yield consistently, or at least consistently enough, it could come to be reenacted each time before hunting or gathering and then transmitted from generation to generation. Thus, the action gradually emerged as custom.

Over time this custom might undergo various degrees of formalization.[4] Once built into a system, in our case, a recurring ritual cycle, it would be preserved in its prescribed state. Religion, the collection of ritual customs, would become the depository and the guarantor of time-honored rites. As such, religion is inherently conservative, and fundamental changes occur rarely, although in Roman religion, its polytheistic composition allowed foreign cults to be integrated. Conservatism shows itself in that the rituals of foreign cults did not change upon their integration. We have what might seem two contradictory strands; first, the inclusive system, polytheism, is inherently dynamic because it allows broad integration. On the other hand, ritual activities tend to be static, determined by tradition; thus, cults that are integrated conserve their formalized action.

If we understand a calendar as making social time concrete, then its purpose is the binding of a group to a system of chronological coherence, which is linear and cyclical, which in turn, because of its codified and recurring features, gives permanent reference points that engage and coordinate individuals as a group. The individual is integrated and the group homogenized. Cultic rituals also marked the progression of time and were the constant as they shaped daily, monthly, and yearly routines. Rituals linked an individual and the group to its past. Furthermore, rituals shaped and continuously reshaped the comprehension of the self and the community in relation to the past, the present, and the future.

What we know of the Roman calendar has been reconstructed from surviving fragmentary inscriptions and literary sources. The three most important days of each month were the 1st day, Kalendae (Kalends); the 5th (or 7th) day, Nones; and the Ides, in the middle of a month (13th or 15th day), which originally coincided with the full moon. In March, May, July, and October, the Nones fell on the 7th day of the month, the Ides, on the 15th; in the remaining months, the Nones fell on the 5th and the 13th day respectively. These three days (Kalends, Nones, and Ides) functioned as points of reference and any day was calculated in reference to them; that is, one calculated the time moving toward them, including the starting and ending day.[5] March, May, July, and October had 31 days; February, 28; and the remaining months, 29 days. Altogether the Roman year had until Julius Caesar's calendar reform 355 days. Earth's elliptical revolution around the sun, however, takes $365\frac{1}{4}$ days, which meant that the Romans had to correct their calendar, as we do today with the addition of a day in February in a leap year. The added days or months were called intercalary.

The Roman year consisted of 12 months and a smaller cycle of 8 days, equivalent to our week, which was marked throughout the year with the letters *A* through *H*. Every 8th day (*H*) was a market day, a *nundinae*. This was, by law, a business day and called a *dies fastus*. The root of *fastus* is *fas,* meaning "right or correct by divine law." The letter *F* identified such a day on the calendar. The opposite of the 42 market days (*dies fasti*) were the 58 nonmarket days, the *dies nefasti,* which were labeled with the letter *N*. On these days, which were religious holidays, sacrifices were prepared in the morning and offered later in the day. Magistrates were not allowed to address public meetings, and citizens could not file lawsuits with the urban *praetor.*

Some other days were a combination of market days and holidays, which were indicated by the letter combination *EN*.[6] There were also a 195 *dies comitales,* labeled with the letter *C,* on which assemblies could meet. Such meetings, however, could not take place on a market day or a holiday. Another letter combination, the ligature *NP,* seems to indicate public holidays. The German scholar Georg Wissowa proposed the reading *dies nefasti publici.* An *NP*-marked day was a public holiday on which everyday life was put on hold and religious ceremonies were performed (*feriae publicae*).[7]

The months September (the 7th month), October (the 8th month), November (the 9th month), and December (the 10th month) indicate that, at one point in time, there was an underlying system of 10 months.[8] The political year started in March and ended with February, the month of purification. Agriculture determined this yearly cycle, which would make March an excellent choice for the start of a new year. The god Mars gave the month its name. This Mars, however, was not the god of war but the divine guardian of fields.[9] Yet ancient sources also declare that January was, since earliest times, the year's 1st month. The easiest explanation would be that a 12-month solar cycle was grafted onto a 10-month seasonal system, which itself might have replaced a lunar system of marking time.[10] The 2 months that were introduced were January and February, by first assigning them to eleventh and twelfth position and later moving them to first and second place. The original introduction happened in the sixth century BCE when Rome was in Etruscan hands, and the later change occurred in 153 BCE at the latest, when the beginning of the new and civil year was moved from the Ides of March to the Kalends of January.[11]

The god Janus, the two-headed god, who looked backward as well as forward, was believed to be the god of beginnings. This understanding of Janus moved January into its present position at the beginning of the year. Although the Romans had a 12-month calendar, they periodically had to add an additional month (an intercalation) of 22 or 23 days to keep in line with the solar year. The college of pontiffs was in charge of this intercalation. By the end of the late Republic, however, the calendar was so hopelessly off that it needed to be readjusted to correspond to the solar year. Julius Caesar introduced calendar reforms based on the Egyptian solar calendar in 46 BCE, which were implemented on January 1, 45 BCE. With one additional readjustment, the reform introduced by Pope Gregory XIII in the sixteenth century, and the switch from an 8- to a 7-day week, is the calendar system we use today.[12]

JANUARY

The Carmentalia was the first festival of the 12-month year that involved women. Before its celebration, however, the Romans celebrated Janus' festival, the Agonium, on January 9th. This festival had the calendar marking

NP. On this public holiday, the *rex sacrorum* (the king of sacrifices) sacrificed a ram in the *regia,* thought to have been the home of Rome's second king, Numa. The *regia,* located northwest of the temple of Vesta (*aedes Vestae*) at the east end of the *forum Romanum,* held the office of the *pontifex maximus* (head pontiff). It was the meeting place of the pontifical college and most likely held its archive during the Republic. Augustus moved the locale to the Palatine where he lived, and because eventually he, and all *princeps* after him, held the position of *pontifex maximus,* the headquarters remained with the emperor. The *rex sacrorum* was the priest of Janus and belonged to the college of pontiffs. He took first position, before the *flamen Dialis,* in the *ordo sacerdotum* (the order of priests). This is interesting insofar as the *flamen Dialis* was the priest of Jupiter,[13] the highest god in the Roman Olympian-based pantheon. After the ousting of the last king (*rex*) of Rome, in whose position political, military, and religious powers were united, the title *rex* was retained only in the religious sphere.

The temple of Vesta, located at the foot of the Palatine hill at the southeast corner of the *forum Romanum,* was close to the water pool of Iuturna, the *lacus* (lake) *Iuturnae,* and the temple of Castor and Pollux. Most intriguingly, the temple of Vesta, whose priestesses, the Vestal Virgins, tended the sacred flame that symbolized the Roman state, stood outside the *pomerium,* the religious boundary that defined the parts of the city of Rome that lay within this boundary.[14] Furthermore, the *palladium,* an emblem endowed with protective force, was stored in the temple of Vesta.[15] Just as had been the case with the *regia,* Augustus appropriated Vesta in part when an altar of the goddess and a statue were, by the decree of the Senate, placed on the Palatine in 12 BCE, the year he became *pontifex maximus.* Livy records that Postumius, Rome's dictator, vowed a temple to Castor and Pollux during the battle of Lake Regillus in 493 BCE and then again when the twins appeared watering their horses at the water pool of Iuturna after Rome's victory over the Latins. The dictator's son dedicated the temple in 484 BCE.[16] This structure belongs to one of the earliest temples of Republican Rome.[17] Although the dedication date of the temple of Vesta eludes us, most ancient sources link it to the time of the Sabine king Numa, simply indicating that the foundation was laid before records were kept. There was also no cult image of Vesta in this temple until the time of Nero. Vesta was linked to Janus in two ways. First, when Romans invoked gods, Janus was called upon first and Vesta, last.[18] Second, there was a ritual connection between the Vestals and the *rex sacrorum,* priest of Janus, which also connects this festival, the Agonium, with the Carmentalia.

The Vestal Virgins fetched water at the spring of the Camenae (*fons et lucus Camenarum*) on the foot of the Caelian hill near the *Porta Capena*.[19] Frontinus, in his treatis *On the Water Supply of the City of Rome,* writes that "the memory of the springs is still considered holy and revered; indeed they are believed to restore sick bodies to health, such as the spring of the Camenae, and . . . that of Iuturna."[20] A question arises, however, as to why the Vestals did not fetch their daily water at the closer *lacus Iuturnae.* Two reasons come to mind. First, the Vestals, walking through the city to fetch water, must have made quite an impression. They were recognizably different from other women, but at the same time, they were doing women's work. Most likely, fetching water would be only one aspect of their daily duties, but it was one that took them outdoors, thus making them visible. Since it was part of a routine, the water fetching might have taken place at the same time every day. Second, before its springs fed into a marble basin, the *lacus Iuturnae* was, as the Latin word *lacus* suggests, a pool. The whole *forum Romanum* area was prone to floods, and one can but imagine rather swampy and unhealthy conditions. This fact did not, however, seem to impede the water quality of the *Iuturna.* Like the *Camenae,* according to Frontinus, it had salutary effects. According to tradition, the Dioscuri, Castor and Pollux, watered their horses at the *Iuturna.* Indeed, like any creature, thirsty horses drink stagnant water when no other water is available, and so the poor condition of the water might not have been a deterrent. The *Camenae,* whose water was considered especially good,[21] was linked to Numa. According to tradition, in the grove (*lucus*) where the spring (*fons*) of the *Camenae* was, Numa conversed with Egeria, a water nymph with mantic powers. She became the king's major inspiration. Water flowing (*fons*), rather than standing water in a pool (*lacus*), moved spirits and intellects. For the Romans, Numa was first to organize Roman religion, and this he did with the help of a prophesying nymph.

In addition, an *ancile,* an ancient shield in the figure of an eight, fell from the sky into Numa's hands in this special grove.[22] He realized it as a token of kingship and to protect it from thieves had eleven copies made. These twelve shields were stored in the *regia* and carried by the Salii in religious processions. These Salii were priests of Mars, who performed ritual war dances. The verbal root of Salii is *salire,* which means "to leap or spring."[23] Of the Salii there were two groups, the Salii Agonenses or Collini and the Salii Palatini. The first group's epithet, Agonenses, has the same root as the festival name Agonium. The suffix *-enses* of Agonenses points to a location. Festus states that the Agonus was the old name for the Quirinal.[24] *Collinus* is the adjectival form for the *collis* (hill) *Quirinalis.* Ovid, in his *Fasti,* collected the ancient linguistic arguments and tried to explain the word. He discusses formation based on the verb *agō* (to lead) and points to *agōn,* which means struggle or competition. Ovid also mentions that *agōnia* was an ancient word for sheep.[25] A ram, after all, was what the *rex sacrorum* sacrificed on this January holiday.

Whatever the original meaning of the word, there is a geographic explanation that sheds some light on the problem. The two groups of dancing warrior priests, one from the Palatine serving Mars and the other from the Quirinal serving Quirinus, point to a past when independent ethnic groups populated Rome's hills. Roman tradition assigned the Sabines to the Quirinal and the original core group of Romans to the Palatine. The coming together of the priest-warrior dancing groups ritualistically merged the two, presumably largest, ethnic groups, a practice we will encounter again in the Lupercalia. The god Quirinus, however, poses a bit of a problem. He belongs, together with Jupiter and Mars, to the group of indigenous gods (*di indigetes*).[26] These gods had a special priest, a *flamen,* who in the hierarchy of priests came after the *rex sacrorum.*

While we can easily fit Jupiter and Mars into the Olympian (Greek) system, that is, Jupiter/Zeus (the father of gods) and Mars/Ares (the god of war), Quirinus has no immediate place. Quirinus was thought to be the deified Romulus, an idea especially prominent in Augustan literature and a Sabine version of Mars. Roman citizens were collectively called *Quirites,* especially in solemn address and appeal. The ancients connected the word with the Sabine town of Cures and the Sabine word for spear, *curis.*[27] In connection with the Salii the explanation associating Quirinus with Mars makes most sense, because Quirinus also gave his name to the hill. Thus, the two warrior-dancer groups were, although not necessarily originally, rationally, and maybe subsequently, equivalent. Quirinus was also used as a title for Janus. The temple of Janus functioned as an indicator of war and peace (*index pacis bellique*). In peacetime the doors were closed, something of a rarity, and in wartime the temple doors were open.[28] The god of the door or the gateway (*ianua*) had a clear connection with war.

The Carmentalia was celebrated on two days, January 11th and 15th, with a three-day interval. In the calendar, both days were marked with *NP,* which made them public holidays. The linguistic root of Carmentalia is *carmen* (song, magic utterance), and it is also akin to Camena (Muse).[29] In Vergil's epic, Carmentis is a prophetess who foretold Rome's glory.[30] The calendar (*Fasti*) of Praeneste (now Palestrina), a city southeast of Rome, records that a successful Roman general established the festival on January 15 to celebrate the capture of Fidenae. Fidenae, on the salt route (*Via Salaria*), was Rome's first colony.[31] As Rome expanded, colonies guaranteed a continued Roman presence in newly acquired territories. The ancients had trouble explaining the three-day interval between the two festival days, but it may be that a festival with a similar content, potentially from a different group than the Romans, was added to an already existing one.

Ovid gives what H. H. Scullard termed a "wilder explanation,"[32] but then the poet's treatment of the Roman festival calendar is a rather curious affair anyway.[33] Ovid explains that when women were forbidden to drive in carriages (*carpentae*), they simply refused to bear children. The poet often empowers women, as he does here, in his work. When the elders, the *patres,* after scolding the women, gave them back the right of using carriages, the women sponsored a second festival (1.621–1.628). Ovid suggests, in what turns out to be a false etymology, that *carpenta* (carriage) is to be linked to Evander's mother, Carmentis. But this kind of linguistic connection is not necessary at all.[34] Carmentis was most likely a goddess of childbirth. Having a special priest, a *flamen,* only emphasizes Carmentis' importance. The women in Ovid's story had stopped giving birth in protest and thus imperiled the state. Carmentis also had two additional names: Prorsa and Postverta. These names were based on the position of babies to be born: head or feet first. Consequently, the supplementary names generated a plurality of deities, the Carmentes, and a duality, a Januslike entity, that looked back as well as forward.[35] Augustine combined Carmentis' mantic powers, which she derived from being a water nymph, with that of being the protector of child bearing. In his opinion, the Carmentes were goddesses who sang the fate of infants at birth.[36]

Scullard noted that "the month of January may seem a curious time of year for a festival concerned with birth, but many births probably occurred at this time, since we know that marriages were favored in April."[37] Differently from Scullard, it can also be argued that winter months provide ideal conditions for conception. The argument is one of seasonality, and, consequently, fall months have higher birth rates than others.[38] January was thus an ideal month to have a festival in honor of a goddess of childbirth or a goddess who prophesied Rome's greatness, which depended on continuous generations of Romans.

The shrine of Carmentis was at the foot of the Capitoline hill near a gate that took its name from the shrine, the *porta Carmentalis.* Outside the gate lay the *forum Holitorium,* Rome's original provision market.[39] Nothing is known of the ritual that took place there, except that the *flamen Carmentalis* gave a sacrifice, and no animal skin (leather) was permitted in the shrine. This follows Greek as well as Roman sacred law that prohibited anything made from animal hide to be brought inside a sacred place. Varro, discussing the word *scortum* (skin, hide), records that "in some sacred ceremonies (*sacris*) and shrines (*sacellis*) we have the written law (*scriptum*): Let nothing be brought in contact with something made of hide (*scorteum*). The idea behind it was that nothing dead should be there (*ne morticinum quid adsit*)."[40] Cicero informs us that in the third century BCE, the consul Marcus Popillius Laenas, a plebeian, and the *flamen Carmentalis*[41] had to mediate a dispute between the orders.[42] Livy adds an important insight when he notes that women often put up an altar or a shrine to this goddess after patricians and plebeians had resolved their differences over a particular matter. If conflict is seen as halting the generation of new life, then it is only through reconciliation that life can properly continue.

FEBRUARY

February was, as its name based on the word *februa* suggests, the month of purification.[43] February 1st was dedicated to Juno Sospes (or Sospita) Mater Regina.[44] Inscriptions from Lanuvium (*CIL* XIV 2088, 2089, 2091, and 2121) record the goddess' full name: Iuno Seispes (Sospes, Sispita, Sospita) Mater Regina. Her name Iuno and her attributes *mater* and *regina* position her as parallel to Jupiter. The ancients construed the goddess' cult title, Sospes, to mean preserver or savior. Juno Sospes was the guardian deity of Lanuvium,[45] which the Romans incorporated as a city with Roman rights in 338 BCE. Although integrated into the Roman calendar, and under the auspices of its *pontifices* (priests), the cult of Juno Sospes was never moved to Rome. The festival, guided by a *flamen,* remained solely in Lanuvium, the city of its origin, though Rome exerted its superior position by having its two consuls officiate in the annual sacrifice to the goddess.[46]

Inscriptions of imperial times inform us of a college of priests comprised of Roman knights, the *sacerdotes Lanuvini.*[47] During a battle against the Gauls in 197 BCE, the consul Cornelius Cethegus vowed to build her a temple. Three years later on February 1st, when he was *censor,* he dedicated the promised temple, which was located in the *forum Holitorium.*[48] Ovid made Juno Sospes a neighbor of the Great Mother (Mater Magna) on the Palatine, most likely, maybe even deliberately, confusing Mater Magna with Mater Matuta,[49] the same inaccuracy we find in Livy's narrative. Both deities embodied the notion of fertility and thus facilitated syncretism, which led to confusion about the actual location of the temple.

The elegiac poet Propertius provides a description of an ancient Lanuvian custom (4.8.3–4.8.14). The primordial guardian of Lanuvium was a snake (*draco*) of immemorial age (*annosus*). Every year, girls entered a grove and brought food for the snake that lived there. If the snake accepted the offerings, the girls were vouched to be virgins, and the fertility of the year was assured. Ancients had already explained that the appearance of a snake in a dream, especially in women's dreams, meant that the child born from a union would be an exceptional leader.[50] In antiquity, the snake was considered an earthborn (chthonic) being with magic and apotropaic (protective) powers. The guardian of the temple in Eleusis, the major cultic center of Demeter, the goddess who gave humankind food and laws, was a snake.[51] Like Demeter, Isis, considered to be the original giver of food to humankind, has in her Hellenistic manifestations snakes curled around her right wrist. Pliny writes that "the *draco* (snake) is without poison. Its head put underneath thresholds . . . will bring good fortune to the house."[52] The *genius,* existing in the *pater familias* or oldest male of a clan (*gens*), contained the whole concept of man and his procreative force. *Genius* was a man's life force, the female equivalent was called *iuno,*[53] and its artistic rendering was in the form of a snake. The Lanuvian ritual, which Propertius described, can be explained as an attempt at activating earth's fecundity from within. The virgins went into the cave of the Lanuvian *draco,* where they encountered the symbol of the male procreative force. The snake's acceptance of their offerings, food, denoted procreation; or as the farmers exclaimed: "The year will be fertile! (*clamantque agricolae: 'fertilis annus erit!'*)."[54]

Cicero described some attributes of the cult statue in Lanuvium.[55] Juno Sospes wore a hide of a goat (*pelle caprina*) and shoes with a flattened back (*calceolis repandis*). She also had a spear (*hasta*) and little shield (*scutulum*), which gave her a warriorlike character similar to the Greek goddess Athena. As such, one assumes, Juno Sospes served as protectress of the city. The shoe type points to an Etruscan origin of the deity. The goat hide, which plays a pivotal role in the Lupercalia, Rome's premier procreation rite, signifies fertility. What E. M. Douglas postulated as two incongruous cults, Juno Sospes on the *arx* (the highest point of the city) and the serpent in the cave, which were awkwardly combined,[56] are in fact aspects of one and the same cult: a cult that projected female and male procreative forces onto a divine and ritualized sphere.

Much of February dealt with appeasing the dead. During this time, Ovid reports, houses were cleansed, graves decorated, temples closed, altar fires were extinguished, magistrates laid aside their insignia, and marriages could not take place.[57] The community focused on the past and readied itself for a new agricultural cycle. All seemed dormant, and yet hidden elements connected to fertility remained active. Ovid loosely and humorously connected these elements in his *Fasti*. "The *flaminica*," he says (2.27–2.28), "I have seen myself demanding a *februa;* for her demand a *februa* in the form of a pine twig was given." Pine has antiseptic properties, and as such it was the "band aid" of antiquity. Pliny the Elder noted that pine stopped the outpouring of blood.[58] When one thinks of abortion and childbirth, a theme of the Lupercalia (discussed below), the most community-oriented festival in February, one could say that the pine twig (*pinea virga*) functioned simultaneously as purifying agent and as antiseptic necessary to the child-bearing woman's health and, indeed, her life. In ritual, pine was used to purify.

When Attis, the crazed companion of Cybele, the Great Mother, castrates himself, flowers grow from his blood, dripping onto the earth, and he himself turns into a pine tree. The myth around Cybele and Attis is complex; in its essence, however, it recounts the agricultural cycle: nature's death and rebirth. The primordial procreative force resides in Cybele, the ruler of nature. Attis' castration (and in the myth his subsequent death) is the ultimate sacrifice: the renunciation of potential (male) fertility to ensure the fertility of the larger community. The virgins feeding the snake in Lanuvium did just the same. Another myth tells of the virgin Pine whom Boreas, the north wind, and Pan loved. As Boreas pursued Pine, she fell from a cliff and changed into a pine tree.[59] The north wind was believed to be the bringer of health, while Pan, the goat-human, signified uncivilized nature and unbridled sexual appetites. The latter needed to be tamed to guarantee the continuation of civilized life.

The Parentalia, the commemoration of dead family members, which was a private affair, began on midday of February 13th. The fourth-century calendar of Philocalus notes that "a Vestal Virgin performs rites."[60] There is also an inscription that connects this festival with Tarpeia (*CIL* I², p. 258), and since Varro (*Ling.* 5.41), Propertius (4.4.18), and Silius Italicus (13.448) made Tarpeia one of the first Vestals, it seemed only appropriate to think it at least a possibility that a Vestal performed a rite on the grave of one of her (professional) ancestors. The nineteenth-century scholar Theodor Mommsen, however, proved with another inscription (*CIL* I², p. 309) that there was no such connection. The Tarpeian rock (*Tarpeium saxum*), at the southeast side of the Capitoline hill, had received its name from Tarpeia, the one who had helped Sabine soldiers enter the Roman citadel. But Romans would surely not perform a rite for and commemorate a traitor at a location of their defeat (Dion. Hal. 2.40.3). If, however, we postulate that the place memorialized victory over an enemy and the story of Tarpeia developed from this *tropaion* (trophy) place,[61] then the circular argument based on the name can be avoided. In the end, the Sabines had won the battle with Tarpeia's help; the Romans, however, won the war.

Horace's formula of "the conqueror being conquered"[62] holds true for Rome's earliest history as well. The Sabines were integrated into the Roman cultural weave and with them their rites. There is also the possibility of ritual appeasement. Persons who soiled the community with criminal acts were thrown from the Tarpeian Rock, with the last recorded execution of this kind in 43 CE. A criminal undermined the state's social fabric and as such needed to be eliminated. In eliminating the unwanted person, though, the Roman state incurred blood guilt that required conciliation. The conciliation was in the hands of the Vestals, one of whom was chosen to perform the rite at the location of the criminal's punishment on the first day of the Parentalia.[63] The Vestals were charged with keeping alive the flame that symbolized a state comprised of households and interrelations of social superiors and inferiors. A criminal's activities and his or her execution had jeopardized the social network, which the Vestal with her action reestablished. Whatever the origins of the rite at the Tarpeian Rock, the theme of appeasement fits well with other ceremonies performed in February.

The Lupercalia took place on February 15 in the midst of the holiday cycle concerned with dead family members. The most famous, not the least because of Shakespeare's rendering, was the Lupercalia of 44 BCE, when Mark Antony offered Julius Caesar a crown, which the dictator wisely refused saying: "I am Caesar, not king!" The ceremony started with the sacrifice of goats and a dog, which might have served as a replacement for a wolf, and the offerings of *mola salsa* (sacred cakes) prepared by the Vestal Virgins. These cakes were made with the first wheat of the previous harvest. The Lupercalia has been construed as a fertility ritual, but A. K. Michels has rightly argued that it was a purification rite, fitting nicely within the February appeasement period, the *dies parentales* (days remembering the ancestors). The *luperci,* the wolf-men, ran a race starting at the Lupercal, the place where Faustulus the shepherd found the wolf suckling Romulus and Remus underneath a fig tree, at the southwest corner of the Palatine hill. From there they ran up and then down the *Via Sacra.* Settlements were on the hills, of which Rome had seven.

If the *forum* served originally as a burial site,[64] then the Lupercalia, besides having the purifying aspect, also delineated the living from the dead as a communal act of appeasement. Michel concluded that "the purification given by the beating which the *luperci* administered to those whom they met would free them from the influence of the dead." [65] Since two groups of *luperci* existed, the *luperci Quinctiales* and the *luperci Fabiani,* connected with the Palatine and the Quirinal respectively, one can argue that the focus shifted from the family to the community, which was composed of different groups. The Vestals participated because they as a group guaranteed the continuation of the state rather than because they had any connection between the Lupercalia and the "artificial" infertility of the Vestals. The Vestals' fertility was always present and intended for the whole community, even though it would never give way to new life. A household's future, on the other hand, depended on new family members. In Rome's social construct, dead family members informed the present and the future. Ancestors' memorable actions translated into glory, dignity, and authority (*gloria, dignitas, auctoritas*), and they functioned as examples for family members and citizens.

The poet Ovid records for February, which focuses on fertility rather than purification, that the Sabine women and their Roman husbands came to the grove of Juno Lucina in supplication (2.431–2.446). The victims of rape had not produced children, and a remedy was sought. Terror struck the suppliants when a voice declared: "Let a sacred he-goat go into Italian matrons! (*Italidas matres, inquit, sacer hircus inito!*)" An Etruscan augur helped out, for who could have imagined the reality of the voice's command! He killed a billy goat, and with the thongs cut from the goat's hide, he beat the women's backs. Ten months after the flogging, children were born.

The wolf-men of the Lupercalia ran to chase the wolves from their boundaries, because these animals had long represented a threat to raising livestock, in the period of the year when animals gave birth and the winter was about to end. Stripping down to the basics, the *luperci* displayed their bodies and replaced, for the ritual moment, the actual wolves to hold them at bay throughout the year.

The lore runs deep, and as Mary DiLucia pointedly stated, "Rome is a society with a beast instead of a mother; no wonder why when the sons of this wolf want to make women into mothers themselves, they must procure them in the bestial way of family tradition, through violence and predation." [66] Ritual, lore, and tradition aside, without the women's willingness, procreation and survival of the group was not guaranteed, regardless of men's success and prowess. In DiLucia's words: "The mystery of their (women's) bodies and fertility, if not somehow controlled, kept men at the mercy of their beastly selves. This self, detrimental to civilization in the long term, of which the men themselves need to be freed, and which they can be freed from by being made fathers, by women: yet, this must acknowledge a debt to women (206)." Even in the epic of Gilgamesh, the oldest in our literary tradition, the civilizing force is a woman, Shamhat, who tamed the wild man Enkidu. On the Lupercalia, the Vestals handed out small salted cakes (*mola salsa*) made from husked wheat (*far*) as they did on the Vestalia on June 9th and on the celebration day of the consecration of Jupiter Capitolinus' temple on September 13th. Planting, harvesting, and baking grain form the basis for settled, agricultural societies.

The *lucus* of Juno Lucina and the temple built for her in 375 BCE (Plin. *NH* 16.235) was at the *subura* side of the Caelian hill. According to Varro (*Ling.* 5.49.74), the Sabine Titus Tatius introduced the cult. According to the third-century CE historian Dio Cassius (4.15.5), Servius Tullius, traditionally thought to have been Rome's sixth king, ordered a coin to be put into the treasury of Juno Lucina for every child born. Before Rome existed as a unified city, pre-Roman people inhabited especially the Palatine and Quirinal but also the Caelian hill. In Rome's historical tradition, this hill was named after an Etruscan soldier of fortune, Caele Vibenna, who came to the aid of one of the kings.[67] The procession of the Argei (discussed below), which included in its itinerary the Caelian, in addition to the Palatine, the Quirinal, and the Esquiline, seems to encompass and connect four autonomous districts that did not share a common center.[68] Unified Rome did not exist yet. Ovid's suppliants, the original Romans, were, in his version, outside their historical territory when they asked for an infertility cure, an etiological explanation of the Lupercalia. Through Juno Lucina, the goddess of childbirth, he linked the run of the *luperci* with the women's festival of the Matronalia, celebrated on March 1st.

On February 17th, two days after the Lupercalia, the Romans celebrated the Quirinalia. We do not know what the celebration was about or how it was executed. Quirinus was a god linked to the Quirinal, the Roman hill associated with the Sabines. This association would seem to make the Quirinalia a pendant to the Lupercalia, whose festival route was linked to the Palatine. The origins of Quirinus are lost forever, but Quirinus, like Janus and Mars, had a *flamen,* although of the three *flamines,* the priest of Quirinus held the lowest rank. Since the ancients did not have much more information about Quirinus and the Quirinalia than we have, they focused instead on the last day of the Fornacalia (Feast of the Ovens) of the goddess Fornax, falling on the same day as the Quirinalia.

The last day of the Feast of the Ovens was the "Festival of Fools (*stultorum feriae*)." Ovid (*Fast.* 2.513–2.532) provides two explanations about these *stulti* (fools): first, the ancient ones (*veteres*) burned husked wheat (*farra*) to ash as they roasted it, or even burned down their houses. Second, there were those who did not know to which *curia* (one of the thirty divisions of Roman people) they belonged. They could not read the signs in the *forum* with the names of their *curia* and thus were forced to celebrate on the festival's last day. But why allow these fools to celebrate at all? The festival's components of an oven and roasting wheat make it clear that the Fornicalia had to do with basic sustenance, the survival of a household, and, on a larger scale, of a *curia*. The involvement of the Vestals, the guardians of Rome's eternal flame and distributor of essential food in the form of salted cakes at the Lupercalia, reinforces the notion of survival and continuity. Looking at the Fornicalia in this way then, the festival fits in a period that focused on the past and the future, the dead and the living family members. The fools were young men about to become full-fledged citizens, Quirites.[69] They had not yet received the *toga virilis* (the toga of a man) and so were not entered into the citizen lists. Thus, they did not belong to a curia and when reading the names of the curiae, the names meant nothing to them; in effect, these youths were fools.

The Feralia, on February 21st, ended the cycle that had begun with the Parentalia nine days earlier. In contrast to the latter, the Feralia was considered a public holiday. People went to the graves where they placed gifts and prayed. The dead had to be appeased, because without appeasement the *manes* (spirits of the dead) were believed to rise from the graves and hunt the living. Ovid describes what Scullard labeled "gruesome rites," which "belong rather to private sympathetic magic than to official religion." To Scullard's mind, these rites "well illustrate how witchcraft survived in Ovid's day."[70] The gruesome rites, however, were nothing more than love magic that individuals, not witches, still practiced in early Christian times. Ovid pointed out a couple of lines before that girls could not get married during the Feralia, temples were closed, altars were without incense, and hearths were without fire.[71] Essentially, everything alive was to be inactive, when the slender souls (*animae tenues*) and bodies (*corpora*) left the graves, and the shades (*umbrae*) came to feed from the food placed at the gravesites.[72]

An old hag (*anus annosa*) sat among girls (*puellae*) and performed a broad spectrum of magic in honor of Tacita (the quiet one). The girls could not be married during the Feralia. Tacita retained the notion of inactivity, a major characteristic of the Feralia. Good love magic, however, also produced "quietness," namely, the inability to speak. First, the *anus* marked space by blocking off access, putting three lumps of incense underneath the threshold where a mouse had dug a secret path.[73] Then Ovid describes two kinds of magic: binding magic, indicated by the *anus'* use of threads and lead, and transference magic, when a fish was substituted for a human being. Both magic types were integral elements in love magic and promised the procurement of a lover. Drops of wine, an important component in the appeasement of chthonic gods (gods of the underworld), were sprinkled on the fish. Ovid also hints at black magic, when he noted that the old woman chewed seven black beans.[74] In the end, however, she drank most of the wine and left the gathering inebriated. The whole passage ends with an old drunk woman (*ebria anus*), a seemingly humorous Ovidean twist.

The rites for Tacita move the Feralia into the private realm. Ovid introduces an etiological story about the nymph Lara, who could not hold her tongue and revealed to Juno Jupiter's desire for the nymph Juturna. Jupiter punished Lara by ripping out her tongue, the reason for Lara's new name, Muta (the mute one). Jupiter had Mercury bring Muta to the infernal marsh (*infernae paludis*), where she gave birth to twins, the Lares, deities connected to a home. Ovid then moves to describe the Caristia, not a holiday recorded in the official calendar. He assigned it to February 22nd, on which the living family members gave incense to the *boni generis* (the virtuous ones of a clan) and food to the Lares.[75] Thus, the living family members connected and strengthened their relationship with the best of their family and the land they occupied. This passage culminates in the sacrifice (prayer and pouring wine): "Hail to you (Lares), hail to you (Augustus), father of our country, best Caesar! (*bene vos, bene te, patriae pater, optime Caesar!*)"[76] Without mincing words, Ovid cast Augustus as a superior man and father to his people, thus subtly imbedding the public within the private sphere.

MARCH

March received its name from the god Mars and marked the beginning of the agricultural year.[77] Mars attained land, generated produce, and protected the *pomerium* (the religious border within which a city lay). Attainment and protection of land, that is, property, were the result of successful military campaigns. Land and people were conquered and integrated. The god of attainment and protection of land was transformed into the god of war. Rome, an agriculturally based society, became an extremely successful and efficient conqueror of territory once it began to expand and assimilate peoples. Cato the Elder recorded a prayer in his *On Agriculture* to this agricultural Mars.[78]

Lustration (*lustrum*), a purification ritual, was performed in conjunction with this prayer. The farmer sacrificed an unweaned pig (*sus*), a sheep (*ovis*), and a bull (*taurus*); this sacrifice is called *suovetaurilia*. The private lustration had an equivalent, it can be argued, in the public sphere, when the Salii performed their sacred dance on March 1st and 17th. Again, the Salii were engaged throughout the month. On March 14th, just as on February 27th, horses were consecrated, and on March 19th, weapons. On March 23rd, war trumpets were purified. There were parallel festivals in October. The horse race Equirria and the consecration of the animal of March 14th have their equivalent in the festival of the October horse on October 15th and its sacrifice on October 19th, which was followed by a lustration of arms (*armilustrium*) like the one of March 17th. The rituals of the Salii marked the beginning and the end of the fighting season, which in antiquity started in the spring and ended in the fall. Activities that involved bloodshed needed to be marked as such at the beginning and then purified in the end so as not to incur communal blood guilt. Until Augustus erected the temple of Mars Ultor on the Capitoline hill, all the sanctuaries of the war god stood outside the *pomerium,* for within this boundary military authority (*imperium*) was void.

The Vestals kindled a new fire on March 1st to symbolize the start of the new cycle. All Kalends (first days of the month) were sacred to Juno, and the temple of Juno Lucina on the Esquiline was dedicated to her on March 1, 375 BCE.[79] This dedication day became a public holiday. Women moved as a group to the Cispian side of the Esquiline Hill, where the temple was located. Pliny the Elder records that two lotus trees of great age stood in the sanctuary. Even older was the one on which the Vestals hung offerings of their hair (*HN* 16.235). If this *lotos* tree was a hackberry, the *celtis australis,* its bark might have had, like its North American version, abortifacient and menses-regulating properties. The Vestals' hair, the cutting itself indicating that they were not available as child bearers, on a tree with such properties reinforces this point.

The private and public as well as the agricultural and war-oriented festivals in honor of Mars corresponded to festivals carried out by and in honor of women. Ovid asks Mars: "Since you are more used to manly actions, tell me, why do women celebrate your holidays?" (*Fast.* 3.169–3.170). The reason, Mars answers, was that the Sabine women successfully had stopped the war between their fathers and husbands. In Ovid's poetic rendering, the Matronalia celebrated "both the Sabines' heroic motherhood and the effectiveness of the Lupercalian whipping: the motherhood that results from the Lupercalian cure is also the remedy for the divided state." DiLucia further suggests: "The lash re-enacts the violence by which [the Sabine women] were taken from their families, and which the Romans, by re-enacting it, are not allowed to forget, or forget their part in—and their reason for doing it; that is, their inability to control women." [80]

On March 15, the time of the first full moon of the new agricultural cycle, Romans celebrated the festival of Anna Perenna in her grove (*nemus*) outside the city, at the first milestone on the *Via Flaminia,* close to the river Tiber. There, a sacrifice was given to ensure a good year. [81] Men and women relaxed together, drank, and had a good time. The pitching of tents and leaf huts brings to mind the Thesmophoria, "the principal cult form for Demeter," during which women separated from their husbands and stayed in huts during the festival period. [82] The origin and character of Anna Perenna has eluded scholars so far. Wissowa strongly suggested that Anna Perenna stood for the continuing year, Anna being the feminine form of *annus* (year) and Perenna derived from *perennis* (continuing throughout the year). [83] Roman myth, however, made her an old woman from Bovilla, who provided the starving plebs with food during the struggle of the orders. Ovid, who, as so often, provides us with the most details, also tells the story of Anna deceiving Mars, who believes he has finally gotten the virgin goddess Minerva, his female equivalent, but gets old Anna instead. Since old, probably coarse, jokes and obscenities were related at the festival, Anna's ruse served as an etiological explanation. Lastly, there is Dido's sister Anna, who fled her native land and ended up in Aeneas' and Lavinia's house, only to be urged on by a Furylike Dido to throw herself into the river Numicius. [84] Ovid included every possibility.

Besides the latter two explanations that closely follow a Hellenistic etiological tradition, I do not think it far-fetched to think that Anna Perenna, whatever her origins and beginnings, was bound to the agricultural cycle as a fertility-procuring entity celebrated by men and women together outside the city in great merriment and without the usual societal restrictions. This very theme was picked up again on March 17th, when old women crowned with ivy offered sacrifice to Liber Pater, a fertility god, throughout the city, and the populace simply had fun. Liber became equated with Dionysus and his indigenous Italic characteristics overlaid with Hellenistic attributes of the Greek god. [85] Old women like the Vestals stand in opposition to the women of childbearing age and ability to bear children. Yet, through them the request for fertility was channeled.

APRIL

The ancients already contemplated the meaning of the name *April*. Some, like Varro, proposed a derivation from *aperire* (to open)[86]; others suggested a connection with Venus, that is, through the Etruscan *apru,* which might have been formed from *aprodita* (Aphrodite). This was not the name, however, that the Etruscans used for this month, which they called Cabreas. We most easily connect Venus with love, but Venus had many aspects, among them the power of creation. The late Republican poet Lucretius put it this way: "Mother of Aeneas and his descendants, delight of men and gods, nurturing Venus . . . through you every kind of living creature is conceived and springing up to live looks to the light of the sun."[87] In myth, Venus and Mars were lovers, thus providing an additional dimension to Rome's divine parentage. Both deities encapsulated procreation, fertility, and growth. Unlike the previous two months, most of April was filled with games (*ludi*), the *ludi Megalenses, Ceriales,* and *Florales.* All three *ludi* were linked to temple consecrations in honor of female fertility deities, the Great Mother (Mater Magna), Ceres, and Flora, and were introduced shortly after the Second Punic War. The *Megalenses* and *Florales* were, foremost, play productions (*ludi scaenici*). Such a clustering of "game" days is not found again until July, September, and particularly in imperial times, October and November.[88]

On April 1st, the dedication of the Venus Verticordia (Changer of Hearts) temple was remembered. The shrine was built to atone for the unchaste behavior of three Vestals at the behest of the Sibylline Books (*libri Sibyllini*) in 114 BCE.[89] Almost a century earlier, Sulpicia, the daughter of Servius Sulpicius Paterculus and the wife of Quintus Fulvius Flaccus (consul four times between 237 and 209 BCE), dedicated, together with a hundred other women, a cult statue (*simulacrum*) to the same goddess. Sulpicia, declared the most chaste among Roman women, followed the order of the Sibylline Books.[90]

In both cases, the Sibylline Books were consulted, which suggests that the original cause for the consultation was of statewide importance. In the case of 114 BCE, it is clear. Three Vestals had trespassed and violated their oath. Their trespasses affected the whole state, and appeasement was necessary. The construction and dedication of a temple was the remedy. Venus Verticordia ensured that Vestals, and Roman women in general, obeyed the rules assigned to them by society. All Vestals focused on their duties as keepers of the flame and guarantors of a flourishing state; Roman women, in general, focused on being wives, mothers, and daughters.

Sulpicia's dedication nearly a century before fell within the period of the Second Punic War. This was, without doubt, a period that required women to perform their duties properly so that the survival and continuation of the state would be guaranteed. Since there was no temple for Venus Verticordia yet, her cult statue might have been set up in the temple of Venus Obsequens or Venus Erycina.[91] The cult of Venus Erycina, a goddess from Sicily,[92] had just been introduced in this period, in fulfillment of a vow given by the dictator Fabius Maximus after the disaster of Lake Trasimine in 217 BCE. The oldest temple of Venus in Rome was the one of Venus Obsequens. It may, possibly, have stood at the southeast end of the *circus maximus* at the foot of the Aventine. Sources speak of the proceeds from fines levied on women convicted of adultery that paid for the building of this temple. This would fit very nicely with Venus' additional name Verticordia. The temple was dedicated after the Third Samnite War, that is, after 290 BCE, when great amounts of spoils had reached Rome, and as a result nine new temples were built.[93]

The unchaste behavior of two Vestals and consultation of the Sibylline Books are also part of the traditional tale that surrounds the bringing of the Great Mother (Mater Magna) from Asia Minor to Rome.[94] After Trasimene, Fabius Maximus urged the Senate to order the Sibylline Book consulted because Rome's sound defeat was due to "neglect of the traditional ceremonies, especially the taking of the auspices" (Livy 22.9.7). The *decemviri,* the ten men in charge of the Sibylline Books, concluded that the Romans, the most religious people (*religiosissima gens*) whose city was founded by auspices and augury (*auspicio augurioque*), had failed to perform the rites for Mars properly, and the relationship between humans and gods was disturbed. To correct this, the rites for Mars had to be performed anew and on a greater scale (Livy 22.9). It is also in this context that the Romans introduced Venus Erycina and Mens,[95] the personification of mind (Ov. *Fast.* 6.241–6.248).

Mid-month, April 15th, pregnant cows (*fordae*) were sacrificed and offered to Tellus (Cultivable Soil). Each *curia* (clan grouping) offered a cow in addition to the one sacrificed on the Capitol. The oldest Vestal then burned the unborn calves, and the ashes were used at the Parilia on April 21, also the foundation day of Rome (*dies natalis Romae*). The burning of the unborn calves (*fordicidia*) functioned as purification, whereas the offering itself on April 21st was to incite the soil to produce fruit, since unborn lives contained energy released into the earth to activate its production. The ashes were mixed with the congealed blood of the October horse (see below) and thrown onto burning beanstalks through which participants jumped.

The Pales were celebrated on April 21st, but what they may have been we no longer know. This festival took place privately as well as publicly. Fire and beans convey that the event was to cleanse the inhabitants. Diseases that could diminish potential prosperity were to be parried as the animate and inanimate world was readied for the coming of crops and a new generation of beings.[96] The Vestals, as guardians of the October horse's blood and the ashes of the unborn calves, were the agents in a combination purification/fertility ritual. These priestesses were the constant element that linked festivals and bridged the months.

MAY

Who or what gave May its name is unclear. Ovid's poet admits being at a loss even after the Muses, Polyhymnia, Urania, and Calliope, offered him explanations (*Fast.* 5.1–5.110). Maiestas (majesty), sings Polyhymnia, lays behind the month's name, for after the creation of the world and all the species, no god was more supreme than Maiestas. She then yielded supremacy to Jupiter. Urania's focus is on the history of early Rome, the elders (*maiores*), and the Fathers (*patres*), on whom Romulus conferred his city's government. Calliope points to the nymph Maia, the mother of Hermes, worshiped by the Arcadians. The Arcadian Evander, who founded a city on the spot where Rome eventually would stand, brought his gods, among them Maia, to Latium. If May can be linked to the linguistic root *mag-*, in a sense of increase, then one could further speculate that May was the month of growth.

The Lares *praestites* (procuring household gods) and Bona Dea *ad saxum* (Good Goddess by the Rock) were associated with the first day of May, the Kalends. These Lares were depicted, Dioscuri-like, as youths clothed in dog skins holding spears. Lucius Caesius, who minted Roman coins in 103 BCE, shows the two Lares with a dog between them. Besides being man's best friend, (considered so in ancient times too) the dog, although in a limited way, was used in purification rites, and protection and purification would be aspects that connected the dog with the Lares. It is unclear when the temple of Bona Dea *ad saxum* was consecrated, but before Augustan time, the most intense period of temple construction fell within the third century BCE. Of the two previous centuries, the majority of temples dedicated in the fourth century were to female deities (six out of seven). Festus (p. 60) connected Bona Dea Fauna with the Greek Damia, a fertility goddess. At Tarentum there was a festival in honor of Damia, the Dameia.

The Romans captured Tarentum in 272 BCE; hence, the temple of Bona Dea connected with Damia would have been constructed and consecrated after this annexation. The temple stood in the Remoria at the north end of the eastern part of the Aventine, where Remus was supposed to have taken his foundation augury. This traditional belief alone, whether true or not, makes the temple one of old age whose history is lost in the mists of the past. Wissowa argued that Fauna, the feminine form of Faunus, was the actual name of the goddess with the attribute good goddess (*bona dea*), which eventually became a proper name.[97] Faunus was equated with Pan and Silvanus, the god of fields and flocks (*arvorum pecorumque*). In whatever way Bona Dea might have been related to Faunus, it seems clear from other evidence that the goddess had something to do with fertility.[98]

The most puzzling festival in May, and one that involved the Vestals, was the throwing of "effigies" (*argei*) from the Sublician Bridge into the Tiber on May 15th, the Ides.[99] Gerhard Radke (1980) and Blaise Nagy (1985) have provided the best explanation of the Argei to date. There were twenty-seven (or thirty, if we follow Dionysius of Halicarnassus) altars (*sacella Argeorum*) within the limits of the city's original four regions, including the regions of the Suburana, Esquiline, Colline, and Palatine but excluding the Capitoline and Aventine hills. There were as many Argei effigies as altars. Plutarch states that the Argei was the "greatest ceremony of purification."[100] The ritual cycle of the Argei began in mid-March (sixteenth and seventeenth) with the *itur ad Argeos,* the procession to the twenty-seven altars. The processional way, going counterclockwise, "encircle[d] and connecte[d] the four [originally] autonomous districts: there [was] no common center."[101] The counterclockwise movement followed the cutting of a city's first furrow, the *pomerium.* There was no need for a center, for the procession's purpose was the binding together of independent communities.

Much has been written about the twenty-seven rush dolls, the effigies, and how they might have been substitutes for human sacrifice; perhaps they had been rush huts put up in March and then tossed into the Tiber in May. How huts could have looked like humans with bound hands and feet defies explanation, unless, of course, they were considered symbolic. Moreover, as long as Argei, by way of a false etymology, are thought to be Greeks (Argives), a major puzzle remains. Radke (1980 and 1993) showed that the root of the word Argei was **argha*, a cognate to the Greek *archē,* beginning, and that the procession was a rite bound to an extra-Roman calendar. The rite was not a public holiday (*feriae publicae*) but was celebrated publicly nonetheless, since it marked the beginning of the year. Nagy focused on the Vestals and noted that they "were busy in early May with the preparation of *far,* or spelt, a primitive type of grain which was, apparently, the Romans' oldest cereal." [102] Spelt was normally harvested in late June,[103] which means that the Vestals were working with premature *far.*[104] There seems to be, in my opinion, a parallel to the Fordicidia (April 15th), when unborn, in other words premature, calves were sacrificed to bring about fecundity to the community.

Nagy (1985) has a good point in thinking of the Argei as a sequel to the Lemuria (May 9th, 11th, and 13th). The *lemures* were deceased family members who were still to receive offerings (*inferiae*), but because they lacked these *inferiae,* the *lemures* were wandering ghosts with nasty tempers. The only way to keep these spirits at bay was collectively to give them something, since they were no longer bound to a family or an ancestral home. A private affair thus became a public one. The Vestals bridged these two spheres, and so their offerings, the prepared *far,* may have been to appease these homeless ghosts. At the twenty-seven altars (*sacella*), the rush dolls could have been stand-ins for humans, decoys so to speak, since *lemures* were bloodthirsty and stupid. On the other hand, they might only have been fashioned for the bridge ceremony and then functioned as scapegoats for the whole community, represented by the original four city areas.

There is still another possibility, that the dolls—Ovid uses the term *simulacra,* that is, cult representations—stood for those members of these communities that made up the city who, in death, were deprived of an ancestral link. The communal throwing of these human representations into the current of the river gave these "lost souls" a burial place, albeit an elusive one, and a link to the living. The community as a whole then provided the necessary ancestral connection that would put the *lemures* to rest. Although not directly related to the Roman world, the bulrush is used in Chinese medicine to help women with uterine fibroids and resulting infertility.[105] If the Romans too knew of the bulrush's medicinal properties, then the Vestals were again involved in an act of rejecting infertility (throwing the rush dolls from the bridge into the river) and ensuring the opposite, fertility.

JUNE

Ovid proposes three explanations in a mythological context for the name of the month.[106] The goddess Juno argued that her name was the origin for the month's name. Juventas (Youth) claimed the same. Concordia (Mutual Agreement) claimed that she had joined the Romans and Sabines; the verb *iungo* (to join) is the basis for Concordia's claim. Linguistically, Juno has nothing to do with Jupiter. The root *iun-* goes back to the Sanskrit *yuvan-* (*yun-*), young, which can be found in *iunix* (heifer) and in *iuvenis* (youth). Hence, both Juno and Juventas could serve as the name giver for the month. An Etruscan connection through the Etruscan goddess Uni cannot be, due to the lack of evidence, further developed. The explanation with Concordia, on the other hand, is a false etymology but within a historical context, the joining of Romans and Sabines. Various communities made up Rome and, along with the historical tradition, the various festivals and festival routes attest this merging. Religion was inherently conservative and retained ritual and cultic systems that coexisted within Rome's polytheistic structure. The basic tenet of the rituals and cultic actions was to ensure the goodwill of the gods.

In June, two women-oriented festivals took place, the Vestalia in honor of Vesta on June 9th and the Matralia in honor of Mater Matuta on June 11th. Women had access to the innermost sanctum of the temple of Vesta, the *penus,* when it was opened on June 7th. The *penus* was closed again on June 15th after being thoroughly swept. The rubbish was carried along the incline of the Capitoline hill to an assigned spot. Since Vesta did not have a cult representation, it is most likely that the fire in the *penus* of the temple represented the goddess. Ovid mentions in his *Tristia* (3.1.29) that Aeneas was believed to have brought the *palladium,* the founding token of Rome, to Italy and stored it in the temple of Vesta. Other authors also mention implements and sacred objects the Vestals used.[107] A Greek connection can be seen by the title or epithet Pallas, which also was a title or epithet of the goddess Athena, the Roman Minerva.

Pallas, however, was also a mythological being. He was thought to be the father of Minerva and believed to be a giant. There was also a Pallas, son of Pandion, brother of Philomela and Prokne (Ov. *Met.* 6.438–6.674), and brother of Aegeus, all very much within an Athenian context. There was Pallas the great-grandfather of Evander, and Pallas the son of Evander, which suggests an Arcadian connection. Alexandrian scholars had brought Evander to eminence in a scholarly context, but Rome's "eagerness" was not scholarly, but culturally, to have a Greek pedigree. Evander came from Pallantion in Arcadia; Pallas was a name in Evander's family; and the Roman Palatine, an alignment of Pallantion to Palatine, was the place of his settlement. Both Evander, who was in Italy before Aeneas arrived, and Aeneas gave Rome the opportunity to wedge itself into the Greek cultural continuum. Interestingly enough, both mythological figures are minor, one could even say obscure, but they are heroes and demigods nonetheless who gave

Rome its mythological founders and, above all, legitimacy in the admired Greek cultural context.

The Vestals were the keepers of the *palladium* and the *ignis perpetuus* (the perpetual fire). The festival day of Vesta, June 9, was also a special day for bakers (*pistores*). Pliny records that Romans did not have bakers until the early second century BCE.[108] Each citizen (*quiris*) prepared his own bread, but baking was women's work (*mulierum opus*). During the Vestalia, the donkey, usually bound under terrible conditions to millstones, was freed from work. The Vestals were not related to the bakers through the element of fire but through the use of wheat, the main ingredient for bread. The Vestals prepared special salted cakes (*mola salsa*) on June 9, thus ritually carrying out the socially and culturally assigned task of women.

In art, the donkey occurs most often with Dionysus-Bacchus and his entourage or with Vesta. The connection between Dionysus and the donkey is reinforced by the wanton character traits ancients attributed to this animal. If we think of rejuvenation and fertility associated with Dionysus, we can associate at least fertility with Vesta as well. Although fire was the goddess' element, which symbolized home and nourishment and guaranteed human survival, the steady, dependable, and efficient donkey involved in the milling of wheat represented fertile potency, a potency very much in the symbolic purview of the deity.

On June 11th, Mater Matuta was honored during the Matralia.[109] The goddess' name is formed from an adjective, whose basic Indo-European root is **ma,* which translates "good, timely." The Great Mother (Mater Magna), for example, displays the same combination of noun and adjective (*mater* and *magna*) as does Bona Dea (Good Goddess); the basic name and implicit meaning enlarged by a basic modifier. Mater Matuta was a mother and birth deity.[110] She was a nourisher of children. As with all Italic or indigenous gods, there is no known myth connected with her. The equation of her with the Greek Ino-Leukothea, the sister of Semele, who was the mother of Dionysus, comes to prominence in the Late Republic and especially in the Augustan age. Ino took care of Dionysus after Semele's death. Through archaeological finds (votive statuettes), Matuta can be linked to the Etruscan Uni and the Phoenician Astarte, and as such she is a sky goddess as well as a goddess of love.[111] The cosmic aspect of the goddess is emphasized by the discs that the statuettes have mounted on their heads. The disc symbolizes the sun, an aspect Lucretius explored in his poem (5.656), in which he etymologically connects Matuta through *matutina* (early light) with Aurora. A universality is embedded here, because this kind of disc can also be found on depictions of the Egyptian

Hathor (sky goddess) and Isis, for example. Both goddesses were all powerful, henotheistic mother deities who created and ruled the whole world (*kosmos*).

The temple of Mater Matuta stood in the *forum Boarium,* a market area stretching from the Aventine to the Capitoline hill. The temple structure, part of a larger complex that included a sanctuary of Fortuna, has been dated as belonging to the sixth century BCE, the traditional date of Servius Tullius' reign. The consecration of both temples (Matuta and Fortuna), the *natalis templi,* fell on June 11th. Fortuna was not only the goddess of chance, she was also goddess of prosperity and of favorable outcome; for married women that would have meant giving birth to children and surviving childbirth (*CIL* I² 60).

On the festival day, Matuta received special cakes that had been baked in earthenware pots (*testuacia*).[112] Roman women prayed for their sisters' children, the only ones who could prove to be related to the sisters' families, and then for their own. It is possible that the cognative relationship was stressed because in times when the *in manu* marriage was more common—marriage by which a Roman woman would come under the *potestas* of the family head of her husband's family—this would be one of her few ritually enforced links with her original family. Maurizio Bettini (1991) suggested a binary explanation. The cognatic relatives (*matertera* and *avunculus*) provided their nieces and nephews with warmth and affection, in contrast to the agnatic ones (*amita* and *patruus*), who were, like the father, there to discipline.[113] A *univira* (woman who has had only one husband) decorated her statue. One female slave was allowed into the temple, where she was slapped on her head and beaten and chased out by Roman women in attendance. Ovid explains that one of Ino's servants used to submit to her husband's embraces, and this is the reason for the ritualized treatment of female servants.[114]

Scullard suggests that the action might have been "a warning to others or the survival of a fertility rite?"[115] He does not, however, explain the reason for the warning, unless, of course, we are to think of Ovid's etiological explanation. The fertility-rite aspect is indeed problematic if left without explanation. Why should female slaves be privileged or singled out? Ovid's explanation stresses the slave woman as a rival to the legitimate wife. The slapping, beating, and chasing out would then be a reenactment of a punishment and a symbolic warning. If we, on the other hand, interpret the action in using the Lupercalia, the February festival during which women were struck, as a guide, then the *matronae* striking the female slave can be read as: may you be fertile—instead of me.[116]

It is possible to see this in anthropological terms as well, which postulate the constant replenishment of a strong genetic pool by the introduction of new genes. This is made possible by the existence of a societal structure porous or flexible enough to allow the procreation of members of different groups (ethnic, class, or other groups). Allowing a sexual relationship between a married Roman man and his slave women, who were after all family members, would bring new genes into Roman society. In addition, jurists described children from concubinage, who were not Roman citizens but had a recognized legal status, as "natural children." [117] A child would always receive the legal status of its mother and could be, despite being legally illegitimate, designated heir.

JULY

July is the first month for which we do not have Ovid's *Fasti,* as it ends abruptly with June. July was named in honor of Gaius Julius Caesar. Before this name change, however, July was the fifth month (Quintilis) of the civic year that began with March. The agricultural year reached its climax with the harvest in July, and so there is no agriculturally oriented celebration recorded for July. The major festival was the *ludi Apollinares* (games in honor of Apollo), which lasted from the sixth until the twelfth day of the month. Drama and music performances, introduced in consultation with the Sibylline Books in 212 BCE, were given. The origins of the prophecy prompting the festival's introduction were unauthorized utterances by a prophet named Marcius, which "the fifteen men in charge of the Sibylline Books and the ceremonies prescribed in them (*quindecimviri sacris faciundis*)" had deemed authentic. [118]

The first festival in July that involved women was the Nonae Caprotinae,[119] held on July 7th. Varro explains that in Latium women offered sacrifice to Juno Caprotina under a wild fig tree (*caprificus*).[120] Wissowa stated that the obscene meaning of the fig linked the festival with Juno, who functioned as protectress of female genitals.[121] While there is certainly a connection with fertility, it is not, as Wissowa suggested, by means of the fruit of the fig, which might or might not remind us of genitals. The antiquarian Varro gives us a little hint when women, he says, "use a branch from the wild fig tree," a comment upon which Varro, unfortunately, did not expound further. Horticulturalists know that wild fig trees are needed to pollinate the cultured fig in order to bring about the production of edible fruit, since the fruit-producing fig tree has only male flowers. The wild fig tree, in contrast, has male and female flowers. Using a branch from a wild fig tree and touching a cultured tree for pollination may have been what lay behind Varro's statement. It is worth noting that in Rome's foundation myth, the fig tree plays an important role as the place where the she-wolf found the twins, Romulus and Remus, and suckled them until they were found by Faustulus, the shepherd.

Plutarch offers a more detailed version on these Nonae (*Rom.* 29). He relates the story of *poplifugia* (flights of the people), which the calendar set for July 5. The story is to serve as a historical explanation for the festival. Rome, still weak after the Gallic invasion, came under attack by its neighbors. A female slave named Philotis (or Tutola) devised a ruse that brought victory to the Romans. She and other slave women, dressed as respectable Roman matrons, went to meet the enemy. Once the attackers were asleep, the slave women signaled the Romans with a burning wild fig-tree branch. The Romans attacked and thus overcame their enemy.[122] In commemoration of this feat, Romans called the day Caprotinae, the Nones of July, from the wild fig tree (*caprificus*). On this day, Roman men "feasted women outside the city in huts made of fig-tree branches."

At the Athenian festival, the Thesmophoria, in honor of Demeter, women stayed in huts and slept on willow branches. The willow "was supposed to work as a strong antaphrodisiac and hence to prevent all sorts of undesirable sexual impulses."[123] For three days married Greek women suspended their socially assigned roles, performing neither wifely nor motherly duties and were, in fact, transported back to their virginal, premarital, state, which was "the nymphal prelude to marital fecundity."[124] They recaptured the moment of fecundity potential in this fall festival; symbolically they were like the fallow fields ready to bring forth the new crops the following year. The Caprotinae also had an element of reversal. Female slaves pretended to be Roman matrons. Plutarch also reports that the slave women "ran about and played, after which they stroke and threw stones at one another, in token that on that earlier day they assisted the Romans and shared with them in their battle."[125] In essence, the slave women were doing men's work. But because they were slaves, their actions were in no way threatening. The actions were further circumscribed within a ritual.

Plutarch's "flights of the people," however, remain mysterious, though he explained it (*Rom.* 29) as the flight of the Roman people after Romulus disappeared. The first king's disappearance brought such confusion to his people that they ran out, calling names like Marcus, Lucius, and Gaius, typical Roman names. In commemoration of this, Romans gave sacrifice in the "Goat's Marsh" on the Nonae Caprotinae. Plutarch made the linguistic link between the word for female goat (*capra*), the place of sacrifice (*caprae palus*), and the *Nonae*, whose epithet Caprotinae could also be written as Capratinae. It is assumed that the "Goat's Marsh" was the lowest point of the *campus Martius*, the basin where Hadrian's Pantheon stands. The voting area, the *Saepta*, was to the south of the *campus*. The historian Livy has Romulus review his army before his disappearance.[126] The *campus Martius* outside the city limits, and especially the *Saepta*, was where a *contio*, such as an army review, traditionally took place. All this is, of course, anachronistic. There would be no women in the *contio*, nor would the people have to run out, since they were already outside the city.

It is only Ovid who points to the *Capreae*, the Goat's Marsh, as the exact place of Romulus' disappearance.[127] February 17th, the day dedicated to Quirinus, who was understood as the deified Romulus, followed two days after the Lupercalia. There is a resonance between February, the month of cleansing and making ready, and July, the month of harvest. In July, the thongs of a billy-goat hide used during the Lupercalia to ensure procreation and fertility brought results in the form of a harvest. The male goat embodied the procreative force.[128] The word *capreae* points to a female goat, which can be understood as connected to a woman's sex life. Again, fertility and procreation is the theme. Moreover, Juno Caprotina of Latium thus became connected to Juno Sospita of Lanuvium, whose iconographic marker is a goat hide over her shoulders. The Lanuvian as well as the Latin Juno were linked to fertility.

On July 19th and 21st, Romans celebrated the Lucaria.[129] Both days were public holidays (*NP = dies nefasti publici*). All we know about the celebration is that it took place in a grove located between the Tiber and the *Via Salaria*. As with the *poplifugia*, the Gallic sack was thought to be the origin of this festival, in this case because the battle of the Allia had taken place on July 18th. Wissowa suggested a possible connection between the Lucaria and the Neptunalia, a festival in honor of Neptune, which was celebrated on July 23rd. Bulls were sacrificed and leaf huts built to shelter the festival participants from the July sun. The poet Horace relates the story of the merry character of the *Neptunalia* (*Carm.* 3.28) but, in essence, we know nothing about the purpose of this boisterous event. Was the Neptunalia a celebration of the harvest not yet complete? Was it a festival to avert water shortage?

Two goddesses, Salacia and Venilia, were joined to Neptune in this festival; unfortunately, nothing much is known of either goddess. Salacia was most often connected with *salum* (salt) and the sea, while Venilia was thought of as a nymph or identified as Venus.[130] Fresh water is, of course, indispensable for crops. Venus and the sacrifice of bulls, the premier animal to embody fertility, have an agricultural context. Even Salacia points in that direction, for if we follow Varro,[131] we see the etymology of her name based in *salax* (eager for sexual intercourse). As long as we think of Neptune solely as the god of the (salt) sea, a problem remains. The Romans were a land-based people who came to seafaring late,[132] and it could be that Neptune was originally a god of (fresh) water sources.

July 25th was a public holiday for the goddess Furrina. This goddess had her own priest, a *flamen,* and the festivities took place in a grove on the slope of the Janiculan hill. Cicero associated Furrina with Furia (fury) and also speaks of a shrine not far from his birthplace in Arpinum. Plutarch thought that she was a nymph.[133] An inscription from Rome (*CIL* VI 36802) records *Nymphae Furrinae* and confirms Plutarch's understanding. A temple of the Syrian god Jupiter Heliopolitanus was built in the grove sometime in the mid part of the first century CE.[134] This Jupiter's iconography (thunderbolts on his cloak, bulls flanking his throne, a basket [*kalathos*] on his head, and wheat ears and lightning bolts in his left hand) make him a god of weather and agriculture.

It seems that all the festivals in July were held in groves outside the city and began in times so ancient that their origins and purposes were unknown even to Varro. Conjecturally, one can say that these festivals were agriculturally based, celebrating the potential of Nonae Caprotinae (and possibly the Furrinalia) or the rejoicing in fecundity (Neptunalia). These festivities, however, took place outside the city, making them, in a sense, liminal. In Greco-Roman mythology, sexual encounters between gods and humans take place in liminal spaces. Mars and Rhea Silvia, the parents of Romulus and Remus, for example, met when Rhea Silvia was out fetching water at a spring.[135] She had left the civilized sphere, the city, where she was protected and impervious. The festivals in July may have recreated an environment in which men and women could meet unimpeded by social and political constraints.

AUGUST

Harvesting and storing were the primary agricultural activities in the month of August. While religious activities in July took place in groves outside the city and the *pomerium,* in August there was a movement back toward the city and cultivated land. The religious rites took place "in the neighborhood of the Aventine Hill, the *circus maximus,* and the bank of the Tiber, which . . . was in earliest times part of the cultivated land nearest the city."[136] The two festivals of the oldest order, the Consualia and the Opiconsivia, were strongly grounded in the agricultural cycle. Both celebrated the end of the harvest season.

On August 21st, the Romans honored Consus, god of harvested fruit, in general, and wheat, in particular. The god's name is believed to be related to either the verb *condere* (to put, store up, found) or the noun *consilium* (deliberation, counsel, advice).[137] Ancient writers preferred the latter explanation,[138] which appears in connection with the rape of the Sabine women, although the first explanation (*condere*) is more convincing. The original focus of the festival was on storing agricultural produce. Ovid mentions Consus in the month of March, when Mars recounts the heroic action of the Sabine-turned-Roman wives. The poet also noted that the god spoke on the Consualia, the very festival during which Romulus' men snatched the Sabine women.[139] The Consualia featured horse races. Since the horse was associated with Neptune's Greek equivalent, Poseidon, this was reason enough to think the festival was in honor of the equestrian Neptune (Livy 1.9.6).

It is another ancient writer, Dionysius of Halicarnassus, whose description of the festival gives us information that leads us toward an understanding of the Consualia as a harvest-related occasion. He described the festival as follows:

> A subterranean altar, erected in the vicinity of the hippodrome (*circus maximus*), is uncovered by removal of the earth around it and honored with sacrifices and burnt first fruits and a course run both by yoked and unyoked horses. The god to whom these honors are given, the Romans call Consus, being the same, according to some who render his name into our language, as Poseidon Seisichthon (the Earthshaker); and they say that this god was honored with a subterranean altar because he holds the earth.[140]

Dionysius then addressed the problem of the equation of Consus with Poseidon the Earthshaker. He learned from hearsay of another tradition that understood the Consualia as a festival with horse races for Poseidon. A subterranean altar to a divine guardian of hidden counsels, whose name could not be uttered, was added later. This version tried to reconcile the combination of Consus and Poseidon within the traditional Greco-Roman Olympian system of gods. Consus did not have a place in it and thus was the odd god out, although he, rather than Poseidon, was originally honored. After all, the festival was called Consualia and did not have a name based on Poseidon or Neptune. Scullard suggested that the connection with horses "may well have developed during the Etruscan period at Rome, since the Etruscans were much given to horse races, and they may have associated his underground altar with the spirits of the dead and the horse was regarded as funerary animal."[141] If we recall, however, that in Greek, Plutos, the Enricher, is another name for the god of the underworld, then we are back in the world of agriculture. Indeed, the dead were buried and believed to inhabit a space below the arable earth, and from below sprouted plants and crops year after year.

Consus seems a very old, pre-Etruscan deity. The *flamen* (priest) in charge of the Consualia was the *flamen Quirinalis,* and the Vestal Virgins were in attendance.[142] Because the priest of Quirinus and the Vestal Virgins participated in the ceremony, agriculture and the fertility of arable land seem to have been the focal points of the Consualia. The covered subterranean altar suggests earth hiding its fruits. Then, as the subterranean altar was uncovered, the earth opened up and produced sustenance. Finally, first fruits were burned in a thanksgiving for a successful harvest, for which there was never a guarantee. Bad weather and pests often destroyed crops and left people without food. It is not surprising then that the Consualia took place in an ambiguous place, neither city nor agrestial land, where the city abutted arable land outside the city limits. The altar was located at the southeast end of the *spina* of the *circus maximus,* where the first turning post was placed.[143] Even the Latin word for turning post (*meta*) connotes a boundary, a limit.

The circus structure, as we know it, was put into place only at the time of Julius Caesar.[144] Originally, the circus was an open area between the Aventine and Palatine hill, where wooden, removable structures were set up for races after the harvest season. Religious traditions change gradually, and even when a permanent structure like the *circus maximus* was built, the subterranean altar in honor of Consus remained. Furthermore, if Poseidon's name, as some scholars have suggested,[145] means "wheat husband" (the Greek word *posis* meaning "husband" or "lord" and "de" like *De*-meter referring to "wheat"), then the Romans' equation of their Neptune, the Greek Poseidon, with Consus reveals a rationale, which was connected to agriculture.

Another harvest-related festival took place four days after the Consualia. On August 25th, the goddess Ops (Plenty) was honored during the

Opiconsivia at her shrine in the *regia,* which was located "just outside the *forum Romanum* between the *Sacra via* and the temple of Vesta."[146] Besides the sanctuary of Ops, to which only the Vestal Virgins and a public priest (*sacerdos publicus*), whom Wissowa[147] identified as the *pontifex maximus,* had access,[148] there was also a shrine of Mars inside the *regia.* The name of the festival, Opiconsivia, makes clear that Ops and Consus were thought to stand in close relationship to each other.[149] The verb *condere* includes the activity of putting (sowing) and even storing of the harvested crop. A filled storage room signaled a good harvest.

Ops represented the positive outcome of sowing of which the filled storage room was visible proof. It could be said that the festival for Ops concluded the agricultural cycle. Although this is a wrong inference, it is not surprising that the second-century CE grammarian Festus (pp. 203–204) understood Ops as *terra* (earth), "who supplied the human race with all its resources (*omnes opes*)."[150] Scullard proposed that the Ops sanctuary in the *regia* "may well correspond to the store-cupboard (*penus*) of the king (later the *rex sacrorum*); it housed the fruits of the earth and was tended by 'his daughters,' the Vestal Virgins."[151] Without any reference to primary sources, this is only a hypothesis, but one that is not necessary. The Consualia and the Opiconsivia were thanksgiving harvest festivals. Arable land had successfully produced the crops necessary for human survival. The Vestals, the premier guarantors of the state's fecundity, attended both festivals.

SEPTEMBER

September, November, and December do not feature religious festivals of the types we are analyzing in the context of the Roman calendar and the involvement of women. The harvest was in, and the winter months precluded agricultural activities. The Roman Games (*ludi Romani*) in honor of Iuppiter Optimus Maximus (the Best and Greatest Jupiter) encompassed half of the month of September, from the 5th to the 19th. This Jupiter's temple on the Capitoline hill was believed to have been finished under Tarquin the Proud, Rome's last king. The temple was dedicated on September 13th. A nail was hammered into a sidewall of the *cella Iovis* (inner sanctuary of Jupiter) annually (Livy 7.3), indicating a new administrative year (*saeculum*). Triumphs were celebrated under the auspices of Jupiter.[152] The games that were originally held in connection with a triumph became, over time, the independent *ludi Romani.*

OCTOBER

As in September, Romans celebrated a festival in honor of Jupiter in October. Two horse chariots competed in the *campus Martius* on October 15th, after which the *flamen Martialis* (priest of Mars) sacrificed the right-hand horse of the victorious pair at the altar of Mars in the *campus*.[153] Wissowa interpreted the sacrifice as a thanksgiving for a successful campaign and an expiatory sacrifice for spilled blood and that the *equus bellator* (war horse) was sacred to the god of war, Mars. For that reason, one of the victorious horses was sacrificed to him.[154] Two groups, the inhabitants of the *Via Sacra,* and the Subura fought for the severed *cauda* (tail or penis) and the horse head. It seems that whatever each group won, either the *cauda* or head, they affixed it to a prominent marker in their respective area. When victorious, the Subura group fastened the pieces to the *turris Mamilia* (Mamilian Tower), "a familiar landmark [that] could be regarded as the heart of the Subura."[155] Richardson suggests that the contending for the horse's head was "not a religious ritual but an impromptu donnybrook."[156] Since this donnybrook was repeated on an annual basis, there is certainly a question about this assertion that it was impromptu.

The dismembered horse virtually covered the area from the altar of Mars in the *campus Martius,* outside the *pomerium,* to the *turris Mamilia* in the Subura and the *regia* at the eastern end of the *forum Romanum.* The two groups competing for the head and the *cauda* seem to represent very old population areas of Rome. The Subura area, extending north, west, and south of the Esquiline Hill, corresponded to one of Rome's four original tribes, the *tribus Suburana*.[157] The *regia* and *Via Sacra* were part of the *forum Romanum,* which Tacitus claims (*Ann.* 12.24) Titus Tatius added. Dionysius of Halicarnassus labeled this *forum* the political center of Rome (3.67.5).[158]

The affixing of the horse's tail or its head[159] on the most prominent marker of the Subura can be interpreted as a trophy. The horse head was an excellent indicator for the extraordinary (and expensive) sacrifice to Mars. Besides a military aspect, however, there was an aspect of fertility, since the other part of the horse, the *cauda,* was carried to the *regia,* where the blood from the *cauda* was allowed to drip onto the sacred hearth. The Vestals kept some of this blood for use at the Parilia on April 21st, which was also the foundation day (*dies natalis*) of Rome. This, one could argue, had to do with fertility, the agricultural aspect. Blood could purify, but it also meant life, a characteristic that would have been even more pronounced if the *cauda* was the horse's genitals. The horse, partitioned and distributed, comprised a duality, as did Mars, the military and agricultural god. The same could be said of Rome: it was an agriculturally based, militaristic society, and the actions (in this case, performed by the Vestals in a religious context) make clear that women were instrumental in maintaining Rome.

NOVEMBER AND DECEMBER

As with September, the remaining two months of the year did not feature any women's festivals. The agricultural cycle, and thus their involvement in the annual religious cycle, had come to an end in July, at the height of the harvest season. The focus of the year's remaining months was on retention of, and setting the stage for, a new cycle of agricultural and human productivity. Women would again emerge as key participants in the new year, when preparatory rites involving purification and appeasement would start a new sequence of life-giving and life-sustaining festivals. In particular, February and July mark the beginning and the end of more intensive female participation in Rome's annual ritual cycle.

THREE

THE MAKING OF ROME[*]

This chapter focuses on divine beings that were instrumental in shaping Rome and its Empire, in particular, its self-definition. While territorial acquisition was men's business, the preservation of Empire was linked to female entities, among them the Sibyls, the Great Mother (Mater Magna), and Isis. When the Roman state was faced with a portent indicating a rupture in the reciprocal relationship between the Romans and their gods, the Senate instructed the priestly college in charge of the Sibylline Books, which consisted for most of Rome's history of the fifteen men, the *quindecimviri sacris faciundis,* to consult the books. The interpretation of the sayings guided Rome's political elite in the appeasement process. In this way, sociopolitical problems were transferred onto the religious sphere, because religion was the unifier that brought people together to perform actions as a group. New gods and cults were integrated in this process of communal appeasement. Cults thus introduced were performed in Greek manner, which meant that the original mode of execution was not changed. In the period of Rome's advancement to become the premier political and economic power of the Mediterranean, in other words, at the height of Rome's need to define itself vis-à-vis a cultural power such as Greece, appeasing the gods took the form of integration of new religious cults.

The introduction of the Mater Magna (Great Mother) came on behalf of the Sibylline Books. The narrative surrounding the introduction, however, also shows the Romans consulting the Delphic Oracle, Greece's most prestigious oracular shrine. By the end of the third century BCE, before Greece's actual political subjugation to Rome, the Romans strove to define themselves within a Greek cultural context. Mater Magna linked Rome to its Trojan heritage but, at the same time, emphasized as well as encapsulated the unique relationship Rome had with its Greek cultural heritage. The Romans embraced Greek culture, and while this embrace generated

Latin literature, it never incited a redefinition of the political Rome. Troy and Rome shared the same story, connecting them to Greece, namely, the Trojan War. The Mater Magna reaffirmed the Trojan connection, and the steps of her temple on the Palatine served as seats for theater productions. Rome, the political hegemon of the Mediterranean, had found its own literary voice.

The goddess Isis, originally an Egyptian goddess, was, together with her Ptolemaic consort, Sarapis, a guardian deity of the imperial household (*domus Augusta*) and provider of an etiological explanation of dynasty. Often, in secondary literature, the cult of Isis is associated with Romans, especially the lower classes, who were easily swayed to un-Roman behavior. As long as the cult was deemed unlawful and thus, in a sense, un-Roman, the Senate could lash out against cult adherents in times of social or political duress. The notion of the cult's un-Romanness was fueled by the emperor Augustus' strong political stance against Marc Antony and Cleopatra VII, who were cast as the personification of Rome's antithesis of the period, Egypt. Egypt was the exotic other, a country of ancient monuments that spoke of political power beyond historically tangible times. Egypt, however, was also the major producer of wheat in the Mediterranean, and whoever controlled it, controlled Rome's food supply.

Augustus' publicly expressed view of Egypt, however, did not reflect his personal opinion. He was the one who set into motion the development of Isis and Sarapis into gods connected to the imperial household. Augustus overcame Marc Antony and Cleopatra at Actium in 31 BCE. A year later, after Cleopatra's suicide, Egypt became the personal province of Augustus, where he was pharaoh. Augustus brought Alexandria, Hellenistic Greece, to Rome. He used the architecture to establish a link with Ptolemy, general of Alexander the Great and ruler of Egypt after Alexander's death, who had chosen Sarapis, an oracular god of Memphis and consort of Isis, as his dynasty's guardian god. Ptolemy set himself apart from his heroic predecessor who had embraced the Egyptian ram god, Amun Ra.

The temple of Sarapis in Alexandria, the Serapeum, was part of the palace structure and housed the famous library of Alexandria. A sarcophagus containing the body of Alexander was said to have been in this temple-library structure.[1] Augustus connected his villa on the Palatine hill to the temple of Apollo with a portico representing the mythological Danaids, Egyptian-born Greeks. The Greeks had integrated Egypt into their ideological landscape through the gadfly-tormented Io, thought to be Isis, who shed her bovine shape in Egypt when she married the pharaoh. Hellenized Egypt, through Alexandria, found its way to Rome, where it was integrated into the fabric of Rome's founding location. Even more, Augustus moved the storage place of the Sibylline Books to the temple of Palatine Apollo. Again, in the shaping of and the symbolic retelling of Rome, Hellenistic culture played a crucial role.

SIBYLS AND SIBYLLINE BOOKS

Sibyls were divinely inspired women, and their prophesies were highly esteemed (Figure 3.1). The ancients thought them "with gods" (*entheoi*). Varro counted ten Sibyls. The first and oldest was the Persian; the youngest, the Sibyl at Tibur.[2] Persia, forever the nemesis of Greco-Roman city-states, featured prominently throughout antiquity as an accepted source of millennia-old traditions linked to astrology and astronomy. The most prominent oracular shrine for the Greeks, and later for the Romans, was that of Apollo at Delphi. [. . .] The Romans, using Greek explanations, linked Rome's founding to prophetic sayings and to Apollo. The Greek poet Lycophron, about whom nothing is known except that he wrote a poem called *Alexandra*, has Cassandra, a daughter of Priam, Troy's last ruler, prophesy the coming of a new Troy, Rome. Cassandra had refused Apollo's advances, and the god's punishment was that no one could understand the meaning of her prophesies. In the *Alexandra*, the Trojan princess recalls the "memory of ancient oracles" and proclaims that "Trojans must wander till they were forced to eat their tables" and will "found their city where they encountered a white sow with thirty piglets."[3] Dionysius of Halicarnassus has Aeneas receive the same two-part prophesy from "a Sibylla, a local nymph, who was a prophetess dwelling in the red soil of Ida," and then once more from Zeus at Dodona, the oldest Greek oracular site.[4] Dionysius had turned Lycophron's prophesying Cassandra into a Sibyl.

Vergil separates these two prophecies in his *Aeneid*. The greatest of the furies, Celaeno, inspired by Apollo, speaks of the tables.[5] At the moment of the prophesy's fulfillment, however, Aeneas does not recall Celaeno's prophecy but his father's arcane sayings about destinies (*fatorum arcana*).[6] Helenus, one of Cassandra's brothers, relates the prophecy of the white sow and the thirty piglets to Aeneas when he and his companions land at Buthrotum in Epirus.[7] The river-god Tiber, who urges Aeneas to seek out Evander, a Greek from Epirus who had settled in what was to become Rome, reveals the meaning of the white sow and thirty piglets.[8] Aeneas' son Ascanius is to found Alba Longa thirty years after he, Aeneas, saw an outstretched sow with her piglets. The historian Livy reports that Evander's

FIGURE 3.1.
Sibyl, 1726, by Sebastiano Conca, Italian (Roman), 1680–1764. Oil on
Canvas. 96.3 × 85.7cm. Photograph © 2007, Museum of Fine Arts,
Boston, Gift of William Everett. Inv. No. 88.342.

mother, Carmenta, was thought divine. People revered her as a prophetess
before the actual Sibyl came to Italy.[9]

Carmenta was, like the Camenae, a water nymph. Ancient sources
stressed the chthonic nature of water, and because of this, it had mantic
powers.[10] There was also a perceived linguistic link between the name Carmenta and *carmen,* which we translate most often as "poem." Its primary
meaning, however, is "ritual utterance" or "magic spell." [. . .] The Cumaean

Sibyl, the fourth in Varro's list and the one who plays such a pivotal role in Vergil's epic, appeared during the regal period, which was not much more tangible than the time of pre-foundation. By the third century BCE and then once more in the Augustan period (the Principate), however, the various narrative traditions solidified as they evolved into "explanations" of a chronologically coherent past.

Ancient writers perpetuated this consistent chronology of events. For instance: The Augustan elegiac poet Tibullus has a Sibyl, either the Marpessian (Hellespontine) or the Cumaean, describe Aeneas' coming to Italy and the foundation of the *imperium Romanum*.[11] The Sibyl had been connected to Rome's regal period (the time of the Etruscan Tarquin). At the time of Augustus, Campania (Cumae) as well as the Hellespontine region (Troy and Asia Minor) had been under Roman control for generations. Tibullus' artistic innovation was that he moved the foundation prophesy from a classical Greek literary context to a Roman one.

Varro, our earliest source regarding the introduction of the Sibylline Books to Rome, relates the story of an old woman who tried to sell king Tarquin nine books of Sibylline oracles.[12] In his version, this old woman was the Cumaean Sibyl, who, in all the other sources, remains nameless. Tarquin rebuked the woman twice. Each time, she burned three of the nine books. In the end, augurs convinced the king to purchase the remaining three books. He did and had to pay the initial nine-book price for them—no bargain here. Asked to take great care of them, Tarquin chose two men of distinction (*duumviri*)[13] and two public slaves to guard his acquisition. The books were deposited in the temple of Jupiter Optimus Maximus, Rome's premier god.[14]

A Marcus Acilius (or Atilius) is the only *duumvir* (one of the two men in charge of the Sibylline Books) recorded for the regal period. The reason we know about him is due to his failure as a guardian and the example he became. He secretly copied some of the text, a violation of his charge. For this wrongdoing, he received the death penalty. Acilius (Atilius) was sewn up in a sack and thrown into the sea; the same punishment the ancient law code prescribed for parricide. Since the Acilii and Atilii were plebeian families, they could not have held office during the regal period.[15] It eludes us who these original guardians of the books might have been. The only thing that can be said with certainty is that they, like the *duumviri* (two men), *decemviri* (ten men), and *quindecimviri sacris faciundis* (fifteen men in charge of the Sibylline Books and the ceremonies prescribed in them)[16] of later times, must have been members of leading Roman families. The Sibylline sayings (the *oracula Sibyllina* recorded in the Greek language), arranged in acrostic hexameter texts, and their interpretation were to be kept secret, as Acilius' story taught.[17]

The reported Sibylline instructions could be horrific (bury a Greek and a Gaul alive to avert a foreign invasion),[18] but most often they prompted the introduction of a foreign god and the building of a temple. The introduction of new cults, those performed according to Greek rite (*Graeco ritu*),[19] depended on the college's interpretation of the Sibylline Books. The most dramatic introduction of a cult at the behest of the Sibylline Books was that of the Great Mother from Ida (Mater Magna Idaea) in the Troad, Aeneas' home region, at the end of the Second Punic War. The Romans were urged to fetch this goddess, for her presence in Rome would bring an end to the struggle with Carthage.[20] The Romans did as instructed, but they also double-checked with the oracle in Delphi. Rome's victory over Carthage occurred in 201 BCE, one year after the goddess' arrival in Rome.[21] As a consequence of this victory, Rome's hegemonial supremacy over the Mediterranean world was firmly established. Although the war had turned in Rome's favor already in the late 210s BCE, historical tradition linked the final triumph to the coming of the Great Mother. The Sibylline Books had given instructions, the Roman people carried them out, and victory was attained.

The Roman elite was responsible for the consultation of the Sibylline Books, the visitation to the oracle at Delphi, and the transfer of the goddess to Rome. The early war period had been disastrous for the Romans, whom Hannibal had outmaneuvered. The balance between the leaders and the led within Roman society became strained. Because any prophecy questioning the status quo would have been perceived as playing into the hands of the enemy, the Senate ordered an investigation into prophetic books. This inquiry took place in 213 BCE. The Senate was specifically interested in the freely circulating and unauthorized versions that could potentially undermine the strained status quo. In 212 BCE, a two-volume set of prophecies authored by a Marcius was handed over to them. Using Homeric metaphors, Marcius prophesied the battle of Cannae in 216 BCE, a catastrophic moment for the Romans. He predicted Roman success if annual games in honor of Apollo were held and a sacrifice was given. When the Senate asked the men in charge of the Sibylline Books to consult the collection regarding this prediction, the books ordered the same.[22] The unauthorized version had anticipated the disaster; thus, Marcius' collection was judged genuine and incorporated into the existing set of sayings. This is an illustration of how the commission in charge of the Sibylline Books could add newly found sayings to the existing corpus if they were judged to be authentic, that is, if they proved to be true in their prediction. Of course, Marcius could have introduced his prophesy after the fact; there was after all a gap of four years, but authenticity was not bound to a correct prediction of an event. Once the commission had been accepted and agreed upon, any prophecy was genuine.

Although the history of the Sibylline Books is obscure and the books themselves were hardly authentic, they played a crucial role in the legitimization of religious innovations and the formation of Roman religion. The Roman Senate ordered the consultation of these books during political crises to find alleviation from predicaments that had an impact on Roman society. In general, a political crisis was linked to a religious failing that warranted remedy so that Rome could continue to prosper. Even the most skeptical Roman knew and acted within the understanding that religious discipline (*disciplina*) was crucial for the well-being of the state (*salus publica*) and that accurate religious practice (*religio*) provided it. The underlying mythological, albeit actual, belief was that Rome was founded by *auspicio augurioque* (by auspice and augury), which generated a contract between Rome and the gods, above all Jupiter, and that binary reciprocal mechanisms were at work. Thus, the relationship between the divine and the human sphere, the Roman Senate and the Roman people (*senatus populusque Romanus*), was defined. Society, the web of human interactions and interrelations, is a nonmaterial component of culture. "Religion legitimates social institutions by bestowing upon them ultimately valid ontological status, that is, by locating them within a sacred and cosmic frame of reference." [23] Religious rituals remind society of its ontological definition and legitimization. They also link the changing present with a constant, that is, with the timeless sacred and cosmic frame of reference.

Ancient sources report that when Sulla marched on Rome (83 BCE), the temple of Iuppiter Optimus Maximus burned down and, with it, the *original* Sibylline Books. [24] A senatorial commission was instructed in 76 BCE, after Sulla's dictatorship, to put together a new collection of Sibylline sayings. A committee was sent to the Greek East, but not to Cumae in Campania, the home of a local and one of the ten famous Sibyls. The best collection of utterances (consisting of 1,000 lines) was found on Samos. [25] None of the surviving sources speaks of a deception, because the college in charge of the Sibylline Books judged the sayings from Samos to be authentic. [26]

The search for this new set of prophetic utterances had been a legitimate and authorized task. As in earlier times, this new collection prophesied most accurately. In 18 BCE, when Augustus wanted to move the Sibylline Books into Rome's newest temple of Apollo, which was opportunely situated next to his home on the Palatine, the books were deemed "damaged by age."[27] Augustus ordered the college to make new copies. While doing so, a passage was found that prescribed the *ludi saeculares,* games that celebrated the Empire and Augustus' achievements. There is no indication in the sources that this particular passage might have been a contemporary interpolation, a blatant manipulation, to support the emperor's decision. But even as early as 18 BCE, when Augustus' position was not as secure as it would eventually become, no one dared to challenge Augustus on a religious point.

As Caesar's heir, Augustus was accumulating all powers in and around himself, even symbolically appropriating them. His private house on the Palatine nicely demonstrates this. Next to his house complex, which included the villa of his wife Livia, was the temple of Victoria. This structure had housed the Great Mother from the Troad (represented by a sacred stone) until her temple was built and dedicated in 191 BCE. Below the western corner of the Palatine was the Lupercal with the sacred fig tree (*ficus Ruminalis*), where the she-wolf suckled Rome's twin founders, Romulus and Remus. Augustus had surrounded himself with the symbols of Trojan ancestry, Roman foundation, and the victory over the new Isis, Cleopatra VII, and her Dionysian lover, Marc Antony, at Actium in 31 BCE. The victor Augustus, who had embraced cerebral Apollo in contrast to Mark Antony's emotional Dionysus, made the Palatine the center of the world. By a senatorial decree an altar and a statue of Vesta were placed at the end of Augustus' house, opposite the new temple of Apollo. They were dedicated on April 28, the festival day of Vesta, in 12 BCE, after Augustus became the high priest of Roman religion (*pontifex maximus*). The goddess, whose fire was never let go out (*ignis inextinctus*), symbolized the state. Augustus was Rome's central and ultimate political force, as his home was the center of the Roman Empire.[28]

During the reign of Augustus' successor Tiberius, a *quindecimvir* tried to revitalize the practice of consultation after the Tiber had flooded,[29] but to no avail. During the Republican period, the Books had been consulted over fifty times,[30] in contrast to imperial times, when the books were rarely consulted. The Senate had faded into rubber-stamping oblivion, Roman religion was established, and internal strife had ceased under Augustus' leadership. A secure Rome ruled the world. Famine, plague, and prodigies, indicators of political strain, no longer presented themselves as they did during the Republican period. When Rome experienced a crisis in 19 CE, chiefly brought about by Tiberius' designated successor, Germanicus, a burning of unauthorized books was ordered.[31] Like wandering astrologers, prophets, and dream interpreters, prophecies could upset the established order and societal stability. To prevent such perturbation, unauthorized books were burned, and prophesying persons were killed, exiled, or placed under the direct control of the sole ruler, who alone needed to know what the future held in store.

Nero had the Sibylline Books consulted in 64 CE, after a devastating fire destroyed Rome.[32] The destruction gave him a chance to build his dream palace, which also fueled the belief that he had the fire set. After Nero, the sources are silent until the short reign of Julian the Apostate (361–363 CE). He put it to the college to find out whether the auspices were in favor of a campaign against Persia. The answer was negative, but Julian was already on his way. While Julian invaded Persia in the spring of 363 and was killed, the temple of Apollo on the Palatine burned down. The Sibylline Books were saved, only to be destroyed a generation later by Stilicho, the Christian general in charge of the West. The omen of 363 CE had come to pass, and even Julian's attempted pagan reforms could not prevent Christianity's triumph. Prudentius, known as the Christian Vergil, noted that the Sibylline Books would no longer prophesy.[33] The pagan Sibyl fell silent as the Judeo-Christian one began to speak. Like her pagan sister, she spoke Greek.

Greek culture, however, cannot completely veil an original Etruscan aspect. Scholars of Roman religion such as Wissowa discussed the Etruscan discipline (*Etrusca disciplina,* the inspection of livers, interpretation of lightning and unnatural phenomena) in connection with the Sibylline sayings. If they were thought not altogether different,[34] the conclusion was that the *disciplina* sought to explain the phenomena while the books suggested expiation.[35] Indeed this is true. Ancient sources make it clear that the Sibylline Books were a collection of nothing but Greek oracular sayings. Since 1,000 lines were discovered on Samos immediately after Sulla's dictatorship, this certainly is accurate. Nevertheless, one can argue that they were grafted onto an Etruscan root that Greek layering had obscured until the Etruscan root eventually disappeared. In contrast to the Greco-Roman religious system of rituals and cultic actions, Etruscan religion was one of books.[36] The surviving sources speak of three types: the Books of Divination (*libri haruspicini*), Books of Lightning (*libri fulgurales*), and Books of Rituals (*libri rituales*). The second-century CE grammarian Festus noted:

> *Rituales* are called the books of the Etruscans, in which is described, by which rite cities are founded, altars, shrines are sanctified, by which religious sanction walls, by which legal sanction gates (are sanctified), in what way tribes, *curiae,*[37] centuries[38] are divided, armies are set up, arranged, and other things of this kind pertinent to war and peace.[39]

There were also subcategories to the books of rituals, such as the explanations of prodigies (*ostentaria*) and the books of things destined by fate (*libri fatales*).[40]

Throughout his history, Livy uses the terms Books of Fate and Sibylline Books interchangeably. The most telling episode can be found in Book 5, which deals with the siege of Veii, an Etruscan city, and ends with the destruction of Rome by the Gauls in 390 BCE. Livy ends this book with a speech by Camillus, the Roman general who had brought Veii to its knees in 396 BCE. The historian notes that Camillus particularly moved his audience when he touched upon issues of religion.[41] Rome's strength was its religion and its beneficial reciprocal relationship with the gods. In the summer, three years before Veii's destruction, a grave pestilence afflicted all living creatures. The Senate voted that the Sibylline Books needed to be consulted. The *duumviri* decreed a supplication festival (*lectisternium*), the first ever held in Rome.[42] This was primarily a cultic action with expiation as a consequence. A few chapters later, Livy speaks once more of the pestilence of 399 BCE, but this time he uses the term Books of Fate.[43]

Livy's account, however, continues. More portents were reported. The Romans were at war with the Etruscans, which deprived them of any access to Etruscan diviners (*haruspices,* interpreters of internal organs, lightning, and prodigies). The Delphic oracle, though, was "open for business," and Roman envoys were sent. But then, an old man from Veii, an interpreter of fates (*interpres fatis*), a *haruspex,* presented himself. He declared that "it was written in the books of fate (*libris fatalibus*), thus handed down by the Etruscan discipline (*disciplina Etrusca*), that when the Alban water should overflow, a Roman should draw it with all due formalities, then victory over the Veientes was to be given. Until that should come about, the gods would not abandon the walls of the Veientes."[44] Although the *haruspex* explained the method of drainage, the senators did not follow his advice. Eventually, the Roman envoys returned from Delphi, and the oracle's response corresponded with that of the Etruscan. Delphi, however, was not a cheap oracle. "When you have ended the war of conquest, as victor bring an ample gift to my temple, repeat as well as bring about in customary way the ancestral rites you have neglected."[45] Two points come to the forefront here. One, the Etruscan *haruspex* did not just explain a phenomenon. He referred to a recorded prophecy and then went about expounding it. Second, the Romans consulted the Delphic oracle, which reminded them of their ancestry, and not the Sibylline Books, which were supposedly in their possession at that time. In this story, the Etruscan Books of Fate functioned and were used very much like the Sibylline Books. [. . .]

Even the nameless old woman in the acquisition story might point to Etruscan roots. Women played an important role in Etruscan society.[46] Without the powerful Tanaquil, who was skilled in reading omens, Lucius Tarquin (the Elder) would not have left Tarquinia to find his fortune in Rome, where he became king. Roman historians and antiquarians place the purchase of the Sibylline Books in the time of the Etruscan kings (Tarquins), fusing, in effect, an Etruscan element (king) with a Greek one (Sibyl). For all his details, Livy does not relate the acquisition story at all, although, as we have seen, he speaks about the consultation of Sibylline Books quite often. Why does he keep this story from his readers, when he recounts the one of Numa's sacred books?[47] The king's sacred books were written in Greek, even though Numa was a Sabine, a parallel to the Sibylline Books. Tradition, strongly influenced by Greek sources, had made Numa a learned, Pythagorean, nymph-inspired wise man.[48] The Sibylline Books offer a glimpse of Rome's cultural assimilation, the buried Etruscan and the actively embraced Greek layers. They also unveil how the past was created and how it then, in turn, helped shape Augustan Rome. The books outlived pagan Rome; edited and copied, they were consulted until the Christian god controlled all aspects of life and death.

MATER MAGNA—THE GREAT MOTHER

At the time of Hannibal's military successes in Italy, two Vestal Virgins were accused of sexual offences (*stupri compertae*), for which one was put to death. The other, escaping the fate of being buried alive, committed suicide.[49] The senator Quintus Fabius Pictor was dispatched to Delphi to consult the oracle[50] and maybe even to collect data concerning the state of affairs in Greece. The Sibylline Books ordered unusual rites: human sacrifice and the burial of a pair of Gauls and Greeks.[51] But nothing seemed to stop the Carthaginians. While allied Italian cities withdrew from their relationship with Rome, Philip V of Macedon and Hannibal forged a treaty in 215 BCE. Philip opened a second front in Greece and the Balkans. There was also a war in Spain that required Rome's attention.[52] All in all, Rome's prospects looked grim. Amazingly, though, the city rebounded, all the while introducing new religious rituals and presenting generous gifts to temples in accordance with Sibylline sayings.

As always in the midst of crises, Romans reshaped their religion along the lines of their newly found identity. They were in part the descendants of Trojan Aeneas; their intellectual heritage was Greek. Pious Aeneas suited the Romans well. This wandering Trojan prince existed in the context of Greek myth, a framework the Romans had adopted and were propagating. Aeneas and the Romans shared the same mythological "Greekness." Thus, the militarily successful Romans, armed with an acquired respectable and tangible past, began more intensively to encourage the literary arts, whose major proponent had been the Hellenistic world and whose guardian deity was Olympian Apollo. Ultimately, Romulus and Remus' foundation became the mistress of the Mediterranean. Rome was the political as well as the religious center of an Empire, whose elites prized the arts as much as the successor states of Alexander's empire headed by Attalids of Pergamon (Asia Minor), Seleucids of Syria, and Ptolemies of Egypt. Rome itself was in line to be a worthy successor to them.

Raining stones prompted the last consultation of the Sibylline Books during the Second Punic War period.[53] In Roman terms, the human world was spinning out of control and needed mending. Purification rituals and sacrifices brought the community together while simultaneously reinforcing the bonds between the leaders and the led. The Delphic Oracle, whom Fabius Pictor consulted, concurred with the Sibylline prophecy. Roman victory would come about "if the Idaean Mother from Pessinum was brought to Rome."[54] A Roman delegation was dispatched to Attalus I Soter of Pergamum. He honored the Romans' request and apparently handed over the meteorite representing the goddess from Pessinum.[55]

The Idaean mother, however, most likely came from Pergamum. Ovid hinted at this in his *Fasti,* and the antiquarian Varro suggested it through the etymology of Megalensia: "The Megalensia is called by the Greeks which by the behest of the Sibylline Books was summoned from Attalus, king of Pergamum: there next to the wall was the Megalesion, the temple of this goddess, from there she was taken to Rome."[56] Henri Graillot already pointed out that the association of Pessinus with the epithet Idaea is odd and that Attalus' realm ended about three hundred kilometers short of Pessinus,[57] then still an independent theocratic state. If this is so, why did the priests of Pessinus hand over their deity to the Romans? What could they have gained by doing so? One wonders if Pessinus could have remained the cult's center without its original source of power, the deity.

The Goddess' Place of Origin

The mother goddess was one of the oldest deities in the area. Her sanctuary had existed since remote times. Neither ruler nor high priest of the shrine would have voluntarily handed over such a powerful deity.[58] The goddess' dislocation, the severance of the meteorite from its original place, meant a decrease of religious power and prestige and, in this case, the subjugation of an ancient to a new site. One way to avoid the former problem was to take a representative token, for example, a copy or even a piece of the original, which would possess the same powers and fulfill the same functions as the original. At play here, however, is a form of *evocatio,* the calling out of a deity to come with the Romans to Rome,[59] which demanded the original. Hence, the Romans would have known and cared about what they carried home. The motivation for this cult transfer was to affirm a symbolic connection with the Troad, strengthen a political bond with Pergamum, and signal a "re-foundation,"[60] in this case, a cultural redefinition that involved the Attalids and through them the oldest mythic connections that had defined Greece.

The official name of Rome's divine import was "the Great Idaean Mother of Gods" (Magna Deorum Mater Idaea). There is nothing relating to Pessinus in her name. Erich Gruen suggests that "it was easy enough for an annalistic writer of the late 2nd or early 1st century to assume that the symbol of Magna Mater must have been sought at Pessinus. That assumption need not bind us."[61] Pessinus was and remained the major cultic center, which was not possible without the primary cultic object at hand.[62] It was the Great Mother of Mount Ida who with the help of Attalus came to Rome from the Troad, not from Pessinus.[63] It is even possible that Attalus had moved the Idaean Mother from Ilium (Troy) to Pergamum before learning of Rome's request.[64]

In 205/204 BCE Rome ascertained its Trojan heritage through the mother goddess. Land acquisition was to follow later. Pergamum was in Rome's reach; the theocratic state Pessinus was not yet in its grasp. In essence, Aeneas' descendents had claimed, following the instructions of the Sibylline Books and with the endorsement of the Delphic oracle, what mythologically and ideologically was theirs. Once Rome's political control in Asia expanded with the war against Antiochus III (ruler over Syria, Mesopotamia, and Western Iran), Pessinus and its mother goddess, Cybele, became tangible (Figure 3.2).[65] Romans were shocked when they found out that castrated priests (*galli*) tended this Great Mother. Our sources are mostly silent about this cult aspect, and some scholars attribute this silence to the horror Romans experienced when they saw the actual cult practices in action.[66] This makes the Roman elite, the ones who brought the goddess to Rome, look like buffoons, which they hardly were.

There is, however, another possibility, namely, the ritual around the Great Idaean Mother of Gods differed at first from that of Cybele, whose

FIGURE 3.2.

Seated Cybele with the portrait head of her priestess, ca. 50 CE. Marble.
H: 161.9 × W: 70 × D 64.5cm. The J. Paul Getty Museum, Villa Collection, Malibu,
California. Unknown, Inv. No. 57.AA.19.

cult featured eunuch-attendants. In Greece, the transplanted mother goddess lost her various Phrygian names related to locations and mountains. Even her name, Cybele, was substituted by the title Great Mother (Mētēr Megalē). This reflected the Hellenization of Cybele, whose cult was thoroughly "de-orientalized."[67] Despite this, the *galli* of Cybele did not disappear. Cultic rituals scarcely changed, since a change meant a tampering with what had proved to be effective and thus invited a breach in the mankind-deities alignment. No mode of Hellenization prevented this breaching. On the other hand, there was no loss of divine goodwill, if the neutral and universal concept Mētēr Megalē was sufficiently dislodged from Cybele through associations, for example, with Rhea. In addition, the "Hellenized" Great Mother was represented with the attributes of Cybele, the *tympanon* (tambourine) and the lions. This did not mean that her attendants had to be and behave like *galli*. Syncretism was at work, but not on the level of ritual.

Roman records show that the festival of Cybele was celebrated in March,[68] while the festivities for the Great Idaean Mother of Gods took place in early April. The latter's representation was initially deposited in the temple of Victory on the Palatine on April 4th. A new temple also on the Palatine, Rome's religious center, was not ready until 191 BCE. The first Megalensian Games (*ludi Megalenses*) included theatrical performances (*ludi scaenici*) and were held on the dedication of the temple in 191 BCE.[69] Cicero points out that these *Megalensia* were Greek in style.[70] The Idaean Mother took the iconographic attributes of Cybele, the mural crown, *tympana,* and lions, but her cult did not have orgiastic elements. Support of the argument for an initial division between the celebrations of the two deities comes from the fact that the guardians of the Sibylline Books (the *quindecimviri sacris faciundis*) selected the priest of the Mother of Gods (*sacerdos matris deum*). The Roman state was directly involved in the cult of the Great Mother but not in the cult of Cybele with its castrated priests.

An inscription like *CIL* VI 2183, which features a high priest of the Great Idaean Mother of Gods and Attis (*archigallus Matris deum magnae Idaeae et Attis*), came after Pessinus' entrance into Rome's sphere of control, after the construction of the temple of the Great Mother (*aedes Magna Mater*). At this point, there was a further merger between the goddess of Pessinus, Cybele, and the Great Idaean Mother of Gods. Eventually, both deities were perceived as one, and only the two ritual cycles, in March honoring the Great Mother and in April celebrating Cybele, retained the original difference. Rome had emerged victorious in the East against Philip V and was successful in the West, wrestling control from the Carthaginians in Spain. Further, Hannibal, unable to shatter Rome's alliances in Italy and elsewhere, lost his final battle against Rome. In 205/204 BCE Rome triumphantly looked into the future, claiming and embracing the Greek intellectual heritage, mainly through a link with Aeneas. The religious expression of this was the transfer of the Great Mother Goddess of Ida from the Troad to Rome.

ISIS—THE EGYPTIAN GODDESS AND ROME'S RULING DYNASTY

Isis means "the one who has ruling power." This goddess is one of the most important deities in the Egyptian pantheon. Her headdress is the throne, which is also the hieroglyph for her name. Isis was a daughter of Earth (Geb) and Sky (Nut), who had nine children. Osiris was her brother and husband; Horus was their son. One of the nine children was Seth, who killed and dismembered Osiris. He scattered the body parts all across Egypt. Isis searched and found all the parts, except for the phallus, which a fish had eaten. Isis then reassembled her brother-husband's body and molded a replacement for the missing part. With the help of Thoth, she revived Osiris for a short time. In this period of revival, Isis conceived Horus, who became his father's avenger.

Isis was a healer. She helped women in childbirth. Greco-Roman representations of Isis show her with a knot, which was a sign of life, on the front of her dress. This knot protected pregnant women as well as their babies. When a scorpion stung and killed her son, she revived him. In myth, Isis fashioned a snake that bit the supreme god Re. As Re lay dying, Isis promised to heal him if he gave up his secret name and thus world dominion. Re refused at first but in the end gave in to Isis' request. Thus, Isis became the all-ruler. Greek poems honoring Isis, so called aretologies, emphasize the goddess' powers of creation.[71] Isis was connected to Sothis or Sirius, the Dog Star (Canis Maior), and on representations on temple friezes and reverses of coins, Isis is seen sitting on Sothis.[72] Sothis, envisioned as a female deity, appeared shortly before the annual flooding of the Nile in the morning sky. The Nile's flooding was explained as the tears Isis shed for her dead consort Osiris. The rising waters of the Nile were the key to Egypt's economic success, its agriculture what made it the grain basket of the ancient Mediterranean world.

Greeks, who had economic links with Egypt since the seventh century BCE, explained Egyptian deities by using analogies. Thus, Isis was equated with Demeter.[73] With the advent of Alexander the Great's successors, the Ptolemies in Egypt, a more intensive propagation of the cult of Isis in the

FIGURE 3.3.

Isis with Horus, Egyptian, 1070–656 BCE (Third Intermediate Period, Dynasties 21–25).
Bronze. H: 20.5cm × W: 5.3cm × D: 8cm. Photograph © 2007 Museum of Fine Arts,
Boston. Gift of Mrs. Horace L. Mayer, Inv. No. 1971.749.

Eastern Mediterranean began. Ptolemy I Soter chose Sarapis, an oracular
god from Memphis, as his dynasty's guardian deity. In the Ptolemaic dynastic etiology, the Hellenized version of this god replaced Osiris as Isis'
consort. Together they became the guardians of the ruling dynasty and the
city of Alexandria and eventually the guarantors of Roman emperors' and
their families' well-being (*salus*).

Merchants were instrumental in bringing the Hellenized Isis and Sarapis to the Italian peninsula and the western Mediterranean. In this propagation of the deities and their cult, the island of Delos played a key role.
When the island fell into the hands of Mithridates VI of Pontus in 88 BCE,
Italian merchants returned home, and the integration of Isis and Sarapis
into the Roman pantheon accelerated. In the last decades of the Roman
Republic, the Senate, in control of the integration process of foreign deities,
reacted strongly against the cult of Isis. The Senate ordered the cult and its
adherents expelled. These expulsions took place in 58, 53, and 48 BCE.[74]
The reasons were political in nature. The Senate, losing control to individuals such as Pompey and Caesar, flexed its muscle in the only sphere where
it still exerted some power. The Senate was the authoritative body to accept
or reject a foreign cult. In lashing out against a foreign cult and denying its
introduction, they asserted and exercised their privilege as well as demonstrated authority. With the emergence of Augustus, this picture changed.
The *princeps* was the sole religious authority. In addition, although Augustus
displayed a resolute public stand against things Egyptian, he was, nevertheless, crucial in the introduction of the Ptolemaic dynastic explanation and
Rome's understanding of itself as the Mediterranean's premier hegemony.

Augustus' house on the Palatine had decorations in the private cham-
bers that included Egyptian landscapes. The house connected to a temple
of Apollo, the guardian god of Actium. The connection itself was a portico
of the Danaids, daughters of Danaus. The myth of the Danaids integrated
Egypt into the Greek cultural system, which Romans embraced and had
made their own. The Danaids, like the Romans, were culturally ambiguous; they were Egyptian-born Greeks who, in flight, returned home to Ar-
gos. The portico made a cultural albeit vague statement: Egypt was and yet
was not introduced into Rome's own mythological center. Augustus had
the Sibylline Books deposited in the new temple of Apollo.

Under Augustus' successor, Tiberius, the cult of Isis and her adherents
were banished from Rome in 19 CE. Again, the underlying reason was
political. Tiberius' designated successor, Germanicus, had brought about
political instability with his rash actions in Egypt. He had opened the granaries and thus flooded the market with grain. Middle men bought the
grain at rock-bottom prices, cornering the market. The result was a grain
shortage and famine in the capital.[75] Germanicus also visited Memphis,
whose priests were instrumental in the appointment of a pharaoh. Tiberius
had no choice but to act. Isis, who represented Egypt and its capital Alexandria, became the target through which the emperor demonstrated and
reasserted his power, which Germanicus' actions had not only threatened

with his unauthorized visit to Egypt, in particular, Memphis, but also actually undermined with the opening of the granaries.

Isis and her cult were officially recognized at the end of Caligula's or at the beginning of Claudius' reign. Because Caligula often was portrayed as a ruler who snubbed Roman tradition (after all, he was the great-grandson of Marc Antony) and behaved despotically, modern writers have turned him into an adherent of Isis. The reasoning goes that as a follower, he necessarily must have been the ruler who legitimized the cult. The *aula Isiaca,* "a large vaulted hall in the north corner" of Augustus' villa complex, the *domus Augustiana,* where "Egyptianizing motifs and figures abound, especially those pertaining to the cult of Isis," has been assigned to Caligula's time "because of his known interest in the cult of Isis."[76] But the aula shares a similar decoration style as the Casa della Farnesina, a house often believed to have belonged to Agrippa, which places them in the time of Augustus. Enjoyment of Egyptian motifs and even the embracing of their gods did not depend on a leader's dislike of Rome and its defining traditions.

Wissowa offered a better explanation for the legitimization of the cult. His hypothesis was that the action of legitimization coincided with the building of the temple of Isis in the *campus Martius.*[77] The poet Lucan provides the first concrete literary evidence of this temple, when he alludes to the cultic funeral obsequies for Osiris.[78] These rites were a part of the four-day-long *Isia,* which, according to the fourth-century calendar of Philocalus, began in Rome on the 28th of October and ended on the 1st of November.[79] Wissowa postulated that the finding of Osiris was the most crucial moment in the ceremony, and it fell on the 31st of October. According to the Egyptian calendar, the finding occurred on the 19th of Hathyr, which corresponded to the 15th of November of the Julian calendar. In the years 36–39 CE, however, the 19th of Hathyr and the 31st of October coincided. Since Tiberius had lashed out against Isis and her cult, Caligula had to be the initiator. Unlike Wissowa, Barrett suggested the beginning of the ceremony was the decisive date, the 17th of Hathyr.[80] He concluded that the 31st of October and the 17th of Hathyr coincided in the years 40–43 CE. The official introduction of the cult would then have taken place in the early part of Claudius' reign.

Isis and the domus Augustus

The political connection of Isis with the imperial house (the *domus Augusta*) occurred during the reign of Vespasian. Alexandria had been important in Vespasian's ascension to power since Rome's Eastern troops first proclaimed him emperor there. The night before their triumphal procession into Rome, Vespasian and his eldest son, Titus, are said to have spent in the temple of Isis in the Field of Mars (*Iseum Campense*).[81] This temple was the largest *Iseum* in Rome and may have been built on top of an earlier temple of Isis. The consecration of this temple may be linked to the official introduction of the cult of Isis sometime in the late 30s or early 40s CE. Domitian, Vespasian's youngest son, had many temples of Isis renovated during his reign as a display of piety. There was an increasing interest in Egyptian and Egyptianizing objects at the time of the emperor Hadrian, which had to do with the emperor's cultural interest in Egypt. As a consequence, the *Iseum Campense* received its most elaborate renovation during this time. Hadrian was a philhellene (a lover of Greek culture), and the Alexandrian libraries, the most important ones of antiquity, were the guardians of Greek literature and culture. His villa outside Rome featured an Egypt-inspired area, the Canopus.

Inscriptions asking for the well-being (*salus*) of the imperial household (*domus Augusta*) in the name of Sarapis appear predominantly during Marcus Aurelius' rule. Isis and her consort, Sarapis, were now fully accepted guarantors of the emperor's and the Empire's well-being. Another development aided in making it possible for the emperor's extraordinary sociopolitical position to converge with the concept of the pharaonic Ptolemaic ruler. Since the time of Gaius Julius Caesar, the Senate bestowed deified status for an extraordinary peer, in a process called apotheosis. In time, from Augustus onward, more and more emperors were given this status. The difference between the emperor and his subjects became increasingly marked. The legions of the East had made Septimius Severus, the founder of the dynasty, emperor, just as they had done with Vespasian over a century earlier. There are portraits of Septimius Severus that show him with locks characteristic of Sarapis. The iconography reveals that the Roman dynastic ideology corresponded to the pharaonic-Ptolemaic one. A process that had begun with the emergence of Augustus as the Empire's sole ruler came to a conclusion with the Principate's last dynasty. The guardians of the house of the Ptolemies and Alexandria, Isis and Sarapis, acquired a similar but much more obscured role in the dynastic explanation of Rome's rulers. In a sense, Isis was an integral part of Rome's political ideology, an ideology that was in one way or another anchored in the Hellenistic world.

FOUR

ROME ETERNAL

The six Vestal Virgins dedicated their lives to the goddess Vesta and, by extension, to the Roman state. Though they were "between categories," neither matrons nor priests, they dressed as married women, and for the entirety of their priestly tenure they were to remain in a virginal state. They preserved, as it were, rather than expressing or experiencing, their procreative potentiality, which was controlled by the Roman state. One of the main duties of the Vestals was the upkeep of the fire in the temple of Vesta. This fire symbolized procreation. The Vestals and the fire formed a controllable symbiotic whole of procreative potency. The most atrocious crime a Vestal could be accused of was unchastity (*incestum*), in essence, having turned her attention toward a single man and thus away from the state and the duties that bound her to it. A Vestal convicted of such a crime was punished with death by being buried alive. The failed priestess, thus inserted into the earth, released her life-giving potential in death for the community she was meant to serve.

Vestals could function as portents. When Rome encountered seemingly insurmountable problems, the Romans often ascribed the problems to the religious sphere as a sign of the gods' displeasure with the Romans. Vestals became targets in this transference and found themselves accused of unchaste behavior. The stories of Vestals proving their innocence are highly dramatic and excellent material for narratives that have a moral point to make. Historical veracity, in connection with these accusations, is often difficult to establish.

If we consider that the priesthood existed since Rome's beginning and that Rome faced many internal and external problems in its early history, the number of Vestal Virgins committing the crime of *incestum* is small. Ancient writers record only nineteen cases, starting in the early Republic.[1] It is conceivable that the priesthood did not exist in the regal period and only came about as the need arose to share political power within a larger pool of aristocrats.[2] As with many things connected to Roman religion, the third century BCE, the period of the Punic Wars, and in particular the Augustan age, shaped what we study as the "Vestal Virgins." Thus, it can be argued that with Rome's continued success and its economic growth, women, who consequently would also acquire more liberties, needed to be reminded of their primary functions in society: becoming mothers and devoting their lives to family. The Vestals symbolized these functions in the larger arena. Their service, based on strictly prescribed behavior and ritual, was for the benefit of Rome, the city, and the Empire. In the end, however, the Vestal Virgins defied categories, and, for all their importance to the state, they slipped into the mists of mythic history.

VESTA AND THE VESTAL VIRGINS

The six Vestals were chosen as children between the ages of six and ten to serve the goddess and the state for thirty years. The chosen girl had to be physically and socially unblemished. Her parents had to be alive (*patrima et matrima*), under the control of a *pater familias,* the male head of each respective family (*patria potestas*), and married to each other at the time of their daughter's appointment. The Vestals were Roman citizens, and their social rank was not a factor in their selection. From 5 CE onward, daughters of freedmen were also eligible.[3] The emperor Augustus extended the pool of possible candidates to be able to fill the positions, because there was a shortage of candidates. A Vestal received a sum upon entry into the priesthood and a yearly stipend for her services. Both sums were, every so often, adjusted to interest citizens. The entry sum, for example, reached two million sesterces in the time of Tiberius, Augustus' successor.[4] To put this amount into context, the monetary qualification for senatorial rank, the highest in the state, was one million sesterces. This payment was not a dowry substitution. Jane Gardner suggests that it "should perhaps be regarded as a kind of *peculium,* to compensate for the loss of patrimony."[5] Augustus also gave the Vestals the "right of children" (*ius liberorum*)[6] not as an "exemption from *tutela* (tutelage) . . . but freedom from the restrictions on inheritance which Augustus' legislation had imposed on the unmarried and childless."[7]

Upon becoming a Vestal, "without undergoing *capitis deminutio* [deprivation of civil rights] and without emancipation,"[8] the girl's father ceased to have control (*potestas*) over her. Just like others who were emancipated, the Vestal lost "her rights of intestate succession in her family of origin . . . and

FIGURE 4.IA.

Head of Vesta, depicted on Roman Republican denarius *of Q. Cassius (obverse).
The American Numismatic Society, Inv. No. 1923.150.7.*

FIGURE 4.IB.

Temple of Vesta, curule chair, and inscribed urn tablet, depicted on Roman Republican
denarius *of Q. Cassius (reverse). The American Numismatic Society, Inv. No. 1923.150.7.*

if she died intestate no one had rights of intestate succession. Her property
went to the public treasury."[9] A Vestal had equivalent rights to a Roman
man in making her own testament. Unlike any other Roman citizen,
male or female, a Vestal was free from paternal control (*patria potestas*).[10]
Freedom from *patria potestas,* however, did not bring independence to the
Vestal. She stood in dependence to the *pontifex maximus,* who could exact
corporal punishment, and the judgment of the college of pontiffs in cases of
a Vestal's failure in upholding her chastity.

The ceremony by which the Vestal-to-be was inducted into the college
was called *captio* (capture); it has been interpreted by modern scholars as
something akin to a marriage rite.[11] The *pontifex maximus* called the in-

ductee *Amata*.[12] A Vestal's hair was styled in the fashion of a bride (with linen headbands, *vittae*), but she wore the long dress of a Roman matron (*stola*). The Vestals were not allowed to mill and cook, and yet the three oldest Vestals prepared sacrificial cake (*mola salsa*) for the Roman citizenry. Thus, the Vestal seemed both bride and matron, or neither bride nor matron. Because Rome was originally a monarchy, Vesta's attendants were linked to the king, who had sacrificial duties. The surviving religious title of *rex sacrorum* (king concerned with sacrifices)[13] confirms this aspect of a king's responsibilities. The Vestal's domestic duties were akin to those of an early Roman housewife,[14] but the six priestesses, without any family connections (legally), remained chaste throughout their thirty-year tenure. The "wife-at-home" model simply did not work, and so "daughters of the king" emerged as an alternative though not very satisfying explanation.

Vestals had religious powers that ordinarily belonged to men. A *lictor,* an attendant of praetors and consuls, accompanied them.[15] The priestesses sat with senators at games, another aspect that moved them into the male social sphere and gendered them male. Their priesthood was part of the college of pontiffs. In compensation for holding such powers, however, the priestesses had to remain in a virginal state or, rather, in a perpetual state of being between unmarried and married.[16] "There was something queer about the Virgines Vestales,"[17] and they defied clear-cut categorization. Vesta's priestesses remained in a perpetual "rite of passage" loop, between status (unmarried and married) and a gendered (female and male) sphere.

Once the Vestals were released from their priestly duties, they were well into middle age. They had moved from a premarital to a postmarital state in a world in which a woman's purpose, her socially and culturally determined destiny, was to give birth to (preferably) legitimate children. Who a Vestal was, was thus defined and gendered. The Vestals were anomalies in regard to womanhood, but as if to compensate for their state-ordered asexuality, the state's prosperity and continuity were in their care. These female individuals, severed from their socially determined role, were subordinated to the state for which they were the guarantors of prosperity and continuation, a most extraordinary inversion.

As attendants of the goddess Vesta, the priestesses' duty was to keep Rome's sacred flame alive, prepare and use cultic objects, and perform bloodless sacrifice throughout the year on behalf of and for the Roman people (*pro populo Romano*). Varro lists Vesta as a Sabine deity whose original (Sabine) name no longer was known (Figure 4.1.a.).[18] Hildebrecht Hommel argues that Vesta, like Hestia, signified the hearth.[19] In Rome's earliest times, extended families congregated around the hearths and tables of the oldest male of a large family (*pater familias*); there they ate the food prepared by the daughters and daughters-in-law. Mothers oversaw their daughters' work but did not engage in any kind of food gathering, preparation, and storing, or house cleaning. Their sphere was the preparation and processing of wool; in essence, the making of clothes. The Vestals' ritual work paralleled the duties of these daughters of old. The power of the *pontifex maximus* over the Vestals, especially when they transgressed, corresponded as well to the power of the *pater familias*.[20]

The most grievous offense that brought about the gruesome punishment of live interment was a Vestal's loss (or assumed loss) of chastity. Hommel points to Friedrich Münzer's argument that chastity transgression and letting the fire go out were linked. Both lapses resulted originally in a death penalty. Because the youngest of the Vestals, preteens or teens, were most likely in charge of keeping the fire alive, the punishment was softened to flogging rather than flogging to death, which was and remained the punishment for a Vestal's seducer.[21]

Beyond being a goddess of the domestic hearth,[22] with the Greek Hestia as her equivalent, Vesta incorporated the notion of procreation. Radke suggests that the cultic actions attributed to the goddess' attendant, the Vestal Virgin (*virgo Vestalis*),[23] points to a linguistic root formation *$\u{u}ers$-tā*, meaning procreation. Hommel notes that making fire by friction, using a wooden drill on a wooden surface, does have an everyday (Greek and Latin) linguistic analogue in the erotic sphere.[24] Pliny the Elder also mentions in his *Natural History* "a phallus . . . that is worshipped as a god . . . by the Vestals"[25] and several Roman stories of a phallus appearing in a hearth fire, foreshadowing the birth of an extraordinary child, destined for greatness.[26] Servius Tullius, who succeeded Tarquin the Elder, was such a child. His mother, Ocrisia or Gaia Caecilia, a Latin war prisoner working in the household of the Etruscan king as a servant,[27] saw a phallus in the fire as she brought sacrificial cakes to the altar of the *regia,* the royal house. Tanaquil, who was well versed in the art of Etruscan prophecy, interpreted and informed her husband, the king, that a woman who joined herself with this phallus in the fire would give birth to a divine being. Tarquin decided that it was Ocrisia who should join herself thus. As prophesied, Ocrisia gave birth to a son, Servius, who became Tarquin's successor. Furthermore, when Servius was a baby, fire surrounded his head and remained around it until he was awakened.[28]

Gregory Nagy explored this Roman myth, putting it in a clear ritual context, and demonstrated that "like the Hittite *haššu-,* the Italic king *par excellence* is literally 'lit up'."[29] Moreover, the word Vesta is linguistically connected to the word "beget." Nagy argues convincingly for a semantic relationship between "beget," "fireplace," and "king."[30] The premise is to accept that the root *ə₂es- meant something similar to "set on fire." This verb radical survives in Hittite as haš- and can also be found in the Hittite noun for "sacred fireplace," hašša- which is related to the Latin word for "altar or sacriwficial fireplace," āra.[31] It is Italic myth and ritual, as it survives in the story of King Servius, which eliminates the semantic problem that haš- can also mean "beget," the root of the Hittite word for "king" hašša-.[32] It would make sense then that the Vestal Virgins were connected to the king, not necessarily as daughters or daughters-in-law, as a social explanation would postulate, but as those tending a sacred fireplace or nurturing a sacred fire that could "beget, bring forth." A phallus appearing in the fire's cinders visualizes and manifests this very act.

The ancient sources are not clear about whether a cult image of Vesta stood in her temple. Ovid claims that there was none, but Cicero seems to suggest the opposite.[33] Numismatic evidence supports Ovid's claim, because only after the massive fire of 64 CE do Roman coins show a cult statue inside the temple of Vesta (Figure 4.1.b).[34] If we agree that fire in a fireplace was the cornerstone of the cult of Vesta, that the goddess was linked to fire, and that the main purpose of the goddess' attendants was to keep this fire alive, then the absence of a cult statue could be explained: the goddess was originally not represented anthropomorphically. There was no need, because the divine representation was the fire contained in a specific place. Second, if this fire symbolized a procreative force, then the appearance of a phallus in it does not surprise either. Greco-Roman mythology makes it clear that any female, procreative force producing offspring on her own created monsters or malformed beings. For example, Hera, upset with her husband Zeus, produced the lame Hephaestus alone. It was as if Hera's asexual reproduction caused her child's deformity. It is the male joining the female, our biological reality, that myth and cultic action perpetuate as paradigm. The Vestals, whose chastity kept them forever in the potential of giving birth and at the brink of actual womanhood, tended the fire that in their care was a life giver. One could not function without the other; there was a synthesis between the fire and the caretakers. The Vestals functioned as guarantors of the state's fecundity only when maintaining their chaste, virginal standing. Once any of them was even thought unchaste and joined to a male, this synthetic potentiality of fertility gave way to the reality of human reproduction and thus to the ordinary.

Mary Beard used the concept of ambiguity and mediation in discussing the sexual status and the sacredness of the Vestal Virgins. A Vestal was "not looked upon as sterile but as a mediator of stored up, potential procreative power, a fact that can be adduced against the view that the connection of the Vestals with various ancient fertility cults reaffirms their matronal status."[35] What made these priestesses "sacral" was that they were "both/neither virgins and/nor matrons" and "perhaps" their "sacrality was marked also by an ambiguity between the categories of male and female."[36] At the core of the Vestals' gender construction were binary opposites. The priestesses' definition arose from correlations such as man to woman, virgin to matron, and wife to daughter. These binary correlations were based on social, cultural, religious, and legal definitions and locked within Rome's historical framework, that is, the fabric of its particular historical development.

The Vestals existed within (or more pointedly at the center of) a complex system composed of a subset of structures; the political and social system was patriarchal and militaristic; the religious system was polytheistic. If we continue to look at the Vestals in isolation, they remain enigmatic and ambiguous women both/neither wife and/nor daughter, both/neither virgin and/nor matron, equated with men, which presented the ultimate inversion. In short, Vestals simply defy categorization and, ultimately, definition, or, at least, categorizations and definitions we have pasted together from the remaining (mostly literary) sources. Our explanatory pastiche, however, was most likely not the Roman one. But what was the Roman explanation, if there was one? What was the Roman understanding of these priestesses of Vesta who functioned as guarantors of Rome's well-being (*salus*),[37] the continuation of Empire, the very identity of Rome?

A VESTAL'S FAILURE AND ITS CONSEQUENCE

There are no ceremonial or ritual books describing the Vestals' duties.[38] Inscriptions, usually an important source of information regarding family and status, are not extant for Vestals until the third century CE.[39] Livy, Dionysius of Halicarnassus, and Ovid, for example, provide historical accounts, which, however, have to be judged, at least in part, as fictional. Cicero speaks of the Vestals in some of his philosophical treatises and speeches.[40] Seneca the Elder provides hypothetical arguments for rhetorical exercises (*controversiae*) on the topic of Vestals' failures, which led to a charge of unchastity and, if convicted, to live interment. For the Latin literary corpus in general, mentions and descriptions of Vestals fall into two overarching categories: descriptions of Vestals' social and legal status and descriptions of their duties and circumscribed behavior. A convicted Vestal was buried alive, a sentence that garnered the most vivid descriptions and elaborations. Here was human drama at its best and, as Münzer has shown, the political reality of noble families curtailing each other's political power and influence.[41]

Ancient writers provide us with nineteen accounts of a Vestal's loss of chastity (*incestum*), which were discovered by prodigies in time of crisis.[42] A Vestal's misbehavior upset the reciprocal relationship between the Roman state and its gods (*pax deorum—pax hominum*), and the gods revealed this rupture with prodigies (*prodigia*). The only means of expiation was the removal and killing of the transgressor. In her analysis of Vestals, Ariadne Staples begins with Plutarch's description of a failed Vestal's execution:[43]

> The one who had soiled the vow of chastity is buried alive near what is called the Colline Gate. Here, inside the city wall, projects a little earthen ridge for some distance . . . there a chamber, not a big one, is constructed with an incline from above. In this are placed a covered couch, a burning lamp, and some very small portions of life's necessities, such as bread, a bowl of water, milk, and oil, as if they acquitted themselves of the charge of destroying by hunger a life, which had been dedicated to the highest ritual services. Then the one to be punished is placed on a sedan chair. They cover it from the outside and fasten [the coverings] with ropes, so that not even a sound is heard, and they escort the sedan chair through the public spaces. Everybody moves aside in silence, and they attend [it] without any noise and with dire gloom. There is no other spectacle more awful nor does the city experience a more abhorred day than this. When the sedan chair reaches the site, the servants untie the bindings, then, before the punishment, the high priest makes some secret prayers and stretches his hands toward the gods, he brings forth the all-together veiled one and places her on the ladder, which leads down to the chamber. Afterwards together with all the other priests, he turns away. Then, when she has descended, the ladder is pulled up and the chamber covered with earth so that the place is level with the rest of the ground.[44]

Staples states that "the manner of the Vestal's punishment was in fact used to construct a fiction—the fiction that the unchaste Vestal, who was killed for her loss of virginity, was not really killed at all."[45] Of course, the transgressor was killed, but the "fiction of not killing" was that there was no executioner. The failed Vestal did the punishing herself, and no one looked at her; therefore, no one saw her when she was carried in a litter through the streets of Rome and at the end of the route descended down into the subterranean chamber near the Colline Gate. The "fiction" was that while everyone knew, each and every one pretended not to know; here was an open, veiled secret.

The Vestal who incurred this horrendous death sentence by starvation and being buried alive had diverted her potential energies from the state to a single man. In fact, she had forsaken the whole for a single entity and thus jeopardized divine good will, which held the key to Rome's continuing success. The perception was that whatever procreative potentiality a failed Vestal may still have possessed, the state had to procure. This Vestal then became a token, which was inserted into the crop-producing earth to symbolically incite agricultural growth. The action is similar to the Fordicidia on April 15th, when calf fetuses were placed in the ground. The unborn calf symbolized the potentiality of life. It is also possible, however, that the transgressor, the convicted Vestal, was treated like a fertile seed and as such was planted in the earth.

In either case, the priestess had, with her action, interrupted the reciprocity between the Romans and their gods. Because the ancients thought of all actions and phenomena as sympathetically linked and all inexplicable phenomena as expressions of divine power, unnatural events (*prodigia*) informed them of breaks in their relationship with the divine world. When these portents were confirmed, the Roman Senate ordered pontiffs, the ten or fifteen men in charge of the Sibylline Books, and *haruspices* (diviners) to find an expiation that would bring the world back to order. Even in punishment, whatever the Vestals did was made up of binary opposites. The penalty was executed in public, although no one looked at the priestess. She was to starve to death and in starvation she was to bring back the old order, when the gods smiled on Rome, so that Rome and Romans would enjoy the fruits of their conquered territories. Whatever the Vestals guarded in their sanctuary was hidden, but it was critical to Rome's continued existence and its greatness.

The burial ground for the failed Vestals was near the Colline Gate (*porta Collina*), which was located at the north end of the Servian Wall (*murus Servii Tullii*). The rampart (*agger*) served as Rome's promenade. Two important streets lay beyond the gate, *Via Salaria* and *Via Nomentana*. The *Alta Semita* was within. This street ran the length of the Quirinal and was connected to the *vicus Iugarius,* a street that moved "along the shoulder of the Capitoline Hill above the *Forum Romanum* linking the foot of the Quirinal with the Porta Carmentalis."[46] These streets were of economic importance from earliest times, because they were part of the ancient salt route. The Quirinal, according to tradition, the dwelling place of the Sabines, was once called *Agonus*.[47] As we had learned earlier, the Salii of the Quirinal were called Agonenses.[48] Vestals were thus interred in a location of long-standing economic importance, a place linked to Rome's foundation, and an ancient ritual site connected to the god Quirinus. The Colline Gate stressed success as well as failure. It was a perfect place for the interment of a failed Vestal and demonstration of Rome's resolve to restore order in the world.

Livy describes the first recorded punishment of a Vestal in 483 BCE. The date falls within the period of the internal struggle among the patricians and the plebeians (the Struggle of the Orders). Internal strife was repeatedly set aside for external campaigns against the Volsci, Aequi, and the city of Veii, only to return to internal fighting after a successful conclusion of war. Livy states that

> for external wars there was almost an abundance of physical powers (*vires*), and men misused them to quarrel amongst themselves. Celestial prodigies added to the weary minds of all, for there were almost daily warning signs by way of portents. No other reason for the divinity's agitation, the soothsayers explained, after they had consulted publicly and privately, sometimes inspecting entrails, other times the flight of birds, than not having executed the sacred rite properly. These terrors then arrived at a point where the Vestal Virgin Oppia [or Oppima; Dion. Hal. 8.89.4] was accused of unchastity and punished for it.[49]

The historian had his finger on the Roman pulse, for he set the quarreling men with "an abundance of physical power," who were wrecking internal order, in opposition to Oppia, the Vestal who became the scapegoat. She carried the guilt and failing of the men and in death expiated the whole society. Whenever accused, a Vestal had to prove her chastity, because her life depended on it. These priestesses paid the price for men's failings in the political sphere. When the Vestal Tuccia was accused, she took up a sieve and said: "Vesta, if I have always moved chaste hands to your rites, let it be that I may take up water from the Tiber in this, and carry it to your temple."[50] She did, and her innocence was proven. It was Tuccia's courageous and fantastic demonstration of innocence, like those of others, that charmed the ancients, not that she had been targeted as the source of all problems and thus became society's scapegoat.

FIVE

ROME BESIEGED*

A reciprocal relationship between the divine and the human sphere (*pax deorum—pax hominum*) was at the center of Roman understanding of religion. The proper and timely implementation of prescribed rituals translated into territorial rewards or Empire.[1] Rome was successful because of the inhabitants' care for their gods. Whenever the Roman state found itself in trouble, the underlying cause for it was sought in the religious sphere, as we have seen in the previous chapter. This is not to say that Romans did not address and solve political and societal problems within those spheres, but in their resolution process, the reinstatement of *pax deorum—pax hominum* was crucial.

Two occasions, the Bacchanalian and Bona Dea affairs, will serve as examples of political or social problems deflected and turned into religious issues that then warranted senatorial and priestly involvement. Particularly when women or Vestals behaved inappropriately, a system's breakdown threatened the Roman state, and resolute action on the part of Rome's political and religious elite, the Senate and the priestly colleges, was necessary. Both events spurred dramatic narratives, in which women were blamed for troubles faced by the body politic. Women had the destructive power, at least in literary and rhetorical compositions, which cast moments of rupture in moralistic terms, to wreck what men versed in politics and war had built.

THE BACCHANALIAN AFFAIR OF 186 BCE

The harsh suppression of the Bacchic cult in Italy by a decree of the Roman Senate in 186 BCE (*senatus consultum de Bacchanalibus;* Figure 5.1)[2] prompted Walter Burkert to observe that in the degree of its cruelty—over 6,000 executions—"there is nothing comparable in religious history before the persecutions of Christians."[3] Besides the *senatus consultum,* there

FIGURE 5.1.
Senatus consultum de Bacchanalibus. *Kunsthistorisches Museum,
Wien, Inv. No. ANSA III168.*

is Livy's dramatic and engaging account.[4] It is this narrative that brings support to the notion that women must have made up the most influential group within the cultic organization. Any social group (such as the lower classes and slaves) suffering from "fickleness of mind (*leuitas animi*)," that is, lacking an appropriate education, had to be involved in the propagation of the cult from the Greek colonies in the south of the peninsula to Rome. Nothing of that sort, however, not even a predominance of women in the cult, was the reason for the senatorial reaction. Rather, its response was embedded in its role as the guardian of the state. The affair had political implications, which prompted senatorial involvement, and, if not confirmed, established the Senate as controlling force in sanctioning foreign cults.

The decree against Bacchic worship offers valuable insight into the mechanisms of religious control exercised by the Roman Senate. [. . .] The conclusion of the Second Punic War had given Rome supremacy over the western Mediterranean. Remaining external problems (the Gauls in the north and Philip V [238–179 BCE], king of Macedonia, in the East) and internal consequences from the aftermath of the war against Carthage, however, could still undermine Rome's recent political success. Social ties and family relations had been and were being strained under the pressure of Rome's extensive war efforts. At these points of potential social disintegration, some scholars point to the rise of new and unconventional cults because they seemed to be able to satisfy more adequately the Romans' religious and emotional needs than traditional cults. These new cults did not so much displace traditional religious ways as coexist with them. As long as the traditional cultic rituals were properly exercised and the political order and Rome's ideology were not undermined, new cults would not be attacked. Whether they would be legitimized, that is, turned into official Roman cults with specific festival days, depended on Rome's political and religious leadership.

The political situation seemed under control in 186 BCE. The Romans had successfully stopped the expansionist advances of the Seleucid Antiochus III, [and] . . . the victory at Magnesia sealed Rome's supreme position in the Mediterranean area. The most common reason for a foreign cult's expulsion, intense social and/or political distress, is not applicable here. The senatorial decree against Bacchic worship seems to show that any possible threat to the traditional status quo and ideology could force a reaction from the body of the ruling elite at any time. The Senate's refusal had nothing to do with religious or moral scruples, despite Livy's insistence; it was a question of traditional senatorial rights and political power. Gruen concludes that "the episode served to exhibit senatorial vigilance and responsibility for the security of the state and legitimize senatorial authority in the regulation of alien worship."[5] He makes another important observation when he sees in the senatorial reaction an attempt to restrain Hellenism. "Individuals might absorb the teachings of Hellas and transmit the culture of the East. But state policy concentrated on the interests at home and distanced itself from Hellenism."[6] Militarily, Rome could claim dominance over the Mediterranean area and was ready to demonstrate that it had come into its own. Cultural assimilation and Rome's self-definition had reached a new phase.

Like any other Greek cult believed to have spread from the Greek colonies of southern Italy toward Rome, there was also a connection with Etruria. Livy mentions this, and a nine-line Etruscan inscription[7] on a sarcophagus from Tarquinia dated around 200 BCE[8] supports the historian's claim. Names of five men occupy the first two lines.[9] The great-grandfather's cognomen is *creice (Γραῖκος)*. An Etruscan equivalent, *paχana*, for the adjective *Baccheus* appears in the inscription's fifth line, and Jacques Heurgon suggests that the great-grandfather could actually have been the soothsayer and diviner who introduced Bacchus to Etruria.[10] This Tarquinian family with the name *pulena* retained the memory of a Greek diviner, homonymous with their family's founder, who represented the continuation of their fortune.[11] Heurgon's research moves away from Tenney Frank's postulation that captives from early Greek colonies in southern Italy, like Tarentum or Locri, introduced the cult of Bacchus to Rome and that "the rites were carried on in the quarters of the poor near the docks behind the Aventine."[12] [. . .]

The Etruscan name *pulena* can be connected to the Roman name Pollenius.[13] This family, for example, furnished consuls from the time of the emperor Marcus Aurelius until the reign of Caracalla. The cognomen of these consuls was Auspex.[14] This suggests that the Roman family retained (or rediscovered in an attempt to be of ancient stock) the memory of divination, which was originally linked with their Etruscan namesakes. Despite Cumont's powerful depiction of oriental and orgiastic cults flooding the Empire, one can postulate that in addition to Greek colonies, Etruria also played a role in the introduction of Bacchic rites, before the time of an increased foreign presence in Rome. These Etruscan rites seem to have been without any gender preference, that is, open to men and women alike, but just as with other Etruscan contributions to the Roman cultural quilt, the impact was downplayed, even vilified.

Before leading into his colorful narrative of a young man escaping the clutches of an orgiastic cult, Livy presents some background information on the cult (39.8–39.19). He relates that a Greek of humble origin versed in sacrifices and soothsaying introduced people in Etruria to the Bacchic rites (39.8). This hierophant, eager to attract more people to the nocturnal rites, added drinking and feasting to the celebration. His following of men and women grew, and after all moral judgment had been extinguished, there was promiscuous violation of free men and women. Cult members bore false witness, forged documents and wills, perjured evidence, and dealt in poisons and wholesale murders (39.9). Here was a conspiracy that required a judicial inquiry for which the consuls were given extraordinary powers. One concludes from Livy's narrative that those who undermined the social and moral order of the state had to be punished. This is not to say that moral issues were the actual reasons for the cult's expulsion. Moralizing is one of the basic features of Roman history writing. The consular decree of 186 BCE, a more reliable primary source than Livy in this regard, does not mention any moral cause that might have triggered the Senate's reaction.

Livy presents his reader with a dramatic narrative. The chief actors in this drama are Publius Aebutius, a young man about to be initiated into the cult of Bacchus against his will, and his supportive lover, the prostitute Hispala Faecina. Aebutius, having been driven from home, seeks help from an aunt, who in turn suggests that he speak to one of the consuls, Postumius. Aebutius does as suggested. The consul learns that the rites had started exclusively for women and that Paculla Annia of Campania was the first to initiate her sons Minius and Herennius Cerrinius. This woman changed the ceremonies from day to night and increased the initiation days from the original three a year to five days per month. Unlike the Etruscan variant of the cult, which, according to Livy, was open to both sexes, the Campanian version was originally only open to women, and in this it follows the pattern outlined in Euripides' *Bacchae*.

Paculla Annia, whose name Paculla, a diminutive, can be linked with the Etruscan *paχana*, however, changed the rules. As John Scheid stresses in his discussion of the Bacchanalian affair, the initiation of men below the age of twenty caused anxiety among the senators: "For the authorities the most alarming aspect of this gathering of marginals . . . was the fact that very young men were initiated by their mothers . . . In short, women were taking the place of both the father and the city."[15] It should be added that Roman teenaged boys assumed the *toga virilis* and thus full Roman citizenship when they were fourteen to sixteen years old. Ideally they would then serve in the military from the age of seventeen to twenty-seven. After completion of their military service they were allowed to stand for the state's first political office, the quaestorship, if they had the appropriate monetary qualification.

In keeping with Scheid's assumption, one would have to argue for an initiation before a teenager's acquisition of the *toga virilis* and subsequent military service. A cultic organization could have a hierarchical structure that would not reflect the actual social hierarchy in place. Roman religion, the accumulation of various cults, provided membership hierarchies different from that of the state and if the state did not control them they might generate "a second people," which could undermine, even overthrow, the existing state.[16] With this in mind, the fact that teenaged boys were initiated by women had to cause anxiety levels that in turn would warrant an extraordinary judicial investigation headed by the two consuls. Such an initiation undermined Rome's sociopolitical fabric; young men were first and above all to be presented (by taking on the *toga virilis* under the watchful eyes of the oldest male relative) to the state.

Some Bacchants might have been criminals (counterfeiters, perjurers, murderers, etc.), but certainly not all of them. Also, not all Bacchic priests were women, and Livy does not relate that only men were sought out for initiation. This is not to say that Scheid might not have a point in stressing that "the (real or alleged) role of women in the scandal of 186 BCE and the reaffirmation of the authority of fathers, husbands, and guardians point to a larger problem that Rome had to face since the end of the third century: matrons."[17] The impact of the Second Punic War could still be felt in the 180s BCE. Romans had to deal with an ideologically and physically different landscape in which social and gender roles needed redefinition.

After Postumius had informed his colleagues, a senatorial inquiry was launched, and the Senate passed a decree (39.14). Before addressing the people, Livy has Postumius recite a prayer (39.15). Thus the historian sets the tone of Postumius' public speech; ancestral gods were pitched against new and debauched ones: "It is a prayer that reminds us that these are the gods whom your ancestors ordained to worship, to venerate, to entreat not those gods . . . who would drive on every sort of crime and desire." Describing the thousands of worshipers, Postumius tells his audience that "a great number are women, and they are the source of this evil; next there are men most like women." Hence Livy invokes and reinforces the paradigm of the evil, cunning woman so prominent in his first Pentad. "The impious conspiracy still holds itself to private crimes, it is not yet strong enough to overthrow the state," argues Postumius, "but this evil grows and crawls every day." Livy's Postumius (39.16) continues to argue that "nothing is more treacherous in appearance than perverse religion . . . when the whole discipline of sacrificing, apart from the Roman tradition, is destroyed."

Beard, North, and Price put forth the argument that this cult "was based on a highly structured group basis (unfamiliar to the Roman authorities), which, in turn, was genuinely seen as threatening to the social order" and this "threat the Senate wished above all to destroy." Indeed, the senatorial decree must have "tested the loyalty of the allies to the very limit," for Rome meddled in her allies' internal affairs.[18] Even if the internal group structures had been known to the Roman authorities (after all, they had

had reciprocal contact with their Italian neighbors for centuries), Rome was, for the first time, in a political position to dictate successfully its religious and cultural terms. It had come into its own; Marcus Porcius Cato, the *censor,* had made sure of this. Roman tradition, which included the higher magistrates' integral role in state cults (e.g., the discipline of sacrificing), was to be demonstratively privileged over all things nontraditional, non-Roman. In this context it was the Senate's duty to set into motion measures that ensured and solidified its political control over all the peoples it governed in Italy.

The Senate's task was not to stop a Bacchanalian menace but to curtail and subjugate a non-Roman type of worship within the parameters of *pax deorum—pax hominum.*[19] In doing so, the Senate became the authority in deciding the cult's legitimacy. Livy's summary of the senatorial decree (39.18) is very much in line with the inscription recording the *senatus consultum* [. . .] that spelled out who could participate and where and how the worship was to take place. The urban *praetor* enforced and waived prohibitions with the approval of the Senate, provided that no less than a hundred senators be present when the matter was deliberated. There were aspects, though, that did not allow for any alteration. For example, a man could not become priest of Bacchus. [. . .] Women, then, could be priests, but since they were without active political power, their sacral activities did not siphon away state potency.

Cultic and organizational aspect had been moved from the private to the public sphere, that is, the state represented by the urban *praetor,* and ultimately the Senate, was in control. This control extended over Roman citizens, people with Italian rights, and aliens. It has to be emphasized that Bacchants could worship but only in small groups under strict state supervision. All this fits Roman religious/political thinking well. A compromise had been brought about that did not impede the reciprocal relationship between the Romans and their gods, but to keep the cult going, the internal governing structure had to be changed, adapted to something acceptable to the Roman Senate.

Livy mentions the cult leaders among the more than 7,000 male and female conspirators: Marcus and Caius Atinius, Lucius Opicernius of the Falisci, and Minius Cerrinius of Campania (39.17). The Atinii, for example, were a plebeian family from Aricia. This family's importance in Rome's political life faded after the time of the Gracchi.[20] Livy lists several Atinii. An M. Atinius was *imperator* of Thurii (34.46.12), and a C. Atinius was *praetor* in 189 BCE (38.35.2), who subsequently received Further Spain as a province and stayed there as *propraetor* until his death in 186 BCE (39.21.2).

A homonymous military tribune (*tribunus militum quartae legionis*) fought against the Boii in 194 BCE (34.46.12). Maybe this tribune was one of the conspirators of 186 BCE. Since the family's involvement in politics did not fade until a good sixty years after the conspiracy, it was an individual's "wrongdoing" that was punished and that did not have an impact on another family member's political career. The names Opicernius and Cerrinius point to important cultic locales. The Falisci were a people in Southern Etruria, and the Oscan name Cerrinius might point to Pompeii, where it occurs quite often.[21] Even with this scanty detail it is hard to defend the notion of a cult that attracted exclusively women and the less privileged.

Livy reports that initiates who had polluted themselves by debauchery or murder, had given false witness, had counterfeited seals, forged wills, or had otherwise defrauded were condemned to death. Women condemned for any of these charges were handed over to their families for punishment, and if no suitable person was available, the authorities would exact the penalty (39.18). In light of the criminal acts, the ordered punishment was no different for Bacchants than it was for an uninitiated criminal. While Minusius Cerrinus of Campania was sent to Ardea for imprisonment, the heroes Publius Aebutius and Hispala Faecina received appropriate rewards for their steadfastness. Aebutius was freed from military service; Hispala was given the right of giving away or alienating her property, of marriage outside her *gens,* and a choice of guardian, and she was allowed to marry a man of free birth. The prostitute with the golden heart, who was instrumental in weeding out conspirators against the Roman state, was generously rewarded. And the Bacchic rites continued to exist under the auspices of the appropriate civic channels.

In Livy's narrative, the cult of Bacchus represents disorder and madness, while the state, represented by the (all male) Senate, stands for order and sanity. The account stresses moral and even sexual debaucheries committed by Bacchants. If we had only Livy's narrative, we would conclude that the Roman Senate feared and reacted against the cult for the same reasons as Euripides' Pentheus. The inscription from Tiriolo, however, points to a political reason: the Senate wanted control over the cult and demonstrated its political power over all Italy. In Rome, where politics and religion were intertwined, such control belonged traditionally to the ruling elite and, in the case of Bacchic worship, senatorial control over the cult needed to be established. There was a desire to curb Hellenistic influences on public life, a zeal to subdue, bring into line, and structure a "foreign" cult. Or, in terms of power, Rome reigned supreme over her immediate neighbors and allies. The high number of executions leaves the feeling that in 186 BCE, as happens too often in human history, religion served as a smoke screen. Those who were singled out were undermining the ruling authority, Rome, and were executed not for their participation in a cult but so that a political order could prevail.

Women, whether cult adherents of Bacchus or not, were deemed dangerous. Their activities outside their assigned place, the home, had to be curtailed and controlled to ensure society's stability. This was the bottom line, at least in the literary records from antiquity that created narratives anchored in a moral framework that, as we have seen, put forth examples of moral and immoral behavior. We are to believe that Hispala's proper actions brought her exceptional social and legal rewards, whereas her counterparts were punished with death. Every political elite has to fear the breakdown of the societal system that puts at risk the state as a whole; the greater and more diverse the Empire, the greater the possibilities of real breakdown. In the Roman worldview, women became the canvas on which these anxieties and fears were projected and, subsequently, also served as conduits of resolution.

BONA DEA: THE SCANDAL OF 62 BCE

To mention Bona Dea is to invoke the name of Publius Claudius Pulcher, Clodius, who interrupted the celebration in December 62 BCE and was tried for the offense (*incestum*) in the spring of 61 BCE. Clodius came from one of the oldest, most prestigious patrician families of Rome. There is little tangible information about Clodius' youth. This changes with his appointment to Lucius Licinius Lucullus' staff.[22] Lucullus was Clodius' brother-in-law and held the supreme military command in the Third Mithridatic War (73–67 BCE). Clodius appears on the general's staff in 67 BCE, but it is assumed that he was on it from the beginning. Clodius' older brother, Appius, was highly esteemed, a fact, some argue, that pushed Clodius to instigate a rebellion among Lucullus' troops. Although the campaign of 69 BCE had been successful for the Romans, it had failed in capturing Mithridates.[23]

In 68 BCE, Lucullus' troops marched into northern Armenia, but again, Mithridates and the Armenian king Tigranes threatened Roman success. Lucullus decided to attack Artaxata, the old capital of Armenia, but cold weather and the soldiers' refusal to march again stalled this attempt. Lucullus then eyed the city of Nisibis, where Armenia's imperial treasury was housed, as a new target. Again, Tigranes and Mithridates frustrated the

Romans. Tigranes was successful in reestablishing Armenian control in most of the south and Mithridates, moving westward, defeated the Roman army under the command of Fabius Hadrianus in the Pontic region. Lucullus planned to move from Nisibis into Adiabene, but his troops mutinied. The leader of the mutiny was Clodius. Lucullus' political star was fading, Pontus had been lost to Mithridates, and Cilicia had been assigned to another brother-in-law, Quintus Marcius Rex.

Clodius took the opportunity to disassociate himself from Lucullus and attached himself to Marcius, who put him in charge of the fleet. Pirates, however, captured Clodius. Ptolemy, the king of Cyprus, whom Clodius asked to pay the ransom, was tightfisted, and only Pompey's arrival on the scene forced the pirates to give up their hostage. Clodius continued to serve under Marcius, whose command Pompey in essence outranked. Syria was also on Marcius' agenda, which he tried to stabilize by installing Philip II Barypous as its king. Clodius was sent to Antioch in an attempt to bolster Philip, but he was unsuccessful. Circumstances in the East were changing as well; Pompey's military and political star was rising fast. By 66 BCE, Pompey had replaced Marcius. It is assumed that Clodius returned with his brother-in-law to Rome. In 65 BCE, Clodius attempted to prosecute Catiline for extortion in Africa. The prosecution failed, Catiline having garnered enough support to be acquitted of the charge. Clodius then attached himself to Lucius Licinius Murena, the *praetor* of 65 BCE.

Murena had been a successful legate under Lucullus but also had had a falling out with the proconsul. Murena, the *propraetor* of Transalpine Gaul for the year 64 BCE, put Clodius on his staff. We do not know which duties Clodius had to fulfill in the province, but it is fair to assume that Clodius made the best of the assignment, that is, tried to bolster his political career. Upon their return to Rome in 63 BCE, Murena ran successfully for the consulship for the following year. Clodius campaigned for him, but the elections were problematic, to say the least. The most devastating outcome was Catiline's conspiracy, a direct result of a patrician's thwarted attempt at a consulship. The hapless Catiline fell in battle in January 62 BCE, and as his conspiracy overshadowed Roman politics, another disappointed candidate for the 62 BCE consulship, Servius Sulpicius Rufus, accused Murena of corrupt election practices (*de ambitu*). Cicero was among the legal team who successfully defended Murena against this charge. Although one tends to put Clodius in Catiline's camp, following Cicero's guide, Clodius did nothing to warrant this interpretation. He stayed close to Murena and the established elite. His eyes were on the quaestorship, which he obtained for 61–60 BCE. Sicily was the province assigned to him.

Clodius disturbed the Bona Dea celebration on the night of December 4, 62 BCE. On the first of January 61 BCE, Cicero wrote to Atticus:

> I believe that you have heard that P. Clodius, the son of Appius, was caught in women's clothes in the house of Gaius Caesar when a sacrifice for the people was offered; [you have heard] that he made a safe escape with the help of a servant girl, that this is an affair of utter disgrace, which, I know, you certainly think shameful.[24]

This is the first and our only contemporary source that gives an insight into what happened in December 62 BCE in the house of Caesar, where the festival of Bona Dea was celebrated. Caesar was the *pontifex maximus* at that time. On January 25, Cicero writes to Atticus, referring once more to the affair. At this point, the matter had been brought before the Senate, which, in turn, referred the matter back to the Vestals and the college of pontiffs. These two religious bodies decided that a sacrilege had occurred. On the fateful night, after Clodius' discovery, the Vestals had celebrated the ritual (*instauratio*) once more. The Vestals had acted properly by repeating the ceremony to assure the well-being of the state. Clodius' presence had caused a momentary rupture in the reciprocal relationship between the divine and the human world. In retrospect, however, the repetition of the ceremony was not enough. The driving force behind this judgment was not religion but politics. Clodius, who was to hold a quaestorship for the coming year, needed to be curbed.

Clodius stood trial for *incestum* from March 15 to May 15, 61 BCE. The most prominent witnesses for the prosecution were Caesar's mother, Aurelia, and Cicero. Despite Clodius being recognized (Aurelia) and having no alibi (Cicero), a bribed jury acquitted him. Clodius' political ambitions then made him change his family affiliation. He had himself adopted into a plebeian family but did not take the adoptive family's name. Instead he changed the family name Claudius into Clodius. This new plebeian affiliation gave Clodius the chance to hold the tribuneship of the people (59 BCE), arguably the only effective legislative body in the late Republic.[25]

Ever since the Bona Dea trial, Clodius and Cicero had been on adversarial terms. If anything, it was the former's unremitting political and personal zeal that irritated the champion of the Republic. 58 BCE was an excellent year for Clodius to implement policies, in particular helping Caesar and removing Cicero (exile) and Cato (duties in the East) from Rome. The following year, Cicero's return from exile brought violence. Clodius' men attacked the tribune of the people, Titus Annius Milo. As aedile in 56 BCE,

Clodius tried unsuccessfully to prosecute Milo, and Cicero defended himself against the aedile's accusations. All the while, Milo and Clodius' gangs continued to attack each other until Clodius' death at the hand of Milo's supporters in 52 BCE. It was the year Clodius ran for the praetorship.

EXAMPLES OF INSCRIPTIONS

There were two festivals for Bona Dea:[26] one on May 1st and one in December. The May festival was in remembrance of the foundation day of the Aventine temple of the goddess *ad saxum*. Livia, the wife of Augustus, had restored this temple that stood in the area where Remus had taken his foundation augury. Although it was believed that the *patres* surrounding Remus had built the original temple, men did not have access to the temple. In Ovid we read:

> There is a native hill that gives the place its name: they call it Rock (*saxum*); it is a good part of the mountain. There Remus waited in vain, when at the time the Palatine birds gave the first sign to his brother. There the fathers (*patres*) founded a temple on the gently sloping ridge, [a temple] that was hostile to the male eyes. An heiress of the ancient name of the Crassi dedicated it, who did not give her virginal body to any man. Livia restored it, lest she not imitate her husband and follow her husband in everything.[27]

Macrobius relates that a pharmacy was connected with the temple and that there were snakes.[28] Like Asclepius, Bona Dea *ad saxum* was a healing deity in whose sanctuary snakes were kept, and the iconography of the goddess included a snake as well as a cornucopia. There are inscriptions that give emphasis to the goddess' curative quality. For example, an inscription found in Rome close to the third milestone on the Via Ostiense tells of a man named Felix Asinianus, who recovered his eyesight with the help of the goddess.

CIL VI 68 = *ILS* 3513 = BROUWER 44 [29]

Felix Asinianus, the public slave of pontiffs, has fulfilled the vow to Bona Dea Agrestis Felicula[30] willingly and sincerely, sacrificing a white heifer for the recovery of sight. He was healed, after having been given up by doctors, after ten months of taking medicines, through the kindness of the mistress; through her everything was restored during the ministry of Cannia Fortunata.[31]

We have to remember that loss of sight was a much more common occurrence in antiquity than now, but that one of the culprits, the bacteria *Chlamydia trachomatis,* is easily transmitted through contact between people and still blinds many. A base of a small statuette of a seated female connects Bona Dea with Hygia, a goddess of health who appears often as Asclepius' consort. *Salus* (here having the meaning bodily health) is the Latin equivalent to the Greek Hygia.

CIL VI 72 = *ILS* 3514 = BROUWER 21

To Bona Dea Hygia[32]

Since the title Bona Dea in itself is rather vague, it is not surprising that other deities or epithets are attached to this goddess. An inscription on a tablet from the imperial period shows this nicely:

CIL VI 73 = *ILS* 3506 = BROUWER 22

To Bona Dea Lucifera [the bringer of light], Antistia Eur (. . .) the freedwoman of Vetus, gave this as a gift.[33]

Cicero, for example, mentions *lucifera* as an epithet of Diana,[34] and it could be that Bona Dea is simply named in connection with other deities, though a notional correlation was not always necessary.[35] Although only women were allowed to enter the Aventine sanctuary and men who entered were supposedly struck with eye ailments,[36] this inaccessibility did not preclude men from seeking help from the deity, as Felix Asinianus' inscription shows, or thanking and presenting the goddess with gifts. The epigraphic record, in form of dedicatory inscriptions from Rome, shows that men outnumber women in this votive action. While the cult is understood as a women's cult, and men were not allowed to enter the sanctuary of the goddess *ad saxum,* men still could consult the goddess and doctors, some of whom were women, who had chosen Bona Dea as their guardian deity. There may also have been sanctuaries of Bona Dea that were open to men. There are thirty-one dedications to Bona Dea from Rome and only nine of them are by women. Thirteen of the thirty-one inscriptions name men as dedicators. Men and women put up six inscriptions jointly, and the remaining three are without dedicators. Only one inscription, found on a marble altar, can be dated to the Republican period and seems to point to a prominent family, the Mucii Scaevolae, whose most famous members of the latter part of the Republic carried the *praenomen* Quintus.[37]

102

$$CIL \text{ VI } 59 = 30688 = I^2 972 (=816)$$
$$= ILS 3491 = \text{BROUWER } I5$$

Quintus Mucius Trupho, freedman of Quintus, as slave made a vow and freed fulfilled it willingly and deservedly. Dedicated to Bona Dea.[38]

The most famous members of the latter part of the Republic carried the *praenomen* Quintus. If Trupho was a freedman of this family, then his patron could have been Quintus Marcus Scaevola, the augur, who lived 170–87 BCE; Quintus Marcus Scaevola, a celebrated jurist and *pontifex maximus,* 140–82 BCE; or the youngest of this group, Quintus Marcus Scaevola, the grandson of the augur and augur himself, who spent time with Cicero's brother Quintus in Asia Minor in 59 BCE and was a legate of Appius Claudius Pulcher, the brother of the infamous Clodius Pulcher, until 51 BCE. All other inscriptions come from the imperial period with the exception of an altar, on which a serpent is depicted, whose time period cannot be established.[39]

These inscriptions show that Bona Dea was linked to the imperial household, maybe because of the empress Livia's interest in the goddess, as expressed in her involvement in the restoration of the temple *ad saxum.* Imperial employees, mostly freed persons, and high-ranking politicians embraced Bona Dea. One gesture of gratitude not just toward the goddess but also toward the Roman world's most powerful employer, the emperor and empress, resulted in the upkeep of a sanctuary, as we see in the following inscription:

$$CIL \text{ VI } 56 = ILS 5433 = \text{BROUWER } 5$$

Astrapton, the overseer of Caesar [imperial overseer], having made a vow to Bona Dea, restored a shrine, altar, and an enclosing wall [all] that has deteriorated with age.[40]

While Augustus and Livia were instrumental in shaping Rome's sacred landscape, the dated epigraphic evidence comes from later periods, such as the votive inscription of a slave attached to the imperial household of the emperor Claudius:

$$CIL 64 = ILS 3502 = \text{BROUWER } 4$$

Venustus, the deputy slave of Philoxenus, the steward and slave of Tiberius Claudius Caesar, fulfilled his vow to Bona Dea willingly and deservedly.[41]

We have the funeral inscription of Philoxenus, from which we learn more about this imperial steward. He had a historic first name, Ascanius, the name of Aeneas' son, the founder of Alba Longa and imaginary ancestor of the Julians through an etymology based on Iulus.

CIL VI 8719

To the Gods of the Underworld of Ascanius Philoxenus, the slave and steward of the treasury, who lived twenty-seven years.[42]

A shrine that has been dated to the Neronian period mentions the restoration of a shrine in which a cult statue of the goddess (*simulacrum*) stood:

CIL VI 65 = ILS 3500 = BROUWER 10

Dedicated to Bona Dea. Marcus Vettius Bolanus ordered [it] to be restored.[43]

The dedicator, Marcus Vettius Bolanus, owned an apartment complex in the Trastevere, where there was a shrine of Bona Dea. The goddess served as the protector of the tenement. Bolanus was consul for part of the year (*suffectus*) sometime during Nero's reign, and his son of the same name was consul (*ordinarius*) in 111 CE. Cladus, maybe an inhabitant of the Trastevere and the apartment complex, presented the refurbished sanctuary with a pillar and a cult statue, which would mean that a pontiff had consecrated Bolanus' sanctuary.

CIL VI 66 = ILS 3501 = BROUWER 11

To the Restored Bona Dea, Cladus gave [this pillar as] a present.[44]

CIL VI 67 = ILS 3501A = BROUWER 12

To the Restored Bona Dea, Cladus put up willingly and deservedly a cult statue as protector of the apartment building of Bolanus as well as a sanctuary. Left on the stone: of Bolanus[45]

Among the thirty-one inscriptions, six are dedications jointly by women and men. Like Astrapton (*CIL* VI 56 = *ILS* 5433 = Brouwer 5), Zmaragdus was an imperial overseer. He was in charge of the storehouses of Galba and of the three cohorts that might have received their provisions from these granaries:

To Bona Dea Galbilla, Zmaragdus the overseer of Caesar Augustus of the Galban granaries [and] of the three cohorts, gave this as a present together with Fenia[46] Onesime.[47]

Bona Dea is called Galbilla, the little Galba, like the storehouses seemingly connected to the emperor who ruled for a short time after Nero.

A small altar with a ladle (*simpulum*) and a shallow libation bowl (*patera*) on its side mention Bona Dea the Nurse. The main dedicator was an imperial slave who lived during the Flavian to the Hadrianic period. The woman dedicator, Valeria Spendusa, may have been a freedwoman (*liberta*) of Messalina or even a descendant of such a freedwoman:[48]

To Bona Dea the Nurse, Onesimus Faustinus, slave of our Caesar, and Valeria Spendusa and [their] daughter Valeria Pia gave this present.[49]

Nine inscriptions are by women. A white marble piece found on the Caelian behind the military hospital, now lost, had two snakes moving from left to right toward an altar underneath the inscription. The snakes, besides being connected with healing via the imagery related to Asclepius, can also be connected to a family *genius*. Scholars think of *genius* in this context because the snakes are moving toward an altar, an image found in family shrines (*lararia*).[50] This then would speak of Bona Dea the female force connected to the household, which is to prosper.

Dedicated to Bona Dea. Sulpicia Severa Maior gave this present, a sanctuary with a statue.[51]

The inscription has been dated to the first century CE, probably the time of Augustus. The dedicator, Sulpicia Severa, sponsored a sanctuary with a statue. This statue was decorative (*signum*) and not consecrated (*simulacrum*). It is very possible that the sanctuary was a private one.

An inscription from the imperial period speaks of a dedication of a small shrine:

CIL VI 62 = BROUWER 18

Secunda [freedwoman] of Lucius presented as present to Bona Dea for her paternal *genius* of (her) ancestors a small sanctuary, stairs, . . , a roof, a hearth. The fellow-freedwoman to the fellow-freedwoman Flora.[52]

The dedicator, Secunda, may have connected Bona Dea with the *genius* of her ancestors. The confluence of attributes and characteristics or syncretism, which was a vital feature of polytheism, makes this possible, and the snake functions as its expression. There was no prohibition against the building of shrines on private property even for a deity who might not have received official recognition and thus legitimization. Bona Dea, however, was an officially accepted deity. There was a temple with a foundation date (May 1) and a festival in December, but the state version, the healer and the fertility goddess, did not have to be the same for all inhabitants of the Roman Empire. Because Bona Dea was a rather vague appellative, the goddess was perhaps more easily connected to other deities.

The combination of Bona Dea with *conops,* the Greek word *(κώνωψ)* for a gnat or a mosquito, seems at first rather strange when we read the inscription below. But the dedicator, Antonia Hygia, may have been in the medical profession as her cognomen, Hygia, suggests, and Bona Dea Conops was not the goddess responsible for mosquito-borne diseases such as malaria but, just the opposite, involved in the healing of these illnesses.

CIL VI 71 = ILS 3505 = BROUWER 20

Dedicated to Bona Dea Conops, Antonia Hygia made [this altar] from her own (money) [and] gave [it] as a present.[53]

There are also inscriptions that mention office holders. A funerary inscription from the third or fourth century CE mentions a priestess of Bona Dea (*sacerdos Bonae Deae*) and her protégée (*alumna*). Among the extended group surrounding this priestess were women as well as men.

CIL VI 2236 = BROUWER 25

To the Gods of the Underworld. Aelia Nice, priestess of Bona Dea, built [this] while still alive for herself and for her protégée Claudia Nice and Aelia Thalasse and Aelia Serapia and Claudia Fortunata and Luccia Felicitas and Valerius Menander and . . .[54]

One of the persons, Aelia Serapia, carries a theophoric name. We have to remember that the polytheistic religious system allowed people to be engaged in multiple cults and worship different gods simultaneously. Aelia Serapia may have worshiped Sarapis, but it may as well have been the case that she was Egyptian. In any case, if Serapia was her original name, then it was her parents' interest reflected here, not hers.

The *sacerdos* of Bona Dea did not have to be a woman or an adult as a bilingual Greek and Latin funeral inscription attests. Dated to the third or fourth century CE, it presents us with a boy-priest of the goddess:

IG XIV 1449 = KAIBEL 588 = IGRRP I 212
= CCCA III 271 = BROUWER 31

Here I lie, Aurelios Antonios, the priest of all gods, first of all Bona Dea, then the Mother of Gods and Dionysos and Hegemon, having solemnly celebrated the mysteries at all times, I have left the solemn and sweet light of the sun. Hereafter, initiates or friends of whatever walk of life avoid coming close to all the continuous solemn mysteries of life, because nobody is able to escape the thread of fate. For I, this very exalted Antonios, have lived seven years and twelve days. Aurelia Antonia and Aurelios Onesimos have put up this [monument] in the memory of their most sweet child. Dedicated to the Gods of the Underworld.[55]

While it is hardly imaginable that a seven-year-old could have been an active priest of any cult, the son of a freedman and his wife might have held the title as an honorific expressing the community's or the association's appreciation for the parents' dedication. This kind of honor became rather common in the later periods of the Roman Empire.[56] The combination of Bona Dea and the Mother of Gods is not surprising at all, since both goddesses could be perceived as all-creators, generators of life; thus their most basic characteristic overlapped. The aspect of fertility and *mysterion*, the knowing of a divine revelation, connects Dionysus to both.

Who Hegemon was remains unclear. The female form, Hegemone, points to the Charites, the three Graces. Besides being attached to Aphrodite, they were also classed with Charon, the ferryman of the Underworld, and one of them, Charis Hegemone, also with Hermes Chthonios (Hermes of the Netherworld). Along these lines then, Hegemon can be associated with Dionysus. Together the four deities touch upon fertility and afterlife, the major components of any mystery cult. The four deities could easily have been the gods of one cult association; equally, a priest could have been officiating in each cult separately, which would postulate individual initiations into each cult. It is hard to say which form is applicable here; on the other hand, syncretic accumulation, as evidenced in the various epigraphic corpora, seems more likely in the later Empire.

Inscriptions inform us of two positions besides that of priestess or priest, *sacerdos,* namely, that of *magistra* and *ministra.*[57] The *magistra* was the chief officer managing a Bona Dea association, what we today would call an office manager. Her duties may have ranged from keeping accounts to overseeing the execution of routine practices. A *ministra,* on the other hand, carried out religious duties that were assigned to attendants below the level of *sacerdos,* though what these duties exactly entailed cannot be established. Among the epigraphic data there seem to be more *magistrae* than *ministrae.* The former occur most often in inscriptions from or around Rome whereas the latter appear in epigraphic evidence from the provinces.[58]

An inscription from Fidenae, an Alban Hill city outside Rome on the *Via Salaria* (Salt Route), records what seems most likely the dedication of a sanctuary at the behest of two freedmen and a freedwoman, a *magistra* of Bona Dea. The addressee was the *numen* of the imperial household (*numen domus Augustae*). The dedicators gave an exact date of the dedication, September 18 in the consulship of Marcus Clodius Lunensis and Publius Licinius Crassus (after 105 CE),[59] as was usual for dedications that included sanctification of a sanctuary. This dedication is also political, in that a divine force of the imperial house was invoked and the Senate of Fidenae found it appropriate to restore the sanctuary. One of the original dedicators, Secundus, was also a *sexvir,* most likely an *Augustalis,* involved in the municipal worship of the emperor via the *lares* and the *genius* of the Augustus.

CIL XIV 4057 = BROUWER 51

To the Numen (divinity) of the Augustan House. Blastus Eutactianus and Secundus, freedman of Julius Quadratus, consul for the second time, on account of the honor of the sevirate and Italia, freedwoman of the same, on account of the magistracy of Bona Dea, dedicated [this] on the fourteenth day before the Kalends of October [18th of September], in the consulship of Marcus Clodius Lunensis . . . and Publius Licinius Crassus, and on that day they also held a banquet. Destroyed by fire, the Senate of Fidenae rebuilt [it].[60]

Although literary sources classify the cult of Bona Dea as a goddess of women, the inscriptions from Rome show that men were involved as well. With very few exceptions, the inscriptions come from imperial times, that is to say, from the time of Augustus onward until the end of the Principate. Livia's restoration of a major temple of Bona Dea in Rome, the Aventine sanctuary, may indeed have introduced the possibility for nonelites, freedwomen and men as well as slaves, to participate in cultic actions connected to Bona Dea, which did not interfere with the December celebration. This remained exclusively an elite women's occasion with the Vestals, the representatives of the Roman state and religion, in attendance. Within the group of imperial freedmen and women, the men, the *liberti,* outnumbered the women. In general, however, there were more freedwomen than men. The smallest group of worshipers was made up of slaves, most of whom were women. Among privately owned slaves, however, the majority were men.[61]

All in all, the epigraphic evidence presents a different picture of Bona Dea and her cult adherents than the literary sources that predominantly focus on the mythological aspects of the goddess or the scandal of 62 BCE. The cult of Bona Dea of the Augustan and post-Augustan period was in part linked to the imperial household, open to men and women alike, in particular, freedwomen and freedmen. As such, the cult had a political dimension of binding the newest of citizens and those with imperial connections (like imperial slaves) even more closely to the center of power, the emperor and his family.

THE DECEMBER FESTIVAL

Because of Clodius' trespass, the December festival of Bona Dea grew to be infamous and thus became the norm for our understanding of Bona Dea. She was a woman's goddess. As we have seen, however, the epigraphic evidence suggests a more open pool of worshipers. All we can say is that the December festival of the goddess was solely for the elite women of Rome.[62] The ceremony was held in the house of a magistrate with *imperium.* In 62 BCE, the celebrants gathered in Caesar's house. Caesar was *praetor* at the time and had been appointed *pontifex maximus* a year earlier. His wife Pompeia, the daughter of Pompey, officiated in the ceremony. At the culmination of the festivities, Clodius, dressed as a woman, and Caesar's wife enjoyed their own private pinnacle of enjoyment, certainly a good, tantalizing story, one that grew more and more elaborate as time went by. One sure fact we have is that Clodius, for an undisclosed reason, was in the house at the time the celebration took place.

Despite all the secrecy, we know a fair amount of the ritual surrounding the December festival, which was celebrated *pro populo* (for the people).

Men were excluded; the Vestals were in attendance. The presence of the Vestals signals, as always, fecundity and the state's welfare. The ambiguity of their being and not being matrons inserted an element of sociopolitical non-femaleness into the ritual equation. Clodius did the same when he wore women's clothes to mingle with the celebrants. The room in which the celebration took place was decorated with vines.[63] The satirist Juvenal, ever ready to highlight sexual perversion, mentions the sacrifice of a pig.[64] What better offering than an animal that symbolizes fertility and happens to be the most common as well as inexpensive blood sacrifice, in particular in private cults.[65] Where, however, this sacrifice took place is unknown. If satire derives its force from the disjunction of reality and fiction, then setting Vestals opposite sexual depravity brings about the desired effect: a good laugh.

There was music, dancing, and drinking wine;[66] in general, there was merry-making. Having a party was then, as it is now, not an everyday occurrence. It is something special we do in company of friends or associates who share the same values. Since it is something special, one can let go of everyday norms, one can be a-normal and let oneself go within a delineated context. Thus, Roman matrons had fun in a religious context. Besides dancing to music, they drank unwatered wine (*temetum*), which was reserved for gods and men.[67] Rome's elite matrons were allowed to enjoy this sacrificial wine during the festival because they were in a cultic position of being symbolic conduits, guarantors of fecundity and continuation of life, just as the Vestals were throughout their tenure. Macrobius reports that the wine was called milk.[68] The renaming then would make wine not wine, and the women drinking it, notionally, did not overstep their boundaries. In addition, in ritual, milk held a prominent place of a natural libation, and it was a purifying offering. In time, wine took the place of milk.[69] Calling this ritual wine "milk" may suggest that in the earliest phase of this ceremony, milk was drunk before wine replaced it.

There is also an etiological explanation for why wine was called milk. Plutarch wonders why myrtle is absent among the many plants the women bring to the celebration. Myth tellers (*mythologoi*), he states, relate that Faunus found his wife drunk and beat her to death with myrtle twigs. This is why the celebrants exclude the myrtle and in honor of the murdered wife pour libations of wine, which they call milk. The myrtle, Plutarch continues in an etymological vein, was sacred to Aphrodite Murcia, who in ancient times was called Myrtia.[70] Besides the notoriety the myrtle had as an erotic-sexual stimulant, the Greek word *murtos* "also means female pudendum, more especially the clitoris."[71] One can argue, as Versnel does, that erotic lust was simply not part of the ritual, although the ritual itself had "an overtly sexual atmosphere."[72] Macrobius presents an altogether different story. Bona Dea, who is also known as Fauna, Ops, or Fatua, resisted her father's amorous advances. Although made drunk and struck with myrtle twigs by him, she still did not succumb. Faunus then changed form, became a snake, and had intercourse with his unwilling daughter.[73] The symbolic value of the snake does not need much elaboration; it stands for virility and procreation. A man who changes into a snake and thus achieves his goal of forcing himself on a woman is a well-known motif since Hellenistic times, but in this case the story is more extreme; it speaks of incest: a father forces himself onto his unmarried, virgin daughter.[74]

The myth of Faunus, the few things we know about the celebration of Bona Dea in December, and the scandal of 62 BCE all point in the same direction, namely, in its extreme to sexual encounters, which in narratives (myth of Faunus or the elaborations around Clodius' intrusion) become trespasses of acceptable behavior. In its normative configuration the celebration points to fecundity and fertility. The Vestals, however, hold the key that unlocks the secret, at least in part. The senior Vestal, a representative of the state that was controlled solely by men, officiated at this ceremony, which was undertaken in the name of the Roman people. These priestesses, as we have seen earlier, kept alive the fire that represented Rome, the Empire that like a living organism needed to continue. In other words, fields and humans had to reproduce themselves to guarantee this continuation. As with many religious rituals, there are inversions, reversals, and paradoxes of which matrons and virgins are but one set of players.

The surviving epigraphic and literary evidence presents us with two distinct cult patterns. For one, there was the Augustan and post-Augustan Bona Dea whose worshipers were men and women alike, in particular those of the freed class bound to the imperial household. If there was a key occasion that marked the development of this version of the goddess, it was Livia's renovation of the temple on the foot of the Aventine hill, which was recorded for May 1. Bona Dea was associated with healing, but this was certainly not the only aspect of the deity with a name vague enough, the Good Goddess, to allow easy connection with other deities. The goddess, whose rites Rome's elite women and the Vestals celebrated in December, was a fertility goddess, a guarantor of Rome's continued growth and success. Bona Dea was a multifaceted goddess, and like other deities, had ritual cycles and cult aspects that differed from each other, a multivalence that signifies an assimilating polytheistic religious system.

SIX

ROME AND ITS PROVINCES

Rome's administration of its Empire brought religious structures to the provinces and provincial concepts to the capital. We see an example of this exchange process in the female flaminate and the Matres/Matronae, which, although not empirewide systems, allow a glimpse, especially in the case of the female flaminate, at a provincial adaptation of originally capital-specific priesthoods. The Matres/Matronae, on the other hand, show how soldiers carried their ancestral worship outside their original home area to foreign territories and thus broadened the cult's base of worshipers. In both cases, however, religion bound the center and the periphery, and women, either as priestesses or divine entities, represented dynamic forces that shaped societal cohesiveness.

The *flaminicae,* women priestesses, were originally the wives of *flamines,* priests. In Rome, the *flamines* formed the college of the pontiffs with the *rex sacrorum,* the pontiffs, and the six Vestals. On behalf of the Senate, this college interpreted sacred law in the service of the state. The flaminate was believed to be ancient and its beginnings to have arisen in regal times. Augustus revised the flaminate as he did much of Roman religion. He added a *flamen,* a priest of Augustus and the imperial household (the *domus Augusta*), to the list of these priests. This was to offer members of the equestrian class another opportunity to engage in religious activities, which were traditionally in the hands of those of senatorial rank.[1]

The majority of inscriptions honoring women, who held the position of *flaminica,* come from Portugal, Spain, and Roman North Africa. This fact may indicate an indigenous cultural pattern, different from the traditional Roman view, that permitted women in visibly prominent positions. Inscriptions also inform us that holding the flaminate was often a family affair, as these provincial priestesses were either daughters of *flamines* or *flaminicae* or wives of men who held the flaminate.[2] The priesthood was also seen as a reward for a woman who had done something outstanding for her community. This provincial and municipal flaminate allowed leading women in the provinces and their families to display their privileged status while also binding the periphery to the political center, Rome.

The Matres (Mothers) or Matronae (Married Women) had a similar function, although the original periphery-center connection started not in Rome but in the provinces, which was different from the origin of the *flaminicae.* The Matres/Matronae were a unique phenomenon of ancestral mothers of Celtic clans that had turned into deities. Formerly linked to extended families, these mother-deities were dislodged from their original geographical and ideological context and received a Roman interpretation. They took on anthropomorphic form as Roman matrons with broad-rimmed hats and most often were depicted in a group of three. Even when Christianity became the sole religion of the Empire, the Matres/Matronae, who, like other female deities brought about and secured fecundity, and consequently well-being, continued to exist. They became the "Three Maries" of Gaul and may also be the precursor of the Grimm Brothers' Frau Holle. The *flaminicae* and the Matres/Matronae demonstrate that in the provinces, just as in Rome, women as priestesses or female deities were integral components in a religious system that was instrumental in maintaining Empire.

FLAMINICAE

The Romans had fifteen *flamines* (singular: *flamen*). These fifteen were divided into two groups. The *flamines maiores* (the greater *flamines*) formed the first group; the *flamines minores* (the lesser *flamines*), the second. Specifically, the former were the priests of Jupiter, Mars, and Quirinus; *flamen* Dialis, Martialis, and Quirinalis respectively. The office holders had to be patricians. The names of the lower-ranked *flamines* were Carmentalis, Cerialis, Falacer, Floralis, Furrinalis, Lucularis (?), Palatualis, Pomonalis, Portunalis (?), Virbialis (?), Vulcanalis, and Volturnalis. These priests were most likely plebeians and in imperial times came from the equestrian order.

Varro explained the word *flamen* (priest) by suggesting that the *flamines* "were originally called *filamines,* because in Latium they had kept their heads covered and bound their head with a *filium* (fillet)."[3] The linguistics here are fanciful, a kind of syllable transposition that finds its main explanatory reason in the priests' attire. More probable, however, is the linguistic link to the Sanskrit *brahmán* (priest) and the connection to the Anglo-Saxon *blōtan* (sacrifice). The use of epithets, adjectives formed from names of divinities, to describe the noun (*flamen*) seems to suggest that the noun touched or even encompassed the function the office holder performed for the specific deity. The noun *flamen* was originally linked to a neuter noun meaning "cultic actions."[4] A *flamen* then was an agent performing cultic actions specific to a deity such as Jupiter, Mars, or Quirinus. In short, *flamines* celebrated rituals, whereas pontiffs supervised and *augures* interpreted.

The creation of the flaminate was attributed to Rome's second king, Numa. In the Roman mind that meant that the office was so old that tradition, an accepted and continuously upheld norm, stood in place of hard, provable facts. Even without the knowledge of who a deity was or what exact function he or she might have had originally,[5] tradition dictated continued cultic enactment to keep the beneficial relationship between Rome and its gods intact. When Rome's priests were listed, the *flamines* were mentioned after the *rex sacrorum* and before the *pontifex maximus,* whose position was premier in historical times.

We know most about the *flamen Dialis,* the *flamen* of Jupiter, and his wife, the *flaminica Dialis.* This *flamen* of Jupiter had to be a patrician and the child of parents who had been married *in manum farreo* (*confarreatio*).[6] During this wedding ceremony, the couple sacrificed a loaf of spelt bread (*panis farreus*). This kind of marriage removed the wife from her original family and placed her as a dependent in the family of her husband. The *flamen* and his wife had also to be married in this fashion, and, if they were to divorce, they had to lay down their priesthood. If one of them died, the other also had to give up the priesthood. The *flaminica* could be married only once. The couple was at the center of the priesthood as if to promote togetherness and wholesomeness. Dress and appearance distinguished them from their fellow citizens. The *flamen* wore a cap (*galerus*) made of a sacrificial animal's skin. On top of this cap was an olive branch (*apex*). The priest's toga was made of wool (*laena*). The *flaminica Dialis* wore her hair in a *tutulus* (conical top-knot).[7]

There were many prohibitions that further accentuated the difference between the ordinary people and the priest and priestess of Jupiter.[8] The *flamen* sacrificed a sheep on the Ides of each month, and the *flaminica* sacrificed a ram to Jupiter at the *regia* on each market day, which occurred on the ninth day after the eight-day Roman week. The woman sacrificed the male animal, a reversal, but on the whole it was a reciprocal reinforcement of the male-female balance. Ultimately, as with other priesthoods, the most rudimentary purpose was to effect life, which depended on the continued accessibility of foods, earth's products. The *flamen* was in sleep in contact with the earth, the feet of his bed smeared with a thin layer of clay, and his nail parings and hair trimmings were buried under a fruitful tree. Together with his wife, the *flamen* was on duty every day, as if a disruption of duty would interfere with the desired and needed continuation of life.

In Augustan times, a *flamen* was attached to the cult of Augustus and the imperial household (the *domus Augusta*). The flaminate connected colonies and municipalities via their leading citizens to the political center, Rome and the *princeps*. The *flaminicae* were engaged in the provincial, municipal, and confederate cult connected with the imperial household (*domus Augusta*). While the *flamen*'s object of worship was the emperor and his *genius*, the *flaminica*'s was the empress and her *iuno*, which, like the *genius*, included the life force of dead family members. The line of separation between emperor and empress, however, may not have been strictly enforced. The position of *flaminica* was annual, and the title *perpetua* (perpetual) was honorific.[9]

Most of the inscriptions come from the Iberian peninsula (Portugal and Spain), with thirty-four inscriptions, and North Africa, with sixty-eight inscriptions.[10] One can but assume that the indigenous stratum prepared the way for the introduction of such a religious position. Women who held the position seem to have been daughters of *flamines* or *flaminicae*, and they did not necessarily have to be married to a *flamen*, as they did in the province of Gallia Narbonensis.[11] A community could also reward this office to a charismatic woman, one who had made a positive impression, presumably with material resources. The length of her tenure, if more than a year, might have depended on the level of gratitude or the importance of the *flaminica*'s family.

In the province of Africa, the flaminate was a nuclear family affair.[12] It seems that the provincial council (the *concilium*) chose the provincial *flaminica*. Roman Africa provides the greatest number of these municipal priestesses. Most of these African *flaminicae* fulfilled their religious duties on behalf of a city rather than on behalf of the province. The *flaminicae* belong to the equestrian order, and only in a few cases did they come from senatorial families. This very much reflects Augustan policies that targeted the equestrian class for more involvement in religious activities.

As with many things Roman, even the most structured and regulated had some flexibility to allow for modifications. Ramsey MacMullen noted that "at both the top and the bottom of society, women . . . appear to take an active part in the common business of the city . . ."[13] If we look for equality, it can be found among the poor, where married couples worked day in and out, side by side, to survive. Wealthy women, proponents of their families and their class, involved themselves in public life as benefactors and were rewarded with honorific titles and priesthoods. These women had more independence; nonetheless, they did not threaten male power, for their philanthropic work did not translate into political power or social equality.[14] John Nicols noted that for the Latin West that "over 1200 individuals are known from the epigraphical record and can be dated to the period between 50 B.C. and A.D. 327. Among this number, as many as twenty-one cases have been noted in which the patron is actually a *patrona*."[15] Thus, in terms of percentages, women made up 1.75 percent of the patrons, whereas 98.25 percent were men. All being said then, only a few women achieved the highest civic positions as an exchange for their monetary involvement in a city at a time when a completely centralized government controlled everyday life.

EXAMPLES OF INSCRIPTIONS

Generally, it can be said that the majority of the inscriptions from the provinces citing *flaminicae* of a province, a colony, or a municipality date to the second and third centuries CE. Of the eleven inscriptions mentioning *flaminicae* from the province of Lusitania, six name provincial priestesses. Two of them were also *flaminicae* of their municipality, the most common of these priesthoods. All we know of these women, who were once important for their communities, is what personal information we can glean from the inscriptions.

CIL II 114 = IRCPacen 372A

> To Laberia Galla, the daughter of Lucius, the *flaminica* of the municipality of Ebora, the *flaminica* of the province of Lusitania, the freedmen Lucius Laberius Artemas, Lucius Laberius Callaecus, Lucius Laberius Abascantus, Lucius Laperius Paris, Lucius Laberius Lausus [put this up].[16]

An inscription from Salicia (Alaçer do Sal) refers to a priestess of the province who was also priestess of the colony of Emerita (Merida), the provincial capital, and the municipality of Salicia.

CIL II 32 = IRCPacen 183

> To Jupiter the Best and Greatest, Flavia Rufina of Emerita, the daughter of Lucius, the *flaminica* of the province of Lusitania also the perpetual

flaminica of the colony of Emerita and the municipality of Salacia by decree of the town councilors.[17]

We have six inscriptions from Baetica, of which not one mentions a provincial *flaminica*. Priestesses listed are of the imperial household (*flaminica domus Augustae*), of the municipality (*flaminica municipii*), and of an empress (*flaminica Augusta*). Tucci, a city that became a colony at the time of Augustus (also known as *colonia Augusta Gemella*) provides the information for the two priestesses of the imperial household. The link with the imperial household might have had something to do with the city's formation as a colony at the time of Augustus, and the office might have had prestige similar to that of a provincial priesthood. The first inscription from Tucci is undated; the second, a commemorative inscription (*CIL* II² 5, 89), has been dated to the first century CE.

CIL II² 5, 69 = *CIL* II 1663
= *CIL* V 583* = *ILS* 5080

To the Augustan Piety, Lucius Lucretius Fulvianus, the *flamen* of the exempted colonies, the *flamen* of the province of Baetica, the perpetual *pontifex* of the imperial house ordered to be put in place by a will from a unit of silver [. . .] for the honor of the pontificate, Lucretia Campana, the daughter of Lucius, the perpetual *flaminica* of the imperial house, put this gift toward the dedication of dramatic performances for a period of four days and circus games and a public feast to be distributed. Lucretia Campana dedicated [this and] in addition in her name added a golden crown and gave it as a present.[18]

CIL II² 5, 89 = *CIL* II 1678

To Iulia Laeta, the daughter of Gaius, *flaminica* of the imperial household, Lucius Maecius Nativos for his most pious second cousin, next to himself. . . .[19]

Gaius Julius Scaena or Scaeva was a town councilor and a centurion of the Fourth Legion (*CIL* II² 5, 82). This gives us an indication of the social standing of the family that brought forth these priestesses. They were from the municipal elite. An inscription from the municipality of Iliberri Florentia (Granada) mentions the mother of the consul Valerius Vegetus. Two consuls of this name are known, Quintus Valerius Vegetus suffect consul of 91 CE and his son of the same name, suffect consul of 112 CE.

$$CIL\ II^2\ 5,\ 624\ =\ CIL\ II\ 2074$$

To Cornelia Severina, the daughter of Publius, the *flaminica* of Augusta, [. . .] the mother of the consul Valerius Vegetus, by a decree of the town councilors of Florentia Iliberri.[20]

Nearer Spain (Hispania Citerior) provides eighteen inscriptions, eleven of them from the provincial capital, Tarraco. Seven of these mention provincial *flaminicae,* three of whom were married to provincial *flamines.* Two of the eleven priestesses held the flaminate "perpetually." The sampling of inscriptions from Roman Spain shows much the same as Leïla Ladjimi Sebaï had established in her survey of African inscriptions. The priestesses come from the Romanized municipal elite, as the majority of inscriptions come from the most Romanized places. The object of worship was the empress, either alive or dead, in the context of binding the province to Rome, or, more specifically the imperial house, which, in the end, served the same purpose: binding a provincial community to the center of power. In terms of chronology, most of the epigraphic evidence belongs to the second and third century CE, with the occasional inscription from the first century CE. For the first century, the deification of Augustus' wife, Livia, in the reign of Claudius serves as a chronological starting point.

THE MATRES—MATRONAE

Only epigraphic evidence informs us of the Matres (in Gaul sometimes also Matrae, Mothers) or Matronae (Married Women). They were, as their names (*matres* or *matronae*) suggest, originally ancestral mothers who had turned into goddesses.[21] It is the connection with *iuno,* the female equivalent of the male *genius,* that reveals the ancestral aspect of the Matres/Matronae.[22] Mercury accompanied the Matronae, if they were depicted with a male figure. Behind this god was a Celtic god, who had received a Roman interpretation that rendered him as Mercury. Matres/Matronae represented not only families or clans, but whole ethnic groups. Original location as well as family connection played an important role in the attachment of goddesses to groups. Both aspects, location and family, however, have an inherent dynamic; they can change. Settlers, such as veterans of the Roman army, were integrated into already existing groups who worshiped these deities, while those leaving such groups could take their ancestral goddesses with them.

Most often these elaborately dressed women were represented sitting in a group of three (Figure 6.1). In the region of the Ubii, whose main city was Cologne (*oppidum Ubiorum,* which the emperor Claudius proclaimed *colonia Claudia Ara Agrippinensium* in 50 CE), the Matronae wore great brooches, crescent-shaped necklace ornaments or torques, and huge bonnets. In general, though, the goddesses' iconography was that of the traditional Greco-Roman Mētēr (Mother)-type. Around the Matres–Matronae were placed flowers and agricultural products such as wheat and fruits. These offerings made them fertility goddesses or, more generally, mother goddesses. Only the goddesses identified as Matres had child-rearing functions attributed to them, and only altars of Matronae along the river Rhine depict trees. The latter seem to point to an indigenous tree cult. The oak tree played an important role in Celtic religion.[23] The Celtic priests, the druids, were said to have gathered annually underneath a region's oldest oak tree.

Matres and Matronae, who have in general the same characteristics and function, are attested in the northwestern and northeastern regions of the Roman Empire as well as at Rome. Among the Matres of Gaul, the northern part of Spain, and Italy, the earliest mentioned are the ones of southern Gaul of the mid first century CE. The Matronae fall into two groups: those with and those without epithets. The latter group is found mostly concentrated in the region of Gallia Cisalpina, starting in the first third of the first century CE; the former, with more than eight hundred inscriptions, is linked to the region of the Ubii and began appearing in the middle of the second century CE.[24] The Latin, Celtic, or Germanic epithets refer to tribes, areas, and rivers. Ton Derks points out that the names on the inscriptions from the Rhineland reveal about seventy different groups and that some of the inscriptions can be connected to cult places.[25] The Matronae Aufaniae form the largest single group in the area of the Ubii, with seventy surviving inscriptions. The epithet Aufaniae is thought to be Germanic and has been translated as "the givers of abundance."[26] The goddesses' center was Bonn and the *beneficarii,* who formed the corps of noncommissioned officers attached to the treasury in imperial times, were some of the highest-ranking dedicators to Matronae/Matres.[27]

Cisalpine Gaul produced fifty-nine inscriptions dedicated to Matronae, thirty-two to Iunones, and four to Matronae-Iunones. Most Matronae inscriptions come from *regio XI,* the Transpadana, marked by two lakes, the Lago Maggiore (*lacus Verbanus*) and the Lago di Como (*lacus Larius*), and the secondary capital of the later period, Milan (*Mediolanum*). The *Iunones* inscriptions come from *regio X,* the Venetia, with the Lago di Garda (*lacus Benacus*), Brescia (*Brixia*), Verona, and Padova (*Patavium*) as its markers.

FIGURE 6.1.
Matronae Afliae, depicted on an inscription. Römisch-Germanisches Museum der Stadt Köln and Rheinisches Bildarchiv der Stadt Köln, Inv. No. KI150.

Both regions have the highest occurrence of inscriptions for these goddesses, with thirty-four Matronae, two Iunones, and two Matronae-Iunones for the Transpadana and seven Matronae, twenty-nine Iunones, and one Matronae-Iunones for the Venetia. The remaining twenty-two inscriptions (eighteen inscriptions to Matronae, three to Iunones, and one to the Matronae-Iunones) come from the remaining regions. Latium, *regio I,* provides one inscription to the Iunones; similarily Umbria, *regio VI,* has one inscription to the Matronae-Iunones. Aemilia, *regio VIII,* has three inscriptions, one to the Matronae and two to the Iunones. Liguria, *regio IX,* and the Alpes Maritimae each produced four inscriptions to the Matronae. And lastly, nine inscriptions to the Matronae come from the Alpes Cottidae.[28]

The inscriptions from Britain, found along Hadrian's Wall and that of Antoninus Pius, date from the latter part of the second century CE. The latest datable inscription comes from the time of the emperor Gordian (238–244 CE). Two legions are mentioned in connection with these dedications: *legio VI victrix* and *legio XX Valeria victrix.*[29] Prior to their deployment to Britain, both legions were stationed in the province of Lower Germany (*Germania inferior*); *legio VI victrix* at Neuss (Novaesium) and later at Vetura and *legio XX Valeria victrix* at Cologne (Ara Ubiorum) and later at Neuss. It is from the heartland of the Matres/Matronae that the soldiers of the two legions took the local ancestral deities with them to their new home on the British Isle. Thus, they and their families retained a conceptual but not actual connection with their ancestral home. The same can be said in conjunction with the inscriptions found in Rome; they do not point to a transference and integration of these very specific provincial deities into the official Roman pantheon. The dedicators of these inscriptions were *equites singulares* (special horsemen) recruited most often from Gaul and Germany. These horsemen formed part of the emperor's guard and accompanied him into battle.

The time frame of the datable inscriptions of the Matres/Matronae extends from the mid first century CE to the third century CE, with the majority belonging to the second century CE. There was a revival under Julian the Apostate, who was Caesar of the western part of the Roman Empire 355–361 CE[30] and was credited with Gaul's economic recovery. Julian's reign as emperor was short lived (361–363 CE) and fraught with problems, especially the clash between the Christian and pagan ways of life. The triad of Matres/Matronae, who generated and guaranteed well-being, abundance, and fertility, eventually changed into "Three Maries."[31] These Celtic pagan goddesses, made visible when Romanized folk remembered their local ancestral deities in dedicatory inscriptions, continued to exist in a new religious context, that of Christianity.

CONCLUSION

Roman religion was polytheistic and open, conservative yet flexible. Roman religion was not about faith, dogma, or morality; it was about the proper performance of prescribed rituals. Social standing defined the agents who performed the cultic actions on behalf of the state. The aim was a community's prosperity and, by extension, the continued success of the Roman state. In this, its religion and politics were interrelated. The most important Roman citizens held the most important priestly positions. If there was a religious authority, it was the Roman Senate (only notionally from the time of Augustus onward, when the *princeps* was the ultimate authority on all issues) that determined a cult's legitimacy. Rome was a militaristic patriarchy for which the attainment of (military) glory was a crucial determining and defining dynamic. Traditionally, a woman's place was at home, and her aspiration was to give birth and rear glorious Romans, conquerors of nations. More pointedly, a Roman woman was to be silent, and like her Greek sisters, best not spoken about.

The idea of the silent and homebound Roman woman, however, was a created reality propagated predominantly in historical writings by men who put forth examples of proper moral behavior. In other words, what can be called a discourse was to guide every new generation of Romans to do the right thing, which for a woman meant to be a dutiful daughter, a good wife, and a caring mother. While the silent or silenced Roman women of literature, the ideal, stayed home, their actual counterparts were actively involved in everyday life and domestic economies that brought them outside their respective houses. It was the elite woman, in particular, who was vulnerable to criticism and disapproval, since she, as Ronald Syme formulated,[1] was a "seductive topic," and her story was the source material to enliven historical accounts. A woman's public engagement needed to be judged for the good of family and country; if not, then immoral behavior was easily the charge. In contrast, her lower-class sister, who worked side by side and day in and out with her husband or male relative to make ends meet, left sparse records. She speaks to us most often from inscriptions, formulaic as they may be, and from her gravesite, where the physical remains such as offerings inform us about her life.

The chapters of this book focused on women's involvement in religion, in particular, the execution of religious rituals that brought them into the public sphere, and on female deities that were instrumental in shaping Rome's Hellenistic culture. Religion was an intricate part of Rome's cultural tapestry. Through it we are given an opportunity to ascertain the changes in Rome's cultural awareness as it grew from a collection of small hillside communities to a multicultural Empire. The political center exercised supreme control over the periphery, but the periphery also contributed to the power of the capital. What made Rome successful was that the other, the peripheral, was integrated, adopted, or assimilated. Roman religion did as much. It retained traditional practices, adopted and assimilated new ones. This allows us to look beyond the Augustan reshaping of Roman society and learn about women's importance in the creation and preservation of Empire. Women's rituals throughout the agricultural year stressed fecundity and continuation of life. Female deities and priestesses were integral to Rome's self-definition and in its success so much so that when women were found to be beyond their "proper" place, the Roman world was thought to be at the verge of disintegration.

When Rome's gods were thought to have withdrawn their support, the Sibylline Books were consulted in search of a solution that reestablished the goodwill of the gods toward the Roman state. Interpretations of oracular sayings contained in these books often resulted in the introduction of new cults. The utterances of a prophesying woman (or women) then formed the basis of mending the relationship of the Romans and their gods as well as making religious integration possible, such as the incorporation of the Mater Magna, a new deity, and her cult. It was Rome's struggle against Carthage in the last decades of the second century BCE that necessitated the urging of the Sibylline Books to transfer this deity from Asia Minor to Rome. The transference and integration of the deity and the cult emphasized Rome's connection with mythical Troy and Aeneas. The claim to Greek cultural heritage was thus legitimized.

In contrast, the initial introduction of the Egyptian goddess Isis and her cult in the Late Republican period occurred without state approval. Without such endorsement, the cult was subject to state-ordered repression. One can still find in secondary literature that in the time of political rivalry between Augustus and Marc Antony, in what was fashioned as Roman against un-Roman behavior, anything linked to Egypt was categorically rejected or excised. More to the point though, Augustus, who had claimed Egypt as his personal province and was the country's pharaoh, introduced the Ptolemaic dynastic concept into the Roman ideological system. This notion was linked to Isis and her Hellenistic consort Sarapis and was implemented primarily through Augustus' building projects. This implementation was subtle, but it can be detected in the building program surrounding the emperor's private villa on the Palatine hill. The legitimization of the cult of Isis ensued, and by the time of the Flavian emperors, Isis was fully integrated and functioned as an essential, yet admittedly obscure, part of Rome's political ideology, an ideology that had Hellenistic origins.

Although the ideological aspects around Isis are murky, the religious and political importance of the Vestals is clear. The only female priesthood that was part of the college of pontiffs was key to Rome's continued success. The six priestesses tended a flame that symbolized procreation as well as rule, and they carried out religious rituals on behalf of the state that emphasized fecundity throughout the calendar year. The Vestals were instrumental in generating continuance; Rome depended on their proper behavior and correct execution of rituals. Thus, when a Vestal failed, the whole state was at risk. The severest trespass for a Vestal was a shift of her focus or interest away from the state and onto a single man. Her penalty was live burial. But even a failed Vestal served the state as her body, invested with reproductive potential, was inserted into the earth to reassure exactly that very promise of continuance for the whole state.

Every Roman's religious duty was to perform timely and proper rituals to ensure the gods' goodwill. Rome's Empire was proof of proper conduct. Disobedient Vestals and out-of-control female worshipers of Bacchus, for example, turned the gods against Rome. Such an explanation, however, was the interpretative mode based on cause and effect that the ancients employed as they transposed political issues that threatened the fabric of Roman society onto the religious sphere. Conducting religious rituals bound individuals to each other, connected the group as a whole to its gods, and provided a common vocabulary. It forged a transhuman bond between the center, Rome, and its periphery, the provinces. Religion engaged and involved every inhabitant of the Roman Empire.

At the same time as historical narratives and ancient rhetoric have us imagine Roman women of highest morality sitting at home and taking care of their families, the reality was that they were actively involved in religious ceremonies throughout the year. This book has focused on the public aspect of women's involvement in religion and also highlighted divine women as well as female deities that were essential in bringing about Rome. The surviving literary sources may obscure the importance of women, but the reality was that, within the framework of religion, women were understood to be instrumental in the successful maintenance of Rome and its Empire. Women were not only a "seductive topic" but generators of and protectors of life. Romans were reminded of this every time women performed their religious duties.

ANCIENT AUTHORS

APPIAN, END OF FIRST CENTURY—CA. 160S CE

Appian was born in Alexandria. He lived in Rome where he befriended Marcus Cornelius Fronto, the teacher of Marcus Aurelius and Lucius Verus. Appian was a trained lawyer and, through Fronto's connection with the emperor Antoninus Pius, became a procurator (member of the empire's civil administration). Appian wrote a history of Rome from its foundation to the time of Trajan.

GAIUS JULIUS CAESAR, 100–44 BCE

Caesar was born in Rome. He was the most important and prolific statesman of the Late Republic. Caesar's poems and treatise on grammar (*De Analogia*) survive only in small fragments. On the other hand, his *Commentaries* (*Commentarii*), *On the Gallic War* (*De Bello Gallico*), and *On the Civil War* (*De Bello Civili*) are of all the memoirs of antiquity the only extant ones. In the seven books of *On the Gallic War*, Caesar recounts his campaigns against and policies toward Celts in Gaul and Britain and Germans. Aulus Hirtius, consul of 43 BCE, wrote an additional eighth book that was to bridge the time between the Gallic War, 59/8–52 BCE, and the Civil War, 49–48 BCE. *On the Civil War* in three books is incomplete. It is our prime source for the war between Pompey and Caesar. Just like *On The Gallic War,* however, it is a piece of political propaganda as well as justification. Caesar's style is marked by its clarity and simplicity.

(LUCIUS) CASSIUS DIO, CA. 164–AFTER 229 CE

Dio's family came from Nicaea (Iznik in Turkey). Dio had a successful career as senator, which culminated in the proconsulship of Africa and the governorship of Dalmatia and Pannonia Superior. Dio was consul together with the emperor Severus Alexander in 229. Dio's history of Rome covers the city's foundation down to the year of his own consulship.

MARCUS PORCIUS CATO, 234–149 BCE

Cato was born in Tusculum, southeast of Rome. He had a distinguished military and administrative career. Cato was a "new man" (*novus homo*), the first in his family to hold public office. He obtained the consulship in 195 BCE and the censorship in 184 BCE. Cato spoke out against Hellenism and embraced Roman traditions. Unlike his contemporaries, he wrote in Latin. Cato is the originator of Latin prose writing. *The Origins* (*Origines*) dealt with Rome's and Italy's early history; very little of this work has survived. His *On Agriculture* (*De agri cultura*) is the oldest surviving Latin prose piece. This work gives us information about Roman life and economy of the second century BCE. Cato was the first to publish his speeches as well as write on rhetoric. His style was straightforward and plain. In Cicero's time, 150 of Cato's speeches were published. Again, only fragments survive.

GAIUS VALERIUS CATULLUS, CA. 85–CA. 54 BCE

Catullus was born in Verona. He is the one *novus poeta* ("new poet") whose complete work, 116 poems, survived (in one manuscript). The only record of Catullus' public service is that he served on the staff of Gaius Memmius, Lucretius' patron.

MARCUS TULLIUS CICERO, 106–43 BCE

Cicero was born southeast of Rome in Arpinum. He was a successful lawyer and politician who reached the consulship in 63 BCE. Cicero was a "new man" (*novus homo*). As consul, he suppressed the Catiline conspiracy, an attempt by Sergius Catilina to gain the consulship on a program of debt-reduction and rallying Rome's *plebs* (the general body of citizens, the commons), and was hailed "father of his country" (*pater patriae*). Consequently, Cicero was exiled for his actions against Catiline and his followers. Pompey's engagement brought him back to Rome after one and a half years. Cicero served as governor of Cilicia 51–50 BCE, but he never regained the status he had as consul. Politics were shaped by Gaius Julius Caesar and Pompey, with the former emerging as dictator. After the assassination of Caesar in 44 BCE, Cicero emerged briefly in a position of political importance only to be assassinated on behest of Marc Antony whom he had attacked in fourteen speeches (*Philippics*).

The literary works of Cicero, besides establishing the norm for Latin literary prose, are our most important sources for the Late Republic. Fifty-seven speeches dealing with civil, criminal, and political affairs provide an exceptional insight into the years 81–43 BCE. The most famous of these speeches are the ones against Verres, a corrupt *praetor* of Sicily; Catiline; and Marc Antony. Cicero's letters, published after his death, provide us with a glimpse at private and public life from the everyday mundane to political machinations and intellectual pursuits. Cicero also wrote treatises on philosophy, political science, and rhetoric. In his philosophical writings, Cicero dealt with questions surrounding human beings; their nature, their perceptions, and construct of their universe (e.g., *On The Definitions of Good and Evil* [*De finibus bonorum et malorum*]; *Tusculan Disputations* [*Tusculanae disputationes*], which discussed topics related to the human condition), *On Fate* [*De fato*], *On the Nature of the Gods* [*De natura deorum*], *On Friendship* [*De amicitia*], and *Old Age* [*De senectute*]). Cicero's political treatises have practical as well as philosophical shadings. His *On the State* (*De re publica*) and *On the Laws* (*De legibus*) were inspired by Plato. Cicero's *On Duties* (*De officiis*), philosophically more eclectic than the previous two works, reveal the author's idealized view of the Roman Republic. Cicero strongly believed in the "harmony of orders" (*concordia ordinum*). The goal of the rhetorical writings was to present a generally well-educated speaker who knew how to adapt the various rhetorical styles to the circumstances at hand and so convince his audience. The most important works of this category are *On Oration* (*De oratore*), *Brutus,* and the *Orator.*

DIODORUS SICULUS, FIRST CENTURY BCE

Diodorus was from Argyrium (Sicily). He wrote a universal history, the *Library* (Βιβλιοθήκη), which began with mythological times and ended in 60 BCE. The focus of the *Bibliotheke* is the Greek World and Magna Graecia until the First Punic War (264–241 BCE), which brought Rome into the political foreground.

DIONYSIUS OF HALICARNASSUS, 60/55 BCE–CA. 7 BCE

Dionysius from the Ionian (western Turkey) city of Halicarnassus came to Rome sometime around 30 BCE. He was a teacher of rhetoric and a literary critic. Dionysius wrote the *Roman Antiquities* (Ρωμαικὴ ἀρχαιολογία), Rome's history down to the First Punic War. The first ten books and most of the eleventh book survived intact; the rest, only in fragments or in summaries.

SEXTUS POMPEIUS FESTUS, SECOND CENTURY CE

Festus, most likely from Narbo (Narbonne), summarized Marcus Verrius Flaccus' *On the Meaning of Words* (*De verborum significatu*). Flaccus flourished in the time of

Augustus and served as the teacher to Augustus' grandsons Lucius and Gaius. The first ten books, half of Festus' work, are lost. In the eighth century CE, Paulus Diaconus, in turn, abridged the work once more.

AULUS GELLIUS, SECOND CENTURY CE

Aulus Gellius was probably born in Rome. He studied grammar with Apollinaris Sidonius and rhetoric with Antonius Iulianus and maybe with Fronto, the teacher of the emperor Marcus Aurelius. Gellius also studied in Athens. There he wrote the *Attic Nights* (*Noctes Atticae*) in twenty books, which came down to us with the exception of the eighth book. By profession, he was a judge.

MARCUS JUNIAN(I)US JUSTINUS (JUSTIN) CA. THIRD CENTURY CE

Justin, about whom we have no biographical information, wrote an epitome of Gnaeus Pompeius Trogus' 44-volume work *The Philippic History* (*Historiae Philippicae*), which is lost. Trogus wrote during the time of Augustus.

DECIMUS IUNIUS JUVENALIS (JUVENAL), CA. 67 CE–?MID SECOND CENTURY CE

Juvenal was born in Aquinum in Campania. He was a speech giver (*declamator*). His sixteen satires were published most likely during the reign of the emperor Trajan. The themes of the satires are predominantly corruption of morals and hypocrisy.

TITUS LIVIUS (LIVY), 59 BCE–17 CE

Livy was born in Padua (Patavium) in northern Italy. He never held a political or military office. While Livy's work might suffer from this lack of political and military training, it excels, however, in every aspect of style. The aim of *From the Foundation of the City* (*Ab urbe condita*), which spans Rome's foundation to the death of Drusus, the emperor Tiberius' brother in 9 BCE, was not to provide critical historical analyses but to teach moral lessons from a glorified past. The work has not survived intact; of the 142 books, only 35 survive more or less complete. These books are 1–10, 21–45 (spotty from Book 41 onward). There are summaries (*periochae*) of the lost books, except for two books (136 and 137).

TITUS LUCRETIUS CARUS,
CA. 94–CA. 55 BCE

Lucretius, one of the "new poets"(*novi poetae*) wrote *On the Nature of Things* (*De rerum natura*), a didactic six-book poem in dactylic hexameters. Epicurean atomic philosophy, of which he was an adherent, was to remove irrational fears of death and destruction as well as superstitions. The philosophical aim was to reach a state of true happiness free from pain and anxiety. This goal stood in contrast to everyday life in the Late Republic, which was marked by political instability and out-of-hand violence. Lucretius dedicated his work to Gaius Memmius, who was governor of Bithynia in 57 BCE.

AMBROSIUS THEODOSIUS MACROBIUS,
BEGINNING OF FIFTH CENTURY CE

Macrobius may have been praetorian prefect of Italy in 430 CE. He wrote a literary symposium, the *Saturnalia,* in seven books. The symposium took place on the three-day festival in December, the *Saturnalia,* during which masters and slaves exchanged roles. The topic the participants of the symposium embrace focuses, in particular, on Vergil, his knowledge of astronomy, philosophy, augury, and pontifical law. The first book includes a discussion of the Roman calendar (1.12–1.16). Macrobius also wrote a commentary on Cicero's *Scipio's Dream* (*Somnium Scipionis*).

PUBLIUS OVIDIUS (OVID)
NASO, 43 BCE–17 CE

Ovid was born in Sulmo in the Abruzzi mountains. He was educated and lived in Rome until 8 CE. That year, Augustus banished him to Tomi (Constantza), a city at the eastern shore of the Black Sea. The reason for the banishment is unknown. Ovid was Rome's premier elegist. His works are written in the elegiac couplet, consisting of a hexameter and a pentameter line. The *Love Elegies* (*Amores*), *Heroides* (fictitious poetic letters from famous and infamous mythological women), the *Art of Love* (*Ars amatoria*), and the *Remedies of Love* (*Remedia amoris*) are Ovid's early works. The *Metamorphoses,* 250 stories of mythological transformations in fifteen books, and the *Fasti* (*Calendar*), describing the religious and historical background of the months and their festivals as well as the constellations of each day, might be considered Ovid's most important works. The *Fasti* are unfinished, ending with the month of June. In exile, Ovid did not continue the *Fasti* but wrote the *Sorrows* (*Tristia*) in two books and the *Letters from Pontus* (*Epistulae ex Ponto* [Black Sea]) in which he laments his bitter destiny.

TITUS MACCIUS PLAUTUS,
CA. 250–184 BCE

Plautus was born in Sarsina in Umbria. Twenty-one Plautine comedies survive, the oldest complete drama pieces of Latin literature. Titles and some lines of thirty other comedies are known. Plautus' comedies are reworkings of Greek New Comedy pieces.

GAIUS PLINIUS SECUNDUS (PLINY THE ELDER),
CA. 23–79 CE

Pliny the Elder was born in Comum (Como) in northern Italy. Because he was admiral of the fleet, the emperor Vespasian sent him to evacuate people left stranded by the eruption of Mount Vesuvius. He lost his life doing so. A work of 102 volumes on language, education, history, and military science did not survive. Pliny's encyclopedic learning is reflected in his 37-volume *Natural History* (*Historia naturalis*), which is extant. The work is a compilation of scientific and unscientific facts and miscellany.

MESTRIUS PLUTARCH,
CA. 45–CA. 120 CE

Plutarch was from Chaeronea, Boeotia, in Greece. He studied in Athens with Platonic, Aristotelian, and Stoic philosophers. Plutarch was from a prominent Greek family and well connected to Rome's leading senatorial families. He was a celebrated author in his time, and his literary output was immense. The *Greek Questions* (*Quaestiones Graecae*) and *Roman Questions* (*Quaestiones Romanae*) offer antiquarian information about Greek and Roman religion. Among the *Moralia,* a collection of essays and speeches, is the treatise *On Isis and Osiris* (*De Iside et Osiride*), which gives us invaluable information about these Egyptian deities and their cult. Plutarch's *Parallel Lives* (*Vitae*) offer biographical details of famous Greek and Roman leaders.

POLYBIUS, CA. 200–120 BCE

Polybius was a Greek historian from Megalopolis in Arcadia. He came as one of the Archean League's hostages to Rome. There he became affiliated with Scipio, whom he accompanied on the campaign against Carthage in 146 BCE. Polybius wrote a world history that picked up where Timaeus of Tauromenion had left off. Polybius' history covers the period of the First Punic War to 144 BCE. Of the forty books, only the first five survive in their entirety. Book 6 studies Rome's constitution, which Polybius judged to have been the reason for Rome's greatness.

SEXTUS PROPERTIUS,
54/47–CA. 2 BCE

Propertius was born in Asisium (Assisi). He wrote four books of elegiac poetry in which one can detect some criticisms of Augustus' regime, such as the confiscation of some of his property in 41–40 BCE. Propertius poetry makes use of mythology, and a Cynthia is the woman most mentioned in his poems. Propertius was connected to Maecenas.

MARCUS FABIUS QUINTILIANUS (QUINTILIAN),
CA. 35–CA. 90S CE

Quintilian was born at Calagurris (Calahorra) in Spain and may have received all of his education (grammar, rhetoric, and law) in Rome. He was affiliated with the orator Domitius Afer. Quintilian may have been the first rhetorician to receive a salary from the state. Suetonius (*Vesp.* 18) attributes this development of official pay for teachers of rhetoric to Vespasian. Quintilian taught Pliny the Younger and tutored Domitian's heirs, the two sons of Flavius Clemens. He retired in 88 CE. Quintilian is the author of the *Training in Rhetoric* (*Institutio oratoria*) and other works related to oratory, now lost.

GAIUS SALLUSTIUS (SALLUST)
CRISPUS, 86–34 BCE

Sallust was born in the Sabine town of Amiternum (Abruzza region). He held a quaestorship in 54 BCE and a tribuneship in 52 BCE. Sallust was ousted for immoral behavior from the Senate in 50 BCE. Caesar secured a quaestorship for him in 49 BCE, and thus Sallust gained admittance to the Senate once more. During the civil war he was elected *praetor* in 46 BCE, and he received the governorship of Africa. Sallust enriched himself on the backs of the provincials and, consequently, was tried for extortion. Caesar saved him, but Sallust's political career was over. In retirement, Sallust wrote three historical works, *The War of Catiline* (*Bellum Catilinae*), *The Jugurthine War* (*Bellum Jugurthinum*), and the *Histories* (*Historiae*), most likely covering events from 78 to 63 BCE. The two former ones are extant; only fragments remain of the third work.

MAURUS OR MARIUS SERVIUS HONORATUS,
FOURTH CENTURY CE

Servius, whose origins are unknown, was a grammarian. His main work was a commentary on Vergil based Aelius Donatus' work. Donatus was St. Jerome's teacher.

PUBLIUS CORNELIUS TACITUS, CA. 55/56 CE–FIRST PART OF SECOND CENTURY CE

Tacitus' family came from Gallia Narbonensis or Gallia Cisalpina. He married the daughter of Gnaius Julius Agricola, governor of Britain, in 78 CE. Tacitus' public career began under the emperor Vespasian and fully blossomed under Domitian, when Tacitus was either tribune of the people or aedile, became a member of the *quindecimviri sacris faciundis* (the fifteen men in charge of the Sibylline Books), and eventually *praetor*. He held the consulship under Nerva in 97 CE. Tacitus published the *Agricola*, a biography of his father-in-law, and the *Germania*, a kind of ethnography of the German people, at the beginning of Trajan's reign. These two works were followed by the *Discussion Concerning Orators* (*Dialogus de oratoribus*), the *Histories* (*Historiae*) and *Annals* (*Annales*), the latter two major literary sources for the early Empire.

PUBLIUS TERENTIUS (TERENCE) AFER, CA. 195/190–159 BCE

Terence came to Rome as a prisoner of war. His *cognomen,* Afer, hints at Libyan (North African) origins. Six comedies have come down to us. Terence's plays very much follow their Greek originals, in particular the comedies of Menander.

ALBIUS TIBULLUS, 55/48 BCE–CA. 19 BCE

Tibullus was of equestrian rank. Like Propertius, some of his family property was also confiscated in 41–40 BCE. Tibullus wrote elegiac poetry, and his "beloved" is called Delia. Tibullus' "patron" was Valerius Messalla Corvinus.

TIMAEUS, MID FOURTH–MID THIRD CENTURY BCE

Timaeus was the son of the ruler of Tauromenion (Taormina) in Sicily. He lived about fifty years of his life in Athens, where he collected the material for his history of the western Greeks. Only fragments of his work survive, which covered the time from the beginning of Greek colonization in the West down to the death of Agathocles, tyrant of Syracuse, in 289 BCE.

MARCUS TERRENTIUS VARRO, 116–27 BCE

Varro was born in Reate, a Sabine town sixty miles from Rome. He held public office and achieved the rank of *praetor*. Varro fought on Pompey's side during the civil war.

Gaius Julius Caesar, the victor of this struggle, forgave Varro and charged him with the building of public libraries. Varro's literary output was immense and covered practically all fields of ancient learning. Only a fraction of his work survives, and only *On Agricultural Matters* (*De re rustica*) in three volumes survives in its entirety. *On Antiquities Human and Divine* (*Antiquitates rerum humanarum et divinarum*) deals with the beginnings and advancement of the Roman people. *On Latin Language* (*De lingua Latina*), although primarily a source for the development of the Latin language, provides tidbits of Rome's history.

PUBLIUS VERGILIUS MARO (VERGIL), 70–19 BCE

Vergil was born in Andes by Mantua (Cisalpine Gaul). He was educated in Cremona and Milan (Mediolanum) before coming to Rome to study rhetoric and Naples (Neapolis) to study Epicurean philosophy. Vergil's career as a lawyer was short-lived; it existed only of one lawsuit, which he lost. His family's farm was confiscated in 41 BCE, when land was needed to settle civil war veterans. Vergil received compensation for the loss. While living in Rome, he came in contact with Gaius Cilnius Maecenas (ca. 70–8 BCE), a friend of Augustus. Vergil established himself as an important poet with his ten *Eclogues* or *Bucolica,* "shepard" poems in the tradition of Theocritus, interwoven with contemporary historical events. In the *Georgics,* a didactic poem in four books, Vergil praises agriculture and extols Italian lands. His epic, the *Aeneid,* recounts in twelve books Aeneas' wanderings from Troy to Italy, where he concludes a treaty with the Latin king, ultimately defeats the indigenous Italians, and finds a new home for the Trojans and their household gods, the *penates.* When Vergil died unexpectedly in Brindisi upon returning from Greece, some books of the *Aeneid* were not quite complete. Nevertheless, the content and the quality of his verse made it not only a masterpiece of the Augustan period but also a work of art for the ages.

TIMELINE

3000–1000 BCE	Neolithic and Bronze Age
ca. 1700–1100 BCE	northern Italy: Terramaricoli
	Mid and southern Italy: Apennine culture
1000–ca. 750 BCE	Early Iron Age
ca. 1000–800 BCE	Villanovan culture
	Fossa People
	Migration of Illyrian tribes
ca. 800 BCE	Foundation of Carthage
ca. 800–600 BCE	Greek colonization
753 BCE	Legendary foundation of Rome;
	Beginning of monarchy
Late 7th–end of 6th century BCE	Etruscan rule over Rome
509 BCE	Legendary beginning of the Republic
End of Monarchy	
End of 6th century BCE	First Roman-Carthaginian treaty
	Etruscan defeat at Aricia
Beginning of 5th century BCE	Secession of the People
	Creation of the tribunate
	Treaty between Rome and the Latins
Mid 5th century BCE	La Tène culture
509–265 BCE	Roman conquest of Italy
	End of Etruscan sea power in the Tyrrhenian Sea
ca. 450 BCE	Codification of law (The 12 Tables)
445 BCE	Patricians and plebeians allowed to intermarry (*lex Canuleia*)
420s BCE	End of Etruscan rule in Capua (Campania)
Late 5th century BCE	"Servian" centuriate organization
387 BCE	Celtic victory over Rome at the river Allia
367 BCE	Plebeian allowed to hold consulship (Licino-Sextian Law)
348 BCE	Treaty with Carthage

(?)343–341 BCE	First Samnite War
340–338 BCE	War with Latins
326–304 BCE	Second Samnite War
300 BCE	Plebeians receive right to hold important Priesthoods (*lex Ogulnia*)
298–290 BCE	Third Samnite War
	Subjugation of the Sabines
274–204 BCE	Gnaius Naevius (poet)
272 BCE	Conquest of Tarentum
	T. Livius Andronicus (poet) arrives in Rome
265 BCE	Conquest of Volsiniis; conquest of Italy concluded
264–133 BCE	Roman imperialism
264–241 BCE	First Punic War
254–184 BCE	T. Maccius Plautus (playwright)
241 BCE	Roman naval victory off the Aegates Islands; peace with Carthage; Sicily becomes Rome's first province
240 BCE	First showing of a drama (Greek style) in Rome
239–169 BCE	Quintus Ennius (poet)
238 BCE	Occupation of Sardinia
	Sardinia and Corsica, Rome's second province
234–149 BCE	Marcus Porcius Cato the Censor (Roman statesman and writer)
229–228 BCE	First Illyrian War
227 BCE	Beginning of Roman provincial administration under praetors
226 BCE	Carthaginian–Roman treaty (so-called Ebro Treaty)
225–222 BCE	War against Celts in northern Italy
219 BCE	Second Illyrian War
Late 3rd century BCE	Quintus Fabius Pictor (writer)
218–201 BCE	Second Punic War
215–205 BCE	First Macedonian War
202 BCE	Battle of Zama (south of Carthage, North Africa), Roman victory
201 BCE	Rome dictates peace
200–197	Second Macedonian War
197 BCE	Spain established as province
196 BCE	Titus Quinctius Flamininus proclaimed Greece's freedom
192–188 BCE	War against Antiochus III (Syria); Rome victorious
ca. 190–159 BCE	Publius Terentius Afer (playwright)
185 BCE	Slave uprising in Apulia
180–102 BCE	Lucilius (poet)
171–168 BCE	Third Macedonian War

168 BCE	Roman victory at Pydna, Greece
ca. 157–86 BCE	Gaius Marius (politician)
154–133 BCE	War in Spain
149–146 BCE	Third Punic War
148 BCE	Macedonia established as province
146 BCE	Destruction of Corinth
	Destruction of Carthage; Africa established as province
138–78 BCE	Lucius Cornelius Sulla (statesman)
136–132 BCE	First slave uprising in Sicily
133–30 BCE	Late Republic
	Breakdown of system and civil wars
133 BCE	Attalos III of Pergamon bequeathed his empire to the Romans
	Agrarian reform of Tiberius Sempronius Gracchus (162–132 BCE), tribune of the People
132 BCE	Murder of Ti. Sempronius Gracchus
123 BCE	Renewal of Agrarian reform by Gaius Sempronius Gracchus (154–121 BCE), tribune of the People
121 BCE	Murder of Gaius Sempronius Gracchus
	Gallia Narbonensis established as province
116–27 BCE	Marcus Terentius Varro (antiquarian and writer)
113 BCE	Germanic tribes defeat Rome, northern Italy
111–105 BCE	Iugurthine War (North Africa)
106–43 BCE	Marcus Tullius Cicero (statesman and writer)
106–48 BCE	Gnaius Pompeius (Pompey) Magnus (statesman)
105 BCE	Cimbri (German Tribe) defeat Romans at Arausio (northern Italy)
104–101 BCE	Second slave revolt in Sicily
102 and 101 BCE	Marius Victorious over German tribes
100–44 BCE	Gaius Julius Caesar (statesman and writer)
100 BCE	First dispute among Optimates and Populares (political groups)
ca. 96–55 BCE	Titus Lucretius Carus (poet)
95–46 BCE	Marcus Porcius Cato (statesman)
91 BCE	Attempted reforms of Livius Drusus, tribune of the People
90–88 BCE	Social War (war against Italian Allies); allies receive Roman citizenship
89–85 BCE	First war against Mithridates VI (king of Pontus, Black Sea region)
86–34 BCE	Gaius Sallustius (Sallust) Crispus (writer)
ca. 85–54 BCE	Gaius Valerius Catullus (poet)
83–81 BCE	Second war against Mithridates VI
82–30 BCE	Marcus Antonius (Marc Antony, statesman)

82–79 BCE	Dictatorship of Sulla
80 –72 BCE	Quintus Sertorius' resistance in Spain
ca. 75 BCE–5 CE	Asinius Pollio (statesman and writer)
74–64 BCE	Third war against Mithridates
74 BCE	Cyrene (northern Africa) established as province
73 –71 BCE	Slave uprising under Spartacus
70–19 BCE	Publius Vergilius (Vergil) Maro (poet)
68 BCE	Praetorship of Lucius Sergius Catilina
66–65 BCE	First Catilinarian conspiracy
66 BCE	Crete established as province
65–8 BCE	Quintus Horatius (Horace)
	Flaccus (poet)
64 BCE	Bythinia, Pontus, and Syria established as provinces
64–11 BCE	Octavia (Augustus' sister and one of the wives of Marc Antony)
63 BCE–14 CE	Gaius Octavianus (Augustus)
?63–12 BCE	Marcus Vipsanius Agrippa (military commander and Augustus' son-in-law)
63 BCE	Second Catilinarian conspiracy; consulship of Cicero
62 BCE	Defeat and death of Catiline
60 BCE	First so-called Triumvirate (Pompey, Caesar, and Marcus Licinius Crassus)
59 BCE	Caesar's first consulship
59 BCE–17 CE	Titus Livius (Livy, writer)
58–50 BCE	Caesar's conquest of Gaul
58 BCE–29 CE	Livia (Augustus' wife)
56 BCE	Renewal of the so-called Triumvirate at Luca
55 BCE	Consulship of Pompey and Crassus
53 BCE	Roman defeat at Carrhae (Iraq) and death of Crassus
51 BCE	Gallia established as province
ca. 50–17 BCE	Albius Tibullus (poet)
49 BCE	Caesar crosses the Rubicon
48 BCE	Battle of Pharsalus (northern Greece); death of Pompey
48–47 BCE	Alexandrian war (Egypt)
47–15 BCE	Sextus Propertius (poet)
47–46 BCE	War in northern Africa Numidia established as province: Africa Nova
46 BCE	Caesar dictator for ten years
46–45 BCE	Pompeian resistance broken in Spain Battle of Munda
44 BCE	Murder of Caesar
43 BCE–17 CE	Publius Ovidius (Ovid) Naso (poet)

43 BCE	(Second) Triumvirate (Octavian, Marc Antony, Marcus Aemilius Lepidus)
	Deification of Caesar
42 BCE	Battle of Philippi (Greece)
	Death of Caesar's murderers
42 BCE–37 CE	Tiberius Claudius Nero (Augustus' stepson and successor)
39 BCE–14 CE	Julia (Augustus' daughter)
38–9 BCE	Drusus (the Elder, military commander and Tiberius' brother)
37 BCE	Treaty of Tarentum (Octavian and Marc Antony)
	Renewal of triumvirate for five years
	Marc Antony married to Cleopatra VII
36 BCE	Battle of Naulochus, defeat of Sextus Pompeius (Pompey's son)
	Lepidus stripped of political powers
36 BCE–37 CE	Antonia (daughter of Marc Antony and Octavia, wife of Drusus the Elder, mother of Claudius)
36–34 BCE	Marc Antony's Parthian campaign
35–33 BCE	Octavian's Illyrian campaign
31 BCE	Battle of Actium
30 BCE	Death of Marc Antony and Cleopatra
	Egypt established as province
30 BCE–284 CE	Principate
29 BCE	Octavian receives triple triumph
27 BCE	Octavian granted proconsular powers and named Augustus
27–25 BCE	Augustus in Gaul and Spain
25–24 BCE	Roman expedition to Arabia
23 BCE	Augustus granted tribunician powers for life and *Imperium Proconsulare Maius* (authority and power extends to all provinces)
22–19 BCE	Augustus tours the East
20 BCE	Diplomatic victory: Parthian return Roman standards lost at Carrhae in 53 BCE; Armenia established as client-state
19 BCE	Augustus granted consular powers for life, his *imperium* to include Rome and Italy
19 BCE–28 CE	Julia (the Younger, daughter of Julia, Augustus' daughter)
17 BCE	Secular games
16–13 BCE	Reorganization of Gaul
15 BCE	Raetia established as province
15 BCE–19 CE	Germanicus (son of Drusus the Elder and Antonia, brother of Claudius)
14 BCE–33 CE	Agrippina (the Elder, daughter of Julia [Augustus' daughter] and Agrippa, wife of Germanicus, mother of Caligula)

13 BCE–23 CE	Drusus (the Younger, son of Tiberius and Vipsania, daughter of Agrippa)
12–9 BCE	Drusus' (Augustus' stepson) campaign in Germany; Tiberius conquers Pannonia
12 BCE	Death of Lepidus
	Augustus becomes *pontifex maximus*
10 BCE–54 CE	Claudius (Tiberius Claudius Caesar Augustus Germanicus, Caligula's uncle and successor)
9 BCE	Pannonia established as province; dedication of the Ara Pacis (Altar of Peace) in Rome
8–7 BCE	Tiberius' campaigns in Germany
6 BCE	Tiberius receives tribunician power; withdrawal to Rhodes
ca. 4 BCE–65 CE	Lucius Annaeus Seneca (statesman and philosopher, Nero's tutor)
2 BCE	Augustus named *Pater Patriae* (Father of the Country)
2 CE	Death of Lucius Caesar (grandson and designated heir of Augustus)
4 CE	Death of Gaius Caesar (grandson and designated heir of Augustus)
	Adoption of Tiberius and designation as heir, receipt of proconsular *imperium* and tribunician power; adoption of Germanicus by Tiberius
6–9 CE	Uprising in Pannonia
9 CE	Battle of the Teutoburger Forrest (Germany); death of Roman commander Varrus and destruction of three Roman legions
10–12 CE	Tiberius' second campaign in Germany
12–41 CE	Caligula (Gaius Julius Caesar Augustus Germanicus, Son of Agrippina the Elder and Germanicus, Tiberius' nephew and successor)
14 CE	Augustus' death in Nola; deification of Augustus
14–37 CE	Principate of Tiberius
14–16 CE	Roman campaigns in Germany
15–59 CE	Agrippina the Younger (daughter of Agrippina the Elder and Germanicus, sister of Caligula, mother of Nero)
17 CE	Cappadocia and Commagene (Asia Minor) established as provinces
17–24 CE	Uprising in North Africa
21 CE	Uprisings in Gaul and Thrace
23–79 CE	Gaius Plinius Secundus Maior (Pliny the Elder, military commander and writer)
37–68 CE	Nero Claudius Caesar Augustus Germanicus (son of

	Agrippina the Younger and Gnaius Lucius Ahenobarbus, nephew of Claudius)
37–ca. 100 CE	Flavius Josephus (writer)
37–41 CE	Principate of Caligula
39–65 CE	Marcus Annaeus Lucanus (Lucan, poet)
ca. 40–120 CE	Dio (writer)
ca. 40–102 CE	Marcus Valerius Martialis (Martial, poet)
40 CE	Uprising in Mauretania (North Africa); reorganization of the province of Mauretania
41–54 CE	Principate of Claudius
43–44 CE	Conquest of southern Britain and establishment of province
44 CE	Thrace established as province
ca. 46–ca. 119 CE	Plutarch (writer)
54–68 CE	Principate of Nero
ca. 55–ca. 120 CE	Tacitus (statesman and writer)
ca. 60–ca. 127 CE	D. Iunius Iuvenalis (Juvenal, poet)
60–61 CE	Uprising in Britain under Boudicca
ca. 61–113 CE	Gaius Plinius Secundus Minor (Pliny the Younger, statesman and writer)
64 CE	Fire destroys Rome
	Kingdom of Pontus established as province
65 CE	Pisonian conspiracy
66–70 CE	Uprising in Judaea
68 CE	Death of Nero, end of the Julio-Claudian dynasty

ROMAN EMPERORS AFTER THE JULIO-CLAUDIAN DYNASTY TO THE END OF THE SEVERAN DYNASTY

69 CE	Year of Four Emperors
	Galba, Otho, Vitellius, Vespasian
	Flavian Dynasty
69–79 CE	Vespasian
	(Imperator Caesar Vespasianus Augustus)
79–81 CE	Titus
	(Titus Caesar Vespasianus Augustus)
81–96 CE	Domitian
	(Imperator Caesar Domitianus Augustus)
	Antonine Dynasty
96–98 CE	Nerva
	(Imperator Nerva Caesar Augustus)

98–117 CE	Trajan
	(Imperator Caesar Nerva Traianus Augustus)
117–138 CE	Hadrian
	(Imperator Caesar Traianus Hadrianus Augustus)
138–161 CE	Antoninus Pius
	(Imperator Caesar Titus Aelius Hadrianus Antoninus Augustus Pius)
161–180 CE	Marcus Aurelius
	(Imperator Caesar Marcus Aurelius Antoninus Augustus)
161–169 CE	Lucius Verus
	(Imperator Caesar Lucius Aurelius Verus Augustus)
180–192 CE	Commodus
	(Imperator Caesar Marcus Aurelius Commodus Antoninus Augustus)
193 CE	Year of Five Emperors
	Pertinax, Didius Iulianus, Septimius Severus, Clodius Albinus, Pescennius Niger
	Severan Dynasty
193–211 CE	Septimius Severus
	(Imperator Caesar Lucius Septimius Severus Pertinax Augustus)
211–217 CE	Caracalla
	(Imperator Caesar Marcus Aurelius (Severus) Antoninus Augustus)
211–212 CE	Geta
	(Imperator Caesar Publius Septimius Geta Augustus)
217–218 CE	Macrinus
	(Imperator Caesar Marcus Opellius Macrinus Augustus)
218–222 CE	Elagabal
	(Imperator Caesar Marcus Aurelius Antoninus Augustus)
222–235 CE	Severus Alexander
	(Imperator Caesar Marcus Aurelius Severus Alexander Augustus)

MAPS

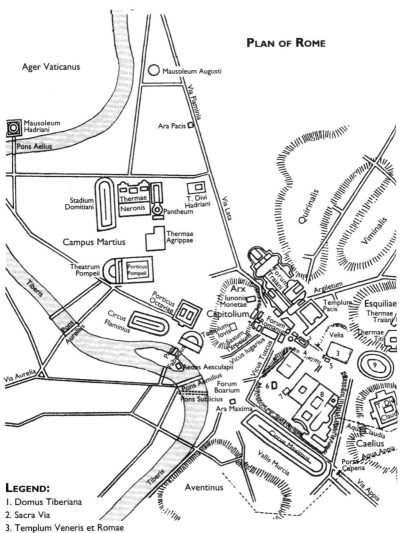

PLAN OF ROME

Ager Vaticanus

Mausoleum Augusti

Via Flaminia

Mausoleum
Hadriani

Ara Pacis

Pons Aelius

Stadium
Domitiani

Thermae
Neronis

Pantheum

T. Divi
Hadriani

Via Lata

Quirinalis

Viminalis

Campus Martius

Thermae
Agrippae

Theatrum
Pompeii

Porticus
Pompeii

Tiberis

Porticus
Octaviae

Arx
T. Iunonis
Monetae

Capitolium

Argiletum

Templum
Pacis

Esquiliae

Thermae
Traiani

Forum
Traiani

Circus
Flaminius

T. Iovis

Saxum
Tarpeium

Forum
Romanum

Velia

Thermae
Titi

Pons
Aurelius

Vicus Tuscus

Vicus Iugarius

Via Aurelia

Pons
Fabricius

Aedes Aesculapii

Aemilius

Forum
Boarium

9

Pons Aemilius

Pons Sublicius

Ara Maxima

T. Divi
Claudi

Aqua Claudia

Caelius

Aqua Appia

Circus Maximus

Vallis Murcia

Porta
Capena

Via Appia

Tiberis

Aventinus

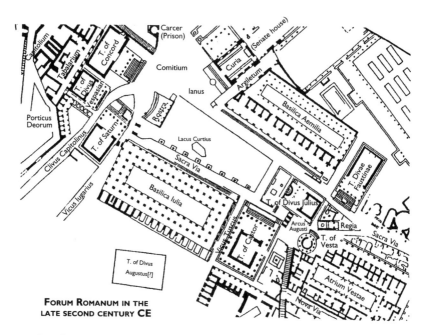

Plan of Rome (145) *and the* Forum Romanum (this page). *From* Roman Religion: A Sourcebook *by Valerie Warrior, 2002* © *Focus Publishing, R. Pullins Company, Newburyport, MA. Reproduced by permission.*

Italy. Map by Rachel Barckhaus, Mary T. Boatwright, Alexandra Dunk, Tom Elliott, Daniel Gargola, Andrew Hull, and Richard Talbert. Courtesy Ancient World Mapping Center, University of North Carolina at Chapel Hill (http://www.unc.edu/awmc).

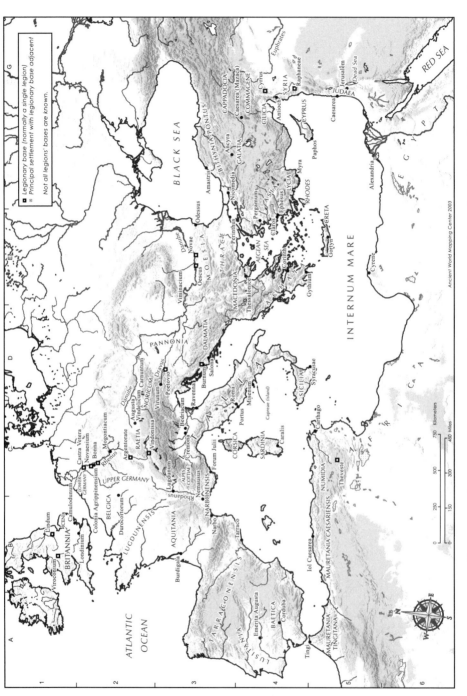

The Mediterranean World. Map by Rachel Barckhaus, Mary T. Boatwright, Daniel Gargola, Andrew Hull, and Richard Talbert. Courtesy Ancient World Mapping Center, University of North Carolina at Chapel Hill (http://www.unc.edu/awmc).

NOTES

CHAPTER ONE

1. For a survey of Latin literature, see Kenney (1982).

2. Plut. *Rom.* 12.1.

3. Bömer (1951).

4. Timaeus of Taormina in Sicily wrote a thirty-eight-book history of the Western Greeks living in Sicily and southern Italy (Magna Graecia). His description of the history of early Italy, including the story surrounding Aeneas, formed a basis for Rome's foundation myth.

5. Gaius Julius Caesar exploited the linking of Iulus to the name Julius (Iulius). Thus, the divine ancestor of the Julian family (*gens*) was Venus.

6. There is a conceptual but not an immediate linguistic connection between *penates* and *penus* (food, provisions).

7. Verg. *Aen.* 2.776–789.

8. Verg. *Aen.* 4. 621–629.

9. In addition to Vergil's account in the *Aen.,* see also Justin's *Epitome* 18.4–6.

10. Varro *Ling.* 5.143 and Robinson (1992), 5–32.

11. Livy 5.52.

12. Linderski (1993), esp. p. 56.

13. See Chapter 4.

14. Women who fetched water left the secure sphere of home and ventured into the unknown, the liminal. This was also the sphere of nymphs. Myths often recount that women fetching water outside their homes were raped. See Larson (2001).

15. Cato *Orig.* frg. 68; Dion. Hal. 2.67.4; Plut. *Num.* 10 and *Mor.* 286–287.

16. Quint. *Inst.* 7.8.3.

17. "[M]ilitary success or the safety of a city dependent on the sacrifice or voluntary self-oblation of a person of especially high value—the fairest Virgin in the land, the king's daughter, or even the king himself. This might in origin be a quite distinct conception, since death rather than expulsion is here essential; but, if so, a contamination of the two forms seems early to have occurred. Late sources speak of virgin sacrifice as a 'purification'" (Parker [1983], 259).

18. Livy 1.9; Ov. *Fast.* 3.199–3.234 and *Ars* 1.116–1.131.

19. Ov. *Fast.* 2.425–2.441.

20. Livy 1.26.

21. Livy 1.34–35.

22. Livy 1.46.7: "The initial source of throwing everything into confusion was a woman (*initium turbandi omnia a femina ortum est*)."

23. Calhoon (1997).

24. Livy 1.57–59 and Ov. *Fast.* 2.720–2.758.

25. Cornell (1995), 293–313.

26. Cornell (1995), 293–326.

27. Livy 2.12–2.13.

28. McCarthy (1994), esp. 106.

29. Mitchell (1986).

30. Archer (1994).

31. Livy 3.48.5.

32. Cornell (1995), 313–318.

33. Bettini (1991) and Flower (1996).

34. Livy 34.1.3: "*ne qua mulier plus semiunicam auri haberet neu vestimento versicolori uteretur neu iuncto vehiculo in urbe oppidove aut proprius inde mille passus nisi sacrorum publicorum causa veheretur.*"

35. Briscoe (1981), 39.

36. Ridley (1997). Ridley implies that females (especially those of a young reproduction age) are more likely to wander and cross territory lines that males establish and are sometimes killed for crossing. Females not only wander across, but they mate with others.

37. Livy 34.3.1.

38. Voconian Law of 169 BCE.

39. Gel. 17.6.8.

40. Treggiari (1991), 378.

41. Plut. 31.26.

42. Polyb. 31.26–31.27.

43. Cornelia was the daughter of Scipio Africanus, the wife of Tiberius Sempronius, and the mother of Tiberius and Gaius Gracchus. Both sons were tribunes of the people who were murdered for their engagement in social reform in the 130s and 120s BCE.

44. See Chapters 3 and 4 below.

45. Hallett (1984) and Beard (1980), 14–15.

46. See Chapter 4 below.

47. Cic. *Att.* 12.18.

48. Cic. *Cael.* 63. The Latin is: "*quadrantaria illa permutatione.*" The *quadrans* was a quarter of an ass (the smallest monetary unit) and considered a token of minimal value (*OCD*). See also Geffcken (1973).

49. This Ptolemy was Cleopatra's father and pro-Roman. In 58 BCE, he fled to Rome as a consequence of Rome's conquest of Cyprus, which his brother ruled. Caecus served Roma as *censor* (312–307 BCE) and was one of Clodius' and Clodia's most esteemed ancestors.

50. Apul. *Apol.* 10, and for a list of modern studies, see *OCD* "Catullus, Gaius Valerius."

51. See Chapter 5 below. The Bona Dea Affair (62 BCE) had caused the rift between Clodius and Cicero. In 58 BCE, Clodius introduced a bill exiling any Roman who had put fellow Romans to death. The bill passed, and Cicero, who as consul in 63 BCE, had encouraged and approved the elimination of Catiline and his followers, was exiled. Cicero was allowed to return to Rome in 57 BCE. His villas and his house on the Palatine, however, had been destroyed (Cic. *Dom.*). On the site of the Palatine house, Clodius had a temple to Liberty built (Cic. *Dom.* 111 and 116; Dio Cass. 38.17.1, 39.11.1, 39.20.3; Plut. *Cic.* 33.1; Richardson [1992], 234).

52. Sall. *Cat.* 24.3–25.5, 40.5–40.6.

53. Sall. *Cat.* 23.

54. Octavian used this honorific name after January 27 BCE, when it was given to him by the Roman Senate in appreciation for his devotion to the restoration of the Roman Republic.

55. The *lex Titia* was passed on November 27, 43 BCE. Unlike the first triumvirate, this one was legal.

56. See Cicero's speeches the *Philippics.*

57. Brutus' mother was Servilia, daughter of Quintus Servilius Caepio and stepsister of Cato Uticensis, grandson of Cato the Censor. Servilia is said to have been Caesar's lover (Suet. *Caes.* 50.2). After Caesar's murder, Servilia seems to be active in discussions with Cicero, Brutus, and Cassius (Cic. *Att.* 15.11, 12.1).

58. Bauman (1992), 81–83.

59. App. *B. Civ.* 4.32–4.34; Val. Max. 8.3.3; Quint. *Inst.* 1.1.6.

60. In the battle of Mutina, legions headed by the two consuls, Aulus Hirtius and Gaius Vibius Pansa, and Octavian who, because of Cicero's demand, received senatorial rank and pro-praetorian power, came to Brutus' aid. The two consuls died in battle but Octavian marched on and entered Rome. Octavian and Quintus Pedius, a distant relative, finished Hirtius' and Pansa's consulships.

61. Castellani (2001); Gurval (1995).

62. Verg. *Aen.* 696–713.

63. Livia Drusilla was born in 58 BCE. Her father was Marcus Livius Drusus Claudianus. The Livii were a plebeian family that came to prominence in the second half of the fourth century BCE. Drusus is a cognomen of the family. Members of the *gens Livia* with this cognomen belonged to the leading plebeian families in the second and first century BCE. The famous tribune of the people of 91 BCE, Marcus Livius Drusus, who tried to implement agricultural and judicial reforms as well as extend Roman citizenship to Italian allies, seems to have adopted Livia's father from the family of

the Claudii, perhaps the branch of the Pulchri. The latter is the family of the notorious Clodius Pulcher and infamous Clodia. The Claudii were originally a Sabine family that immigrated, supposedly, in 504 BCE to Rome. The family was patrician. Livia's extraordinary ancestry boosted Octavian's, who lacked such pedigree. Octavian's father, Gaius Octavius, was an equestrian from an undistinguished family. His mother, Atia, was a niece of Caesar. When Octavian was four years old, his father died and Atia married Lucius Marcius Philippus, *praetor* in 60 BCE.

64. Augustus had received tribunician sacrosanctity in 36 BCE, and six years later he was voted full tribunician power. Augustus offered to surrender all his extraordinary powers given to him on January 13, 27 BCE. In return, the Senate voted him the honorific name Augustus and gave him proconsular powers for ten years over the provinces with the largest number of legions (Spain, Gaul, Syria, and Egypt). A laurel wreath was placed above the doorposts of his house, and a golden shield inscribed with four virtues (valor, clemency, justice, and piety) was placed in the *curia*, the Senate house. The latter made Augustus, based on his military and political virtues, the most important Roman citizen. The arrangements between the Senate and Rome's first citizen on January 13, 27 BCE, are also known as the First Settlement. The Second Settlement came on July 1, 23 BCE, when Augustus resigned his consulship. Augustus' continuous occupation of one consulship slot year after year gave Rome's elite less and less a chance to hold the state's highest political office. In return for his resignation, Augustus received full tribunician power (*tribunicia potestas*) and *imperium maius* (greater *imperium,* the power of a consul). Augustus could convene the Senate, present legislation, and command all legions. All political and military powers were in his hands without his occupying the magisterial positions. See Eck (2003), 52–66.

65. Damon and Takács (1999), 31–32: "That as far as the case of Plancina was concerned, against whom numerous weighty charges had been lodged . . . the Senate deemed that both Julia Augusta, who was most well deserving of the Republic not only because she gave birth to our *princeps* but also because of her many and great kindnesses to men of every order—although she rightly and deservedly should have the greatest influence in what she requested from the Senate, she used it most sparingly—and the very great devotion of our *princeps* to his mother should be supported and indulged; and that it was [the Senate's] pleasure that the punishment of Plancina be remitted" (lines 109–120).

66. Tac. Ann. 1.3 and passim. See also Barrett (2001, 2002).

67. Wood (1999), 78, with references to Flory (1984); Kleiner and Matheson (1996), 32; Galinski (1996), 98; and Purcell (1986), 88.

68. The story was outlined in Livy 2.40.1–2.40.12 and Dion. Hal. 8.39–8.62; these are the ancient sources for the women's heroic action.

69. Tac. *Ann.* 1.14.

70. A *lictor* was an attendant of high magistrates who held *imperium* (supreme military power, supreme authority) and some priests. Lictors carried *fasces,* a bundle of rods with an axe.

CHAPTER TWO

1. Kaster (1996).

2. Newlands (1995) suggested that Ovid "plays with time (12)," but he also plays with politics.

3. This is actually the rotation of the earth around its axis and its elliptical path around the fixed star of our solar system, the sun.

4. Cf. Konrad Lorenz' observation of Martina, the goose. See Lorenz (1996). Lorenz observed that newly hatched birds spontaneously followed their mother. He discovered that an arbitrary stimulus introduced during this period after hatching could bring about this response. Lorenz called this process "imprinting." Each new generation of birds would display this imprint; their behavior and action patterns were thus fixed.

5. Romans calculated inclusively.

6. *EN* standing for *endotercissus,* an archaic form of *intercissus,* "having fallen between."

7. Wissowa (1902), 436.

8. There were two other months with names based on numbers: the fifth month (Quintilis), which Julius Caesar renamed to July to commemorate his birth month, and the sixth month (Sextilis), which Augustus renamed to August to commemorate his victory over Egypt, which took place in early August 30 BCE.

9. Cato *Agr.* 141.

10. On the calendar, see Michels (1967); Samuel (1972), 153–188; Scullard (1981), 41–48. The newest, and in many ways, most thought-provoking monograph is that of Rüpke (1995).

11. Hauben (1980–1981), esp. 253.

12. Archer (1941); Zerubavel (1989).

13. Dialis is formed from *dies* (*piter*) and the adjectival ending *-alis.* The link to Zeus/Jupiter can be found in the genitive singular form of Dios.

14. A Roman city was founded by Etruscan rite (*Etrusco ritu*). At a designated day (by augury), a cow and a bull were harnessed to a plow. A furrow was cut within which the city would lay. Generally, we can say that this originally cut furrow is the *pomerium.* Boundary markers, *cippi,* delineated the *pomerium.* The historian Tacitus (*Ann.* 12.23) recorded that the emperor Claudius extended the *pomerium. Cippi* support this claim, while such archaeological proof does not exist for the extensions by Augustus, Nero, and Trajan, which Aulus Gellius mentioned.

15. The *palladium* was an image or a statue of Pallas, which Odysseus was said to have stolen from the Trojans; subsequently, the image was brought to Italy.

16. Livy 2.20.12 and 2.42.5.

17. See Orlin (1997).

18. The song of the Arval Brethren.

19. Plut. *Num.* 13 and *Rom.* 21; Juv. 3.10–20, 6.10; Vitr. 8.3.1; Livy 21.3; Frontin. 1.4.

20. Frontin. 4, however, with a textual problem.

21. Vitr. 8.3.1.

22. Verg. *Aen.* 8.664.

23. The *OLD* gives as a second category "to move suddenly or spasmodically especially under the stress of emotion"; third, "(of water and other fluids) to be ejected with some force, gush, spurt, discharge"; and fourth, "(of male animals) to mount, cover."

24. Festus (1913), 9.

25. Ov. *Fast.* 1.317–1.336.

26. The expression is problematic. The title of these gods is obscure; *indiges* might be the archaic form (*indu*) of the preposition *in* and the verb *ago* (to move, bring, bear, be in motion, etc.).

27. Ov. *Fast.* 2.477; Festus (1913), 43.

28. The most dramatic description in Verg. *Aen.* 1. The antiquarian Varro quotes the annalist L. Calpurnius Piso and renders Numa's formula as: "that it always be open, except when there is no war (*ut sit aperta semper, nisi cum bellum sit nusquam*)."

29. The name of the muse addressed in Livius Andronicus' *Odyssia* (*Od.* 1.1), the earliest Latin poetry ("tell me, Camena, of the skillful man, *virum mihi Camena insece versutum*").

30. Verg. *Aen.* 8.338–8.341. Carmentis was thought to be the mother of Evander, king of Arcadia, who founded the city Pallanteum at the side of the Palatine Hill (Ov. *Fast.* 1.471ff.).

31. Scullard (1981), 62; *CIL* I^2, p. 307 (Mommsen). *Inscr. Ital.* 398 suggested Romulus; Livy on the capture of Fidenae in 426 BCE names Manlius Aemilius as general (4.31–4.34).

32. Scullard (1981), 62.

33. Newlands (1995), 1–26.

34. Some editions bracket the line (1. 620): "*haec quoque ab Evandri dicta parente reor* (I believe that these things were also said by the ancestor Evander)."

35. Macrob. *Sat.* 1.7.20; Ov. *Fast.* 1.635f.

36. Dio Cass. 4.11. The fairy tale Sleeping Beauty retains this aspect of (wise) women prophesying the child's future.

37. Scullard (1981), 64.

38. Lam and Miron (1991).

39. Varro *Ling.* 5.146.

40. Varro *Ling.* 7.84.

41. There is only one inscription from Rome that records a *flamen Carmentalis* (*CIL* VI 3720 = 31032).

42. Cic. *Brut.* 57. Münzer (1999), 198–204 passim, expounds on the Popillii Laenates, whose "ancestor had probably been one of the leading men from plebeians who immediately after the Licinian-Sextian laws had been recognized by the patricians to be their equal, but only his son held the consulship in 316."

43. Ovid explained that *februa* was the word the Roman fathers used for purification (*Fast.* 2.29).

44. Latte (1960), 166–168, on the name and with Douglas (1913) as a basis on the Etruscan influence.

45. A Juno Curritis, a Juno with a spear (Sabine word: *curis*), was also the guardian deity of Falerii (*CIL* XI 3126 and Ov. *Am.* 3.13.7). A *pontifex sacrarius* (*CIL* XI 3100, 3125) was assigned to take care of her cult.

46. *CIL* XIV 2088, 2089, 2091, 2092, 2121, I^2 1430; Livy 8.14.2; 21.62.4; Cic. *Mil.* 27.45, *Mur.* 90.

47. *CIL* XIV, p. 192; Livy 32.30.20, 34.53.3.

48. Livy 32.30.10 and 34.53.3.

49. Ov. *Fast.* 2.55–2.58.

50. In modern times, the father of psychoanalysis, Sigmund Freud, developed explanations for snake dreams that seem to have underlying sexual tensions.

51. Strabo C393.

52. Plin. *HN* 29.20: "*draco non habet venena. caput eius limini ianuarum subditum propitatis adoratione diis fortunatam domum facere promittitur. . . .*"

53. Wissowa (1902), 154–155. Mater Matuta was a goddess of dawn and of childbirth. Scullard (1981), 150: "The festival of Mothers, Matralia, was held in honour of Mater Matuta, who was an old Italian goddess, worshipped in many places in central Italy."

54. See also Gellius 11.16. The snake is depicted on silver coins (*denarii*) issued by L. Roscius Fabatus in the late Republican period. Crawford (1974), no. 412/11; Sydenham (1952), no. 915.

55. Cic. *Nat. D.* 1.29 [82].

56. Douglas (1913), esp. 71; Shields (1926), 67–70.

57. Ov. *Fast.* 2.533–2.570.

58. Plin. *HN* 23.142(74).

59. Geopon. 11.10.

60. Salzman (1990), 129.

61. Reinach (1908), 223–224.

62. "*Graecia capta ferum victorem cepit et artes / intulit agresti Latio* (Greece captured the uncivilized victor and brought forth the arts in rustic Latium": Hor. *Epist.* 2.1.156–2.1.157.)

63. Scullard (1991), 75.

64. Cornell (1995), 48: "The first traces of permanent habitation on the site of Rome date back to around 1000 BC, and consist of a handful of cremation graves in the forum."

65. Michels (1953), 48.

66. DiLucia (1998), 204–205.

67. Varro *Ling.* 5.46; Richardson (1992), 62–63; Cornell (1995), with more detail.

68. Cancik (1985/6), 256.

69. Baudy (2001).

70. Scullard (1981), 75. Ov. *Fast.* 2.565–582.

71. Ov. *Fast.* 2.557–564.

72. Ov. *Fast.* 2.565–567.

73. Ov. *Fast.* 2.573–574.

74. Ov. *Fast.* 2.571–582.

75. Ov. *Fast.* 2.631–2.634.

76. Ov. *Fast.* 2.637–2.638.

77. Radke (1993).

78. Cato *Agr.* 141: "Mars, Father, I pray and ask you that you may be willing and favorable to me, our house and family; therefore, for this reason, I have ordered a pig, a sheep, and an ox (the *suovetaurilia*) to be driven around my land and farm so that you will prevent, guard against, and avert seen and unseen illnesses, childlessness and barrenness, calamities and storms, so that if you wish fruits, grains, vines, and shrubs to grow and to come to fruition, so that you may keep healthy shepherds and flocks and give health and strength to me, our house and family. Therefore, for these reasons, for the lustration and expiation of my farm, field, and land such as I have said, accept the killing of this suckling pig, sheep and ox. Mars, Father, accept the killing of this suckling pig, sheep, and ox."

79. Ov. *Fast.* 2.435–2.452; Varro *Ling.* 5.49; Plin. *HN* 16.235.

80. DiLucia (1998), 212.

81. Ov. *Fast.* 3.657–3.674; Mart. 4.24.16; Macrob. *Sat.* 1.12.6.

82. Versnel (1993), 235. One could also point to the Feast of the Tabernacle or Sukkut, which also focuses on fertility.

83. Wissowa (1902), 241–242.

84. Ovid, *Fast.* 3.523–710.

85. Bruhl (1953), esp. 13–29.

86. Varro *Ling.* 6.33; also Macrob. 1.12.1–14; Ov. *Fast.* 4.87–4.90.

87. Lucr. 1.1–1.5.

88. July: *ludi Apollinares* and *ludi Victoriae Caesaris;* September: *ludi Romani;* October: *ludi divi Augusti et Fortunae Reducis, ludi Capitolini,* and *ludi Victoriae Sullanae;* November: *ludi plebei.* Without Caesar, Augustus, and Sulla, we are left with *ludi* lasting several days in July, September, and November, in addition to the block in April.

89. Obsequens 37; Oros. 5.15.21–5.15.22; Ov. *Fast.* 4.157–4.160.

90. This temple was most likely located on the slope of the Aventine behind the *circus maximus.* See Richardson (1992), 411. On Sulpicia, see Val. Max. 8.15.12; Plin. *HN* 7.120; Solin. 1.126.

91. Richardson (1992), 211.

92. Ov. *Fast.* 4.863–4.876. On Venus Erycina and Mens, see Galinsky (1969), 173–180. Bömer ([1958], vol. 2, 284) notes that the cult of Aphrodite points to the Orient, in particular Phoenicia-Carthage. In light of the Punic Wars, the integration of a deity that has a Punic background explains the Romans' behavior in appropriating a deity that came from an area originally controlled by the enemy but that belonged squarely in the Roman sphere. On the origins of the cult of Aphrodite, see Herter (1960).

93. Richardson (1992), 409; Orlin (1997), 127–128.

94. Takács (1996); Chapter 5 below.

95. Bömer (1958), vol. 2, 353, agrees with Altheim (1960), 239–240, that Mens is Roman. On the introduction of this abstract concept as a deity, see also Wissowa (1902), 313–314.

96. Ov. *Fast.* 4. 735ff.; Tib. 2.5.89f.; Prop. 4.4.75ff.

97. Wissowa (1902), 177.

98. For a more detailed discussion of Bona Dea, see Chapter 5.

99. On the question of the festival date as well as a detailed discussion of the festival, see Radke (1980); B. Nagy (1985).

100. Varro *Ling.* 5.45–5.56, 7.44; Dion. Hal. 1.38.3; Plut. *Quaest. Rom.* 86.

101. Cancik (1985/6), 250–265, esp. 256.

102. B. Nagy (1985), 7.

103. Varro *Rust.* 1.32.

104. B. Nagy (1985), 8–9.

105. Mehl-Madrona (2002).

106. Ov. *Fast.* 6.1–100.

107. The most detailed of them is Dion. Hal. 2.66.3–2.66.6.

108. Plin. *HN* 18.107.

109. Dumézil (1996), vol. 1, 47–59; Ov. *Fast.* 6.473–6.562.

110. Pokorny (1989, 2nd ed.) connects the Latin "*Mātūta*" the wife of the early morning, dawn, but also of maturity, with *mātūtīnus* "matutinal," *mātūrus* "timely, in time, and mature" (based on **ma-tu-* approximately "good, opportune time"), Oscan *Maatu'i's*.

111. Heurgon (1966).

112. Varro *Ling.* 5.106.

113. Bettini (1991).

114. Ov. *Fast.* 6.551–6.558.

115. Scullard (1981), 151.

116. In an age without antibiotics, the childbirth death rate of both mother and child was high, as was infant mortality. Miscarriages and giving birth can, even with modern medical advances, be dangerous. It could be argued that to ensure survival, Roman women (and men) exercised birth control to avert medical situations that were potentially deadly. Also, wealthy families tried to maintain small family sizes in order to avoid economic loss and a breakdown of the living standard.

117. Balsdon (1962), 190–199.

118. On the Sibylline Books, see Chapter 3 below.

119. An alternative spelling is *Capratinae*. I am not discussing the ritual surrounding the temple of Fortuna Muliebris recorded by Dionysius of Halicarnassus, because its dedication is not recorded in any calendar. See *CIL* IV 1555.

120. Varro *Ling.* 6.18. Also Macrob. *Sat.* 1.11 and 36.40, attested in Silvius' calendar of 448 CE.

121. Wissowa (1902), 118.

122. Macrobius (*Sat.* 1.11.36–1.11.40 and 3.2.14) has the women give wine to the attackers.

123. Versnel (1993), 237.

124. Versnel (1993), 286.

125. Plut. *Rom.* 29.6.

126. Livy 1.16.1, as well as later writers Florus 1.1.16 and Sollinus 1.20.

127. Ov. *Fast.* 2.491–2.496.

128. For example, Verg. *Ecl.* 3.8; Ov. *Ars* 2.486; Plin. *HN* 26.98.

129. *CIL* I², p. 288; Festus (1913), 106.

130. Wissowa (1902), 250–251.

131. In August. *De civ. D.* 7.

132. Cato's *On Agriculture* gives a good sense of a Roman's aversion to seafaring and trade linked to the sea.

133. Plut. *C. Gracch.;* Varro *Ling.* 6.19; Cic. *Nat. D.* 3.46 and *Q. Fr.* 3.1.4.

134. Richardson (1992), 219–220 and 235.

135. E.g., Ov. *Fast.* 3.11–24.

136. Scullard (1981), 169.

137. Wissowa (1902), 201–204.

138. Just as Plut. *Rom.* 14.3 had done.

139. Ov. *Fast.* 3.199–3.200; Bömer (1958), vol. 2, 156, on Consus.

140. Dion. Hal. 2.31.2–2.31.3.

141. Scullard (1981), 178.

142. Tert. *De spect.* 5.8.

143. Richardson (1992), 100.

144. Plin. *HN* 36.102.

145. Burkert (1985), 159 (Demeter) and 136–139 (Poseidon).

146. Richardson (1992), 328.

147. Wissowa (1902), 168.

148. Varro *Ling.* 6.21; *CIL* VI 32482.

149. Varro *Ling.* 6.21; *CIL* VI 32482.

150. Scullard (1981), 181.

151. Scullard (1981), 181.

152. Versnel (1970), 66–93.

153. See Richardson (1992), 245, for more details on this altar.

154. Wissowa (1902), 145.

155. Richardson (1992), 403.

156. Richardson (1992), 403.

157. Welch (1999), 381.

158. For more detail, see entries under Purcell (1993).

159. Which part of the horse was affixed depended on which part the participating inhabitants of the Subura won in the contest with the inhabitants of the *Via Sacra* (Festus [1913], 372). Where the latter affixed their "captured" horse part is not known (Plut. *Quaest. Rom.* 97; Polyb. 12.4b).

CHAPTER THREE

* The discussion on the Sibyls and the Sibylline Books was originally published in Takács (2003). I adjusted the original article to better reflect the focus and tone of this book. I used [. . .] to indicate to the reader where a section from the article was

omitted. My thoughts on Mater Magna and Cybele (Kybele) can be found in Takács (1996, 1999a, 1999b) and those on Isis in Takács (1995, 1998, 2005).

1. Frazer (1972), vol. 1, 305–335.

2. Lact. *Div. Inst.* 1.6 (quoting Varro *Antiquitates rerum divinarum*) and Dio. Hal. 4.62.4. The second one was the Libyan (Euripides), the third the Delphian (Chrysippus), the fourth the Cimmerian (Naevius and Piso), the fifth the Erythraean (Apollodorus of Erythrae), the sixth the Samian (Eratosthenes), the seventh the Cumaean (Varro), the eighth the Hellespontine (Heraclides), and the ninth the Phrygian. See Parke (1988) for details and discussion.

3. Lycoph. *Alex.* 1250–1262. On the poem as a whole and Vergil's adaptation, see West (1983). These tables turn out to be flat bread on which food was placed. The story of the sow follows Hellenic patterns of city foundations. The city was founded on the spot where a guiding animal found a resting place. The thirty piglets suggest incredible fecundity and may even be interpreted as the future *curiae* (division of Roman people) of the same number.

4. Dion. Hal. 1.55.4. In Dionysius' story, the sow about to be sacrificed runs off and leads Aeneas and his men to the future site of Lanuvium.

5. Verg. *Aen.* 3.230.

6. Verg. *Aen.* 7.123; also West (1983).

7. Verg. *Aen.* 3.359.

8. Verg. *Aen.* 8.42–8.85.

9. Livy 1.6.

10. Ninck (1960).

11. Tib. 2.5.19–2.5.64; Cardauns (1961); Cairns (1970), 73–78.

12. Lact. *Div. Inst.* 1.6 (quoting Varro *Antiquitates rerum divinarum*) and Dio. Hal. 4.62.4.

13. In 348 BCE the number was raised to ten (*decemviri*) and in the late 80s BCE, to fifteen (*quindecimviri*).

14. The temple was located on the Capitoline hill. It was dedicated to the Capitoline triad: Jupiter, Juno, and Minerva. Tarquin the Elder (Tarquinius Priscus) vowed to build the temple during his war with the Sabines. Tarquin the Proud (Tarquinius Superbus), however, is thought to have brought the building project to completion. Tarquin the Elder was Rome's fourth king; Tarquin the Proud was Rome's seventh and last king. Both were Etruscans. See Richardson (1992), 221–224, for more details.

15. Münzer (1999). On Atilii, see pp. 57–59, on Acilii pp. 87–88. An interesting fact is that the Atilii were a very prominent plebeian family from Campania, the region in which Cumae is located. The first Atilius was consul in 335 BCE; another, in 294 BCE. Other Atilii became prominent during the First Punic War, and the clan was instrumental in keeping Campania loyal to Rome when Hannibal had the upper hand in Italy.

16. The *collegium* (college) was originally made up of ten members, five patricians and five plebeians, in 367 BCE. Sulla (dictator, 83–79 BCE) increased the number to

fifteen; Caesar, to sixteen. The name of the priestly college remained the same, even though its membership was over twenty during the Principate. The college in charge of the Sibylline Books was one of the four most important priestly colleges (*quattuor amplissima collegia*) in Rome.

17. The traditional dates of Rome's foundation (753 BCE) and the beginning of the Republic (509 BCE) reverberate in Greek/Athenian dates: the first Olympic Games in 776 BCE and the murder of the Athenian tyrants, Peisistratos' sons (the Peisistratides), in 514 BCE. Because early Roman history is very much a literary invention, these close chronological parallels come as no surprise. The Peisistratides deposited an oracular collection on the Akropolis. The Akropolis was, like the Capitoline hill, the location of the temple of the city's guardian deity. Peisistratos' son employed a diviner (*chrēsmologos*) and an editor (*diathetēs*) of oracles. The editor, Onomacritus, worked on sayings from earlier times. These sayings were attributed to Musaeus. Onomacritus, however, was caught improving the oracles (that is, interpolating) and was fired from his job (Hdt. 7.6). The Peisistratides wanted a coherently arranged set. Unlike the Homeric poems, which received their first standardization during this period, interpolations could not enter the oracular corpus.

18. Plut. *Marc.* 3; Livy 27.37.

19. This in contrast to Etruscan rite (*Etrusco ritu*). The cults Romans introduced were, according to the literary sources, Greek (*Graeco ritu*). For a discussion and primary sources, see Scheid (1995). It is not surprising that new cults were incorporated with their original cultic action. As the Empire encompassed more than the Greek East, new cults kept being performed *Graeco ritu*.

20. Livy 29.10.

21. On the introduction of the cult, see Takács (1996).

22. Livy 23.12.

23. Berger (1969), 33.

24. Plut. *Sulla* 2.7.6; Dion. Hal. 4.62.5–6; see also Richardson (1992), 222.

25. Samos, like Ephesos, did have a Sibyl but not a cult of Apollo. An interesting fact insofar as prophesying women goes, be they the Delphic Pythia or a Sibyl, was that they were thought to be the mouthpieces of Apollo. The myth has Apollo slay the dragon Python, a monstrous son of Gē (Earth) and guardian of her oracle at Delphi. From that moment on, Apollo controlled the oracle. Ov. *Met.* 1.454–462.

26. Latte ([1960], 160–161) and Parke ([1988], 136–137) conjecturally assign the dissemination of Sibylline prophecies from different places to the Mithridatic period (80s BCE).

27. Verg. *Aen.* 6.69–76; Dio Cass. 53.1.3; Suet. *Aug.* 31.

28. Takács (2007).

29. Tac. *Ann.* 1.76.

30. Parke (1988), 212 n. 5.

31. Dio Cass. 57.18.4. Discussed in Newbold (1974).

32. Tac. *Ann.* 15.44; Dio Cass. 52.18.4.

33. Prudent. *Apotheosis* 4.39.

34. Latte (1960), 160–161.

35. Wissowa (1902), 461–475, esp. 470 n. 2. Beard, North, and Price's work (1998, vol. 1) is the first study of Roman religion in English. They do not, unfortunately, give any new insights on the Sibylline Books.

36. Capdeville (1997), 465–466: "Car justement, parmi les traits qui distinquent la religion étrusque—que les Romains appelaient l'*Etrusca disciplina*—, notamment par opposition aux religions romaine et grecque, il y a les deux caractéristiques suivantes: c'est une religion du livre, ou plutôt des livres, ceux-ci étant constamment mentionnés par nos sources dès qu'il est question d'un acte relevant de cette *Etrusca disciplina; c*'est une religion révélée, comme le rappelle avec emphase Cicéron lui-même (*Har. resp.* 20). . . . (For exactly, among the traits that distinguish the Etruscan religion—which the Romans called Etruscan discipline—, notably as opposed to the Roman and Greek religion, there are the two following characteristics: it is a religion of the book, or of several books; these are constantly mentioned by our sources as a question of an act relevant to this Etruscan discipline; it is a developing religion as Cicero himself emphasized. . . .)"

37. There were thirty such groupings. The assembly of the thirty *curiae* voted on issues related to religion. See above, n. 2.

38. A *centuria* was a military unit (nominally, 100 soldiers) but also a unit into which the Roman people were divided for voting purposes. The issues voted in the centuriate assembly had military overtones.

39. Festus (1913), 358.

40. Detailed discussion of ancient sources in Capdeville (1997).

41. Livy 5.55.1.

42. Images of the gods were placed on couches so that they could be part of the banquet in their honor; Livy 5.12.4–5.12.8.

43. Livy 5.14.4. For the Livy commentator R. M. Ogilvie, the term Books of Fate is a neutral, overarching category. He writes in Ogilvie (1965), 658: "The term is wider than and inclusive of the Sibylline Books. It would also include the books of Etruscan discipline."

44. Livy 5.15.11.

45. Livy 5.16.8–5.16.11. The last time a Roman had consulted the Delphic oracle in Livy's account was the Etruscan Tarquin the Proud, Rome's last king, shortly before he was overthrown. The prodigies were such that the most famous oracular site in the world needed to be consulted (Livy 1.56.5–1.56.6).

46. A short and insightful discussion in Bonfante (1994).

47. Livy 40.29.

48. A water nymph called Egeria (Dion. Hal. 2.60; Ov. *Met.* 15.479–484; Plut. *Num.* 4.13).

49. Livy 22.57.2.

50. For the oracle's response, see Livy 23.11.2–23.11.3.

51. Livy 22.57.6.

52. Livy 29.3.

53. Livy 30.38. Dumézil (1996), vol. 2, 458, proposed that "from the religious standpoint there is no crisis in the years between Saguntum and Zama." His focus was on the religious system, which was open and flexible. The statement, however, ignores the human component. There were prodigies and omens that prompted the repeated consultation of the Sibylline Books. The occurrences and the interpretations could be explained as arising from the anxieties of the uneducated masses, which forced Rome's leadership to react.

54. Livy 29.10.5. Ovid presents more baffled Romans and a more hesitant Attalus in his *F.* 4.259–4.272.

55. Of the ancient sources quoted in this respect, I would argue that Cic. *Har. resp.* 27–28 does not connect the Mater brought to Rome to Pessinus. Pessinus is, in fact, still the home of the Mother of the Gods when Cicero wrote. Starting with Diodorus Siculus (34–35.33.2), the goddess is taken from Pessinus (Strabo 12.5.3; Val. Max. 8.15.3; App. *Hann.* 56; Dio Cass. 17.61; *Viri Illustres* 46; Amm. Marc. 22.9.5). While on his way to battle the Persians, Julian (361–363 CE) stopped at Pessinus, where he visited the shrine of ἡ τῶν θεῶν Μήτηρ, the Mother of the Gods, and composed an oration in her honor (*Or.* 5). Julian gives a brief account how τὸ ἁγιώτατον ἄγαλμα the most sacred statue or image arrived in Rome (159c–161a). Although the emperor does not state it explicitly, one can but assume that in his mind the "holiest statue/image" came from Pessinus.

56. Ov. *Fast.* 4.265–272. Varro *Ling.* 6.15: "*Megalesia dicta a Graecis quod ex libris Sibyllinis arcessita ab Attalo rege Pergamo: ibi prope murum Megalesion templum eius deae, unde aduecta Romam.*"

57. Graillot (1912), 45–46, as well as Magie (1950), vol. 1, 25–26, vol. 2, 769–770, and Virgilio (1981), 46–47 and 63–69.

58. Sanders (1981), 276.

59. *Evocatio* is most often seen as a pontifical action in the context of war. The Romans asked the tutelary deity of a city to leave that city and join them. The most famous story of an *evocatio* is the transference of Juno of Veii to Rome. Our main source is Livy 5.19–5.23. For an overview of *evocatio,* see Gustafsson (2000).

60. On these kinds of motivations, see Blomart (1997), 99–111, esp. p. 103.

61. Gruen (1990), 19. The whole chapter ("The Advent of the Magna Mater," pp. 5–33) provides stimulating reading.

62. Bömer (1958), vol. 2, 229, suggested that even if the stone had come from Pessinus through Pergamum, then it was not *the* but *a* stone of Mater Magna. Gruen (1990), 19: "For Romans of the later Republic, the cult of Cybele at Pessinus was the principal functioning shrine of the goddess in Asia Minor."

63. Sanders (1981), 275–276, noted that Aeneas, Rome's founding "father," was born and spent his youth on Mount Ida in the vicinity of Troy. This connected him with Mater Deum Magna Idaea, the "Great Mother Goddess of Mount Ida." Since the region of Troy belonged to Pergamum, and Pessinus was an independent theocratic state until 183 BCE, it may certainly have been possible that the Roman embassy received the goddess. Sanders called this goddess Cybele, who was not from Pessinus but from Pergamum. Along similar lines are the comments of Gruen (1990), 32.

64. Bömer (1958), vol. 2, 229–230, mentions that there were several *baityloi* (sacred stones), but not one was known to be from Ida. He cites Schwenn's article "Kybele" (1922), where, col. 2254, the author refers to Claud. *De rapt. Pros.* 1.201–1.205, which mentions Ida as the home of a "religiosa silex (religious flint stone)." Bömer dismisses Claudianus' reference on the grounds that this is a late source.

65. For background reading on the origins of Cybele and her place in Greece, see the articles of Laroche (1960) and Will (1960).

66. For example, Bömer (1964), 132.

67. Sanders (1981), 266–267.

68. *Arbor intrat* ("the tree enters") March 22, *sanguen* ("blood") March 24, *hilaria* ("cheerfulness") March 25, and *requietio* ("rest") March 26. A *lavatio* ("washing"), March 27, was added in the time of Augustus.

69. Livy 36.36.4. On the problem of dating (194 or 191 BCE), see Briscoe (1981), 276; *CIL* VI 496, 1040, 3702 = 30967.

70. Cic. *Har. resp.* 12.24.

71. Diodorus Siculus (1.13–1.27) and Plutarch (*De Is. et Os.* 12–19) provide the most continuous myths surrounding Isis.

72. For example, a gold coin (*British Museum Catalogue of Coins of the Roman Empire*, ed. H. Mattingly, vol. 4, no. 255) depicts Isis sitting on a dog (Sothis or Sirius, the "dog-star") and holding a rattle (*sistrum*).

73. Hdt. 2.59.2.

74. Tert. *Ad nat.* 1.10; Dio Cass. 40.47, 42.26.

75. Tac. *Ann.* 2.67.

76. Richardson (1992), 46.

77. Wissowa (1902), 353.

78. 8.831–8.833.

79. After the finding of Osiris follow two days of celebration. The whole festival ended November 3. See also Salzman (1990), 169–176.

80. Barrett (1989), 220–221.

81. Joseph. *BJ* 7.123–131. On the *Iseum Campense,* see Lembke (1994).

CHAPTER FOUR

1. Cancik-Lindemaier (1990), 10, n. 50, points out that in a period of circa 750 years, nineteen Vestals had been accused of *incestum* in eleven trials. Six of the nineteen accused killed themselves. The question of historical veracity can often not be resolved. For discussions on the relationship between accused and punished Vestals to the Roman state, see, in addition to Cancik-Lindemaier (1990), 10–12, Rawson (1974); North (1986); Cornell (1981).

2. See Raaflaub (2005).

3. Gardner (1986), 22.

4. Gardner (1986), 24.

5. Gardner (1986), 24. For all legal details regarding the Vestals, see Gardner (1986), 22–27, which was my source here. The *OLD* definition for *peculium* is: "Money or property managed more or less as his own by a person incapable of legal ownership."

6. Augustan legislation, *leges Iulia et Papia (Poppaea),* established that unmarried and childless persons had to pay fines and were curtailed in many ways, such as an ineligibility to receive legacies. The *ius liberorum* (the right of children) privileged the recipient, that is, excluded the person from the state-imposed penalties and restrictions. *Tutela* (tutelage) was a form of guardianship. Women were under lifelong (male) guardianship. Under Augustus, however, in order to increase the birth rate, Roman women who gave birth to three children and freedwomen, to four children were freed from guardianship.

7. Gardner (1986), 24.

8. Gardner (1986), 23. This phrase translates to "deterioration of status." Nicholas (1987), 96: "Three elements may be seen in a man's status in Roman law—liberty, citizenship, and family rights—any changes of status may be analysed accordingly. . . . The most common is the loss merely of family rights by either adoption, adrogation, marriage with *manus,* or emancipation." Nicholas (1987), 80, also noted that emancipation "not only freed the son from *patria potestas,* but also deprived him of all rights of succession."

9. Gardner (1986), 23; Gellius 1.12.

10. Gai. *Inst.* 1.130.145.

11. See Beard (1980), 14, for bibliographical references.

12. Even this name is obscure. Is it to be translated as "Beloved," the past participle of the verb *amare* (to love), or "Acquired" from the verb *emere* (to acquire)? Was it the proper name of the first Vestal (Gell. 1.19) or the Latinized form of the Greek *admēta* (unwedded)?

13. The *rex sacrorum* was a member of the pontifical college and in the order of priests (*ordo sacerdotum*) took the place of primacy. This priest had to be a patrician, and his parents had to be married by *confarreatio.* This was a marriage *in manu* that brought the wife under the control of her husband. This marriage type took its name from a cake made from spelt (*far*). Such a spelt cake was also used in sacrifice given to Jupiter.

14. Beard ([1980], 13) uses the German word *Hausfrau.*

15. A *lictor* carried a bundle, which was made of wooden rods, usually tied around an axe. The content of the bundle symbolized the magistrate's power to punish, either to flog with the rod or to kill with the axe. The magistrates, who held *imperium,* that is, supreme military power and authority, had control over life and death. The latter would seem applicable to the Vestals.

16. Beard (1980) and (1995).

17. Versnel (1993), 269–272.

18. Varro *Ling.* 5.74.

19. Hommel (1972), 399–413.

20. Plut. *Num.* 10.

21. Hommel (1972), 406–407, n. 52; Münzer (1937), 199–203.

22. Radke (1975).

23. Radke (1981).

24. Hommel (1972), 407–414 and esp. 412–413.

25. Plin. *HN* 28.39: "fascinus . . . qui deus . . . a Vestalibus colitur."

26. Hommel (1972), 414–415. In Plutarch's life (*Rom.* 2.7) Romulus is thus begotten, and in a similar manner is Caecilius, the founder of Praeneste, according to Servius' commentary, *Aen.* 7.678. There is also a Greek precedent in the *Hymn to Demeter*. Demeter, disguised as an old nurse, fed Demophoon ambrosia and put him in a fire to make him immortal (248–249).

27. The low class of the mother of the future king is noteworthy as is her ethnicity. The whole of early Roman history as it was revisited and refashioned by later authors as well as leaders such as Augustus is wrought with these occasions of providence.

28. Dion. Hal. *Ant. Rom.* 4.2; Plut. *De fort. Rom.* 10.323A–C; ff.; Ov. *F.* 6.625–6.636; Plin. *HN* 36.204; Livy 10.20.

29. G. Nagy (1974), 100.

30. G. Nagy (1974), 71, noted "some striking convergences in the modes [of cognate languages] of referring to fire and the fireplace."

31. G. Nagy (1974), 71.

32. G. Nagy (1974), 71–72: "I find a further semantic problem in the Hittite word for 'king,' *haššu-,* which seems to be derived from the same Hittite verb *haš-* 'beget.' All we can do at this point is cite an analogous semantic relationship, even if we fail to understand the precise application of the notion 'beget.' The English noun *king* and the German *König* stem from a Germanic formation **kuningaz.* This noun is a derivative of **kun* (as in Gothic *kuni* 'race, family'), a root with cognates in Latin *gēns, genus, genitor, gignō,* etc. Note especially the meaning of *gignō.*" The Latin verb *gignō* means "to beget, bear, bring forth."

33. Ov. *Fast.* 6.295–6.299; Cic. *De or.* 3.10 and *Nat. D.* 3.80.

34. Cody (1973).

35. Beard (1980), 15.

36. Beard (1995), 167–168.

37. Cic. *Font.* 48: "If the gods were to scorn their prayers, there would be nothing healthy (*cuius preces si di aspernarentur haec salva esse non possent*)."

38. Cancik-Lindemaier ([1990], 1–16, esp. 3–6) collected the material and literary sources that mentioned the cult of Vesta in the city of Rome.

39. Beard (1980), 12 n. 3; Hülsen (1928), 192–197.

40. According to the *PHI* 5 CD-ROM: *Pro Fonteio* (thrice), *In Catilinam* (twice), *Pro Murena* (once), *De domo sua* (once), *Pro Caelio* (once), *De haruspicum responso* (twice), *De republica* (twice), *De legibus* (once), *De divinatione* (once).

41. Münzer (1999), 222–224.

42. Mustakallio (1992), 56. E.g., Livy 8.15.7. See also H. Parker (2004).

43. Staples (1998), 131.

44. Plut. *Num.* 10.

45. Staples (1998), 133.

46. Richardson (1992), 302 and 424.

47. Festus (1913), 9 and 304.

48. Varro *Ling.* 6.14; Dion. Hal. 2.70.1.

49. Livy 2.42.9–2.42.11.

50. Val. Max. 8.1.5; Richlin (1997), 357.

CHAPTER FIVE

* The discussion on the Bacchanalian Affair of 186 BCE was originally published in *HSCP* 100 (2000 [2001]). Again, changes have been made to keep with the tone and focus of this book and [. . .] will indicate where I omitted a section of the original article. See also Beard, North, and Price (1998), vol. 1, 91–96 and vol. 2, 290–291. Discussions like those of Bruhl (1953) Gruen (1990), 34–78; Pailler (1988), and Pailler (1995) might be of older date, but they are still of great importance for any discussion of the topic and relevant bibliographical material.

1. Linderski (1996).

2. *CIL* I² 581.

3. Burkert (1987), 52.

4. Livy 39.8–39.19.

5. Gruen (1990), 76.

6. Gruen (1990), 77.

7. *CIE* 5430.

8. Heurgon (1957).

9. A son: *laris pulenas,* a father: *larces clan,* a paternal uncle: *larψal ratacs,* a grandfather: *velθurus nefts,* and a great-grandfather: *prumpts pules larisal creices.*

10. Heurgon (1957), 113. Livy 39.8.3: "A Greek of low birth who first came to Etruria (*Graecus ignobilis in Etruriam primum venit*)."

11. Heurgon (1957), 121.

12. Frank (1927), esp. 130. This argument's persuasiveness in establishing a convincing link between Greece and Rome has vanished.

13. Heurgon (1957), 117.

14. Wolf (1952); *PIR²* 6 (Berlin, 1998), nos. 537–539.

15. Scheid (1992), 398.

16. Burkert (1990), 52.

17. Scheid (1992), 393.

18. Beard, North, and Price (1998), vol. 1, 95 and n. 84.

19. Linderski (1993), 53–64, esp. 54.

20. Klebs (1896), esp. 2105.

21. Münzer (1899).

22. This sketch of Clodius' career is based on Tatum (1999).

23. For more detail on Mithridates and his engagement with the Romans, see Mc-Ging (1986).

24. Cic. *Att.* 1.12.3: "*P. Clodium Appi filium credo te audisse cum veste muliebri deprehensum domi C. Caesaris cum sacrificium pro populo fieret, eumque per manus servulae servatum et eductum; rem esse insigni infamia, quod te moleste ferre certo scio.*"

25. For an introduction to Roman political institutions, see Lintott (1999).

26. See also the discussion for the month of May in Chapter 2.

27. Ov. *Fast.* 5.149–5.158:

est moles nativa, loco res nomina fecit:

appellant Saxum; pars bona montis ea est.

huic Remus institerat frustra, quo tempore fratri

prima Palatinae signa dedistis aves;

templa patres illic oculos exosa viriles

leniter adclivi constituere iugo.

dedicat haec veteris Crassorum nominis heres,

virgineo nullum corpore passa virum:

Livia restituit, ne non imitata maritum

esset et ex omni parte secuta virum.

See also Festus (1913), 464.

28. Macrob. *Sat.* 1.12.25–1.12.26.

29. Brouwer (1989).

30. Bona Dea the rural and little happy one, the latter maybe in connection with Felix's name.

31. Felix publicus | Asinianus pontific(um) | Bonae Deae agresti Felic(ulae?) | votum solvit iunicem alba(m) | libens animo ob luminibus | restitutis derelictus a medicis post | menses decem bineficio dominaes medicinis sanatus per | eam restituta omnia ministerio Canniae Fortunatae. The inscription cannot be dated, but it is thought to belong in the latter part of the second century CE.

32. Bonae Deae | Hygiae. Unfortunately, there is no way of knowing where in Rome this statuette stood in antiquity and to which period it may belong.

33. Bon(ae) Deae | Luciferae | Antistia Veteris lib(erta) Eur (. . .) | d(onum) d(edit).

34. Cic. *Nat. D.* 2.68.

35. A pillar thus reads: Dedicated to Diana, Silvanus, Bona Dea (Sacrum | Dianae | Silvano | Bonadiae, *NS* 1912, 313 = *BullCom* 1916, 204 = *AE* 1917–1918, 94 = Brouwer 8).

36. This in itself echoes the story of the famed seer Teiresias who, in one version, glanced at the goddess Athena bathing, and was struck with blindness (Callimachus, *Hymn* 5, 91-100); another version had Teiresias watch snakes coupling. He killed the female, another time the male, while each time turning into the sex of the animal killed (*Melampodia*, ed. A. Rzach, *Hesiodi Carmina* [Stuttgart, 1967], 191–195 [fragments 160–169]). This experience, having been a woman and a man, inspired Hera and Zeus to inquire from Teiresias which of the two sexes enjoyed love making more. When Teiresias announced that women enjoyed sexual intercourse more, Hera blinded him (Ov. *Met.* 3.316–3.338).

37. Badian and Honoré, *OCD*, 999.

38. Q(uintus) Mucius Q(uinti) [l(ibertus)] | Trupho ser(vus) | vovit leiber solv(it) | l(ibens) m(erito) | Bonae deae | sacr(um).

39. Anteros gave Bona Dea this present (Anteros Bonae Deae | donum dedit, *CIL* VI 55 = Brouwer 2). The name Anteros appears again on a rectangular marble base found in the Trastevere. *CIL* VI 75 = *ILS* 3508 = Brouwer 13: Anteros | Valeri Bonae | Deae Oclatae | d(onum) d(edit) l(ibens) a(nimo) | ᵇᵃᶜᵏ C(aius) Pae[ti]|nius et . . . (Anteros of Valerius gave willingly and gladly this present to Bona Dea Oclata; on the back: Gaius Paetnius and . . . If Anteros is one and the same person, then the undated inscription may also belong in the latter part of the first century CE.

40. Voto suscepto | Bonae Deae | Astrapton Caesaris vilic(us) | aediculam aram saeptum clusum | vetustate diruta restituit.

41. Venustus | Philoxeni | Ti(beri) Claudi Caesaris | servi |⁵ dispensatoris | vicarius | B(onae) D(eae) v(otum) s(olvit) l(ibens) m(erito).

42. Diis(!) Manib(us) | Ascani Philoxeni | Ti(beri) Claudi Caesar(is) | Augusti | servi vic(arii) arcari(i) | vixit ann(os) XXVII. Another imperial slave dedicated an inscription on a small marble piece to a Bona Dea connected to the military (*castrensis*). The precise time frame within the imperial period cannot be established: Dedicated to Bona Dea Castrensis. Gemellus [slave of] the emperor (Bonadiae | Castre(n)si s(acrum?) | Gemellus Au(gusti), *CIL* VI 30854 = *ILS* 3504 = *EE* IV 723 = Brouwer 29).

43. Bonae Deae | sacrum | M(arcus) Vettius Bolanus | restitui iussit.

44. B(onae) d(eae) R(estitutae) | Cladus | d(onum) d(edit).

45. Bon(ae) deae Restitu<t>(ae) | simulacr(um) in tu<t>(elam) insul(ae) | Bolan(i) posuit item aed(em) | dedit Cladus l(ibens) m(erito). Left on the stone: Bol(ani).

46. Brouwer ([1989], 24) reads Faenia.

47. Bonae deae | Galbillae | Zmaragdus | Caesaris Aug(usti) | vilicus | horreorum | Galbianorum | coh(ortium) trium d(onum) d(edit) | cum Fenia Onesime.

48. Brouwer ([1989], 34) does not find this suggestion, put forth by Henri Chantraine (1967, 193–215), convincing.

49. Bonae Deae | Nutrici d(onum) d(edit) | Onesimus | Caesaris n(ostri) | ser(vus) Faustinus et | Valeria Spendusa et | Valeria Pia filia.

50. Duzémil (1996), vol. I, 357–363; Boyce (1937).

51. Bonae Deae s(acrum) | Sulpicia Severa | Maior aedem | cum signo d(onum) d(edit).

52. Secunda L(uci?) | aedicul(am) gradus [. . .] | tect(am) focum pro patr[io?] | Gen(io?) Maior(um?) Bonae D(eae) d(onum) d(edit) [. . .] | Florae conlib(ertae) conl[ib(erta)].

53. Bonae Deae | Conopti | sacrum | fecit | Antonia Hygia | d(e) s(uo) d(onum) d(edit).

54. D(is) M(anibus) Aelia Nice | sacerdos Bon(a)e deae | se biva conparavit sibi et | alumn(a)e suae Cl(audiae) Nice et | Ael(iae) Thalasse et Ael(iae) Serapiae et | Cl(audiae) Fortunat(a)e et Lucciae Felicitati et | Valerio Menandro et [. . .].

55. Κεῖμαι Αὐρήλιος Ἀντώ|νιος ὁ καὶ ἱερεὺς τῶν τε | θεῶν πάντων πρῶτον Βονα | δίης εἶτα Μητρὸς θεῶν καὶ Διο | νύσου καὶ Ἡγεμόνος τούτοις | ἐκτελέσας

μυστήρια πάντοτε | σεμνῶς νῦν ἔλιπον σεμνὸν | γλυκερὸν φοὰς ἠελίοιο λοιπὸ|ν
ὑ μσται εἶτε φίλοι βιότητος ἑ|κάστης πάνθ᾽ ὑπολανθάνετε τὰ | βίου συνεχῶς
μυστήρια σεμ νά | οὐδείς γάρ δύναται μοιρ[ῶ]ν μὶ|τον ἐξαναλῦσαι | ἔζησον
γάρ ἐγὼ Ἀντώνιος οὖ| τος ὁ σεμνὸς ἔτεσιν ζ᾽ ἢ ἐραι|σιν ιβ᾽| ἐποίησαν Αὐρήλία
Ἀντωνεία καὶ Αὐ | ρήλιος Ὀνήσιμος γλυκυτάτῳ τέκνῳ | νή ης χάριν | Θ(εοῖς)
Χ (θονίοις).

56. Brouwer (1989), 385.

57. Other examples of inscriptions mentioning *magistra* are *NS* 1929, p. 262,
no. 10 = Brouwer (1989) no. 53, *NS* 1929, p. 263, no. 11 = Brouwer (1989) no. 54, *EE*
VIII 624 = *ILS* 3495 = Brouwer (1989) no. 69, *CIL* IX 805 = Brouwer (1989) no. 85,
CIL IX 4767 = *ILS* 3492 = Brouwer (1989) no. 95, *CIL* XI 6285 = Brouwer (1989) no.
97, *CIL* XI 3866 = Brouwer (1989) no. 102, *CIL* XI 3869 = Brouwer (1989) no. 105,
CIL V 757 = *ILS* 4894 = Calderini 9 = Brouwer (1989) no. 109, *CIL* V 759 = *ILS*
3497 = Calderini 2 = Brouwer (1989) no. 110; for *ministra NS* 1881, p. 22 = *CIL* XI
4635 = *ILS* 3494 = Brouwer (1989) no. 93, *AE* 1946, 153 = *Inscriptions de Glanum* 18
= Brouwer (1989) no. 133, *AE* 1946, 154 = *Inscriptions de Glanum* 19 = Brouwer (1989)
no. 134, for both *magistra* and *ministra*, *CIL* V 762 = *ILS* 3498 = Calederini 5 = Brouwer (1989) no. 113. For the office (*ob magistratum*), *CIL* VI 2239 = Brouwer (1989) no. 35
and *CIL* XIV 4057 = Brouwer 51.

58. An undated inscription from Rome: Tyche (?) the superintendent of Bona Dea
([Tyc?]he mag(istra) Bonae D[eae], *CIL* VI 2238 = Brouwer 27).

59. Iulius Quadratus was consul for the second time in 105 CE (*PIR*[2] IV, pp. 257–260,
no. 507).

60. Numini domus A[ug(ustae)] | Blastus Eutact[ianus? et] | Secundus Iuli
Quadr[ati] | co(n)s(ulis) II lib(ertus) ob honorem V[Iviratus] |[5] et Italia lib(erta)
eiusd[em] | ob magis[t]erium B(onae) [D(eae)] | dedicaverunt XIIII K(alendas)
Oct[o]b(res) | M(acro) Clodio Lunense. . . . | et P(ublio) Licinio Crasso co(n)s(ulibus) |[10]
quo die et epulum dederunt | incendio consumtum senatus | Fidenatium restituit.

61. Brouwer (1989), 254–296, discusses the various kinds of categories of worshipers in detail.

62. Versnel (1993), 228–288, "Bona Dea and the Thesmophoria," provides a won-
derfully insightful discussion of this festival.

63. Plut. *Caes.* 9.

64. Juv. 1.2.86: "and they placate Bona Dea with a pork belly . . . (*atque Bonam
tenerae placant abdomine porcae . . .*)."

65. Polyb. 2.15.3 and Varro *Rust.* 2.4.9 as well as Wissowa (1902), 411.

66. Plut. *Caes.* 9; Juv. 1.6.314–1.6.317.

67. Versnel (1993), 265.

68. Macrob. *Sat.* 1.12.25.

69. Moritz (1979).

70. Plut. *Quaest. Rom.* 20D–E.

71. Versnel (1993), 262.

72. Versnel (1993), 264.

73. Macrob. *Sat.* 1.12.20–1.12.29.

74. Versnel (1993), 272–274; all literary sources are collected in Brouwer (1989), 144–228.

CHAPTER SIX

1. On the *flamen,* see Vanggaard (1988).

2. Fishwick (2002).

3. Varro *Ling.* 84.

4. Latte (1960), 36, n. 3.

5. Even Varro, for example, could not explain Falacer and Furrina.

6. Gai. *Inst.* 112. At a *confarreatio* marriage ceremony, the *pontifex maximus* and the *flamen Dialis* had to be present. As Warde Fowler (1916), 185–195, put it, p. 187: "For in order to be eligible for the great priesthoods . . . children must be born of a marriage celebrated by confarreatio. . . . We must be perfectly clear as to this object of confarreatio; it was a ceremonial of the most vital importance for the welfare of the State." Boels (1973) provides a more recent analysis of the status and role of the *flaminica.* The general idea is that the *flaminica* complements her husband and she represents the power of fecundity.

7. Esdaile (1911).

8. A summary of prohibitions and duties can be found in Gel. 10.15.1–10.15.25.

9. In addition to Fishwick (2002), see also Deininger (1890); Hardy (1890).

10. Sebaï (1990) analyzed the North African material in detail. There is no equivalent study of the data from the Iberian peninsula, but Panzram (2003) discusses some of these *flaminicae* and their families.

11. Deininger (1965), 109.

12. Sebaï (1990), 655.

13. MacMullen (1980).

14. A very informative discussion of women in the Greek East is van Bremen (1983).

15. Nicols (1989).

16. Laberiae |L(uci) f(iliae) | Gallae | fla|minicae munic|(ipii) Eborensis fla|⁵minicae provin|ciae Lusitaniae | L(ucius) Laberius Artemas | L(ucius) Laberius Callaecus | L(ucius) Laberius Abascantus |¹⁰ L(ucius) Laberius Paris | L(ucius) Laberius Lausus | liberti [posuit].

17. Iovi O(ptiom) M(aximo) | Flavia L(uci) f(ilia) Rufina | Emeritensis fla|minica provinc|(iae) Lusitaniae item col(oniae) |⁵ Emeritensis perpet|(ua) et municipi(i) Salicien|(sis) d(ecreto) d(ecurionum).

18. Pietati Aug(ustae) | L(ucius) Lucretius Fulvianus flamen | col(oniarum) immunium provinciae | Baetic(ae) pontif(ex) perpetuus |⁵ domus Aug(ustae) t(estamento) p(oni) i(ussit) ex arg(enti) p(ondo) (*vac.*) | ob honor(em) pontificatus | Lucr(etia) L(uci) f(ilia) Campana flam(inica) perp(etua) do|mus Aug(ustae) editis ad dedicatio-nem | scaenicis ludis per quadriduum |¹⁰ et circensibus et epulo diviso posuit | huic dono

Luc(retia) Campana amplius nomine suo coronam | auream adiunxit | d(onum) d(edit) d(edicavit).

19. Iuliae C(ai) f(iliae) Laetae flaminicae | domus Augustae | L(ucius) Maecius Nativos consobrinae | piissumae erga se. . . .

20. Corneliae | P(ubli) f(iliae) Severinae | flaminicae | Aug(ustae) (*vac.*) matri |[5] Valerii Vegeti | [c]onsulis | [Flo]rentini | Iliberri[t(ani)] | d(ecreto) d(ecurionum).

21. Derks (1998), 119.

22. An example of this combination is an inscription from Arcisate, *CIL* V 5450: Matronis | Iunonibus | Valerius | Baronis | f(ilius) | v(otum) s(olvit) l(ibens) m(erito), which translates to: To the Matres-Iunones, Valerius, the son of Baro, happily and gladly fulfilled his vow.

23. Plin. *HN* 16.249; Meier (1997), 211.

24. Euskirchen (1999) and esp. Heichelheim (1930).

25. Derks (1998), 120.

26. Heichelheim (1930), 2219.

27. Euskirchen (1999); Heichelheim (1930).

28. This epigraphic data is from Gattinoni Landucci (1986), in particular her table on p. 25.

29. Ihm's (1887) summary, 72–76. The summary of the whereabouts of these two legions follows the article on Roman legions in Campbell (1966). Octavian (Augustus) raised both legions in Spain around 41/40 BCE, the *legio XX* maybe later after the battle of Actium. *Legio VI victrix* was transferred to the Rhine in the early period of Vespasian's reign (69/70 CE) and remained at the camp of Novaesium until its deployment to Vetura in 105 CE. In 122 CE, *legio VI victrix* is moved to Britain, where it was permanently stationed at Eburacum (York). *Legio XX Valeria victrix* stayed in Spain from 30–20 BCE and was then transferred to Illyricum at Burnum, where it stayed until 9 CE. Afterwards Ara Ubiorum is its home until its deployment to Novaesium during Tiberius' reign. *Legio XX Valeria victrix* took part in the invasion of Britain in 43 CE, where it then stayed first based in Camulodunum (Colchester) and then, from 49 CE onward, at Glevum (Gloucester).

30. The earliest inscription and accepted as such is the one from Pallanza (*regio XI* in Cisalpine Gaul, *CIL* V 6641 = no. 75 in Gattinoni), dated to the reign of Caligula (37–41 CE). It reads: "Consecrated to the Matronae for the well-being of Gaius Caesar Augustus Germanicus Narcissus [the slave of] Gaius Caesar (Matronis sacrum | pro salute C(aii) Caesaris | Augusti Germanici | Narcissus C(aii) Caesaris)." The latest inscriptions, from the time of Julian the Apostate, come from Pesch, the sanctuary of Vacallinehae (Heichelheim [1930], B CXX, n. 439).

31. Ihm (1887), 75.

CONCLUSION

1. Syme (1986), 186.

BIBLIOGRAPHY

F. Altheim, *Römische Religionsgeschichte* (Munich, 1960).

J. E. Archer, ed. *Male Violence* (London, 1994).

P. Archer, *The Christian Calendar and the Gregorian Reform* (New York, 1941).

E. Badian and T. Honoré, "Scaevola," *OCD,* 999.

J. P. V. D. Balsdon, *Roman Women* (London, 1962).

A. A. Barrett, *Caligula: The Corruption of Power* (New Haven, CT, 1989).

———, "Tacitus, Livia, and the Evil Stepmother," *RhM* 144 (2001), 171–175.

———, *Livia: First Lady of Imperial Rome* (New Haven, CT, 2002).

D. Baudy, "Der dumme Teil des Volkes (Ov. *F.* 2.531)," *Museum Helveticum* 58 (2001), 32–39.

R. A. Bauman, *Women and Politics in Ancient Rome* (London, 1992).

M. Beard, "The Sexual Status of Vestal Virgins," *JRS* 70 (1980), 12–27.

———, "Re-reading (Vestal) Virginity," in: *Women in Antiquity. New Assessments,* eds. R. Hawley and B. Levick (London, 1995), 166–177.

———, J. North, and S. Price, *Religions of Rome,* vol. 1: *A History* and vol. 2: *A Sourcebook* (Cambridge, 1998).

P. L. Berger, *The Sacred Canopy: Elements of a Sociological Theory of Religion* (New York, 1969).

M. Bettini, *Anthropology and Roman Culture: Kinship, Time, Images of the Soul* (Baltimore, 1991).

A. Blomart, "Die *evocatio* und der Transfer 'fremder' Götter von der Peripherie nach Rom," in: *Römische Reichsreligion und Provinzialreligion,* eds. H. Cancik and J. Rüpke (Tübingen, 1997), 99–111.

N. Boels, "Le statut religieux de la *flaminica Dialis,*" *REL* 51 (1973), 77–100.

F. Bömer, *Rom und Troia: Untersuchungen zur Frühgeschichte Roms* (Baden-Baden, 1951).

———, *P. Ovidius Naso Die Fasten,* vol. 1, *Einleitung: Text und Übersetzung;* vol. 2, *Kommentar* (Heidelberg, 1958).

———, "Kybele in Rom: Die Geschichte ihres Kults als politisches Phänomen," *MDAIR* 71 (1964), 130–151.

T. Bonfante, "Etruscan Women," in: *Women in the Classical World: Image and Text,* eds. E. Fantham, H. Foley, N. Kampen, S. Pomeroy, and H. Shapiro (New York, 1994), 243–259.

G. K. Boyce, *Corpus of the* lararia *of Pompeii* (Rome, 1937).

R. van Bremen, "Women and Wealth," in: *Images of Women in Antiquity,* eds. A. Cameron and A. Kuhrt (London, 1983), 223–242.

J. Briscoe, *A Commentary on Livy: Books XXXIV–XXXVII* (Oxford, 1981).

H. H. J. Brouwer, *Bona Dea: The Sources and Description of the Cult, Études préliminaires aux religions orientales dans l'Empire romain* 110 (Leiden, 1989).

A. Bruhl, *Liber Pater* (Paris, 1953).

W. Burkert, *Greek Religion* (Cambridge, 1985).

———, *Ancient Mystery Cults* (Cambridge, MA, 1987).

———, *Antike Mysterien: Funktionen und Gehalt* (Munich, 1990).

F. Cairns, *The Romans and Their Empire* (Cambridge, 1970).

C. Calhoon, "Lucretia, Savior and Scapegoat: The Dynamics of Sacrifice in Livy 1.57–1.59," *Helios* 24.2 (1997), 151–169.

J. B. Campbell, "Legions," *OCD* (Oxford, 1966), 841–842.

H. Cancik, "Rome as Sacred Landscape: Varro and the End of Republican Religion," *Visible Religion* 4/5 (1985–1986), 250–261.

H. Cancik-Lindemaier, "Kultische Privilegierung und gesellschaftliche Realität: Ein Beitrag zur Sozialgeschichte der virgines Vestales," *Saeculum* 41.1 (1990), 1–16.

G. Capdeville, "Les livres sacrés des Étrusques," in: *Oracles et prophéties dans l'Antiquité,* ed. J. G. Heintz (Paris, 1997), 465–508.

B. Cardauns, "Zu den Sibyllen bei Tibull 2.5," *Hermes* 86 (1961), 357–366.

R.-N. Castellani, *Le testament politique de l'Antiquité : des origines de la mémoire historique à la bataille d'Actium, 31 av. J.-C.* (Paris, 2001).

H. Chantraine, *Freigelassene und Sklaven im Dienst der römischen Kaiser: Studien zu ihrer Nomenklatur* (Wiesbaden, 1967).

T. J. Cornell, "Some Observations on the Crimen Incesti," in: *Le Délit religieux dans la cité antique, Collection de l'École française de Rome* 48, ed. M. Gras (Paris, 1981), 27–37.

———, *The Beginnings of Rome* (London, 1995).

M. Crawford, *Roman Republican Coinage,* vol. 1 (London, 1974).

C. Damon and S. A. Takács, eds. *Senatus Consultum de Cn. Pisone Patre,* in: *AJPh* 120.1 (1999), 13–41.

J. Deininger, *Die Provinziallandtage der römischen Kaiserzeit von Augustus bis zum Ende des dritten Jahrhunderts n. Chr.* (Munich, 1965).

T. Derks, *Gods, Temples and Ritual Practices: The Transformation of Religious Ideas and Values in Roman Gaul, Amsterdam Archaeological Studies* 2 (Amsterdam, 1998).

M. DiLucia (under M. DiLucia Miller), "The Sabine Version" (PhD diss., Harvard, 1998).

E. M. Douglas, "Iuno Sospita of Lanuvium," *JRS* 3 (1913), 61–72.

G. Dumézil, *Archaic Roman Religion,* 2 vols., trans. P. Krapp (Baltimore, 1996).

W. Eck, *The Age of Augustus* (Malden, MA, 2003).

K. A. Esdaile, "The Apex or Tutulus in Roman Art," *JRS* 1 (1911), 212–226.

M. Euskirchen, "Matres/Matronae," *Der Neue Pauly* (1999), 1028–1029.

D. Fishwick, *The Imperial Cult in the Latin West: Studies in the Ruler Cult of the Western Provinces of the Roman Empire,* vol. 3, *Provincial Cult,* part 2: *The Provincial Priesthood* (Leiden, 2002).

M. Flory, "*Sic exempla parantur:* Livia's Shrine to Concordia and the Porticus Liviae," *Historia* 33 (1984), 309–344.

H. Flower, *Ancestor Masks and Aristocratic Power in Roman Culture* (Oxford, 1996).

T. Frank, "The Bacchanalian Cult of 186 B.C.E.," *CQ* 21 (1927), 128–132.

Frazer, P. M. (1972), *Ptolemaic Alexandria,* 3 vols. (Oxford, 1972).

K. Galinsky, *Aeneas, Sicily and Rome* (Princeton, 1969).

———, *Augustan Culture: An Interpretive Introduction* (Princeton, 1996).

J. Gardner, *Women in Roman Law and Society* (Bloomington, IN, 1986).

F. Gattinoni Landucci, *Un Culto Celtico nella Gallia Cisalpina: Le Matronae-Iunones a sud delle Alpi, Edizioni Universitarie Jaca* 23 (Milan, 1986).

K. A. Geffcken, *Comedy in* Pro Caelio (Leiden, 1973).

H. Graillot, *Le culte de Cybèle mère des à Rome et dans l'empire romain* (Paris, 1912).

E. S. Gruen, *Studies in Greek Culture and Roman Policy, Cincinnati Classical Studies,* n.s. 7 (Leiden, 1990).

R. Gurval, *Actium and Augustus: The Politics and Emotions of Civil War* (Ann Arbor, 1995).

G. Gustafsson, *Evocatio Deorum: Historical and Mythical Interpretations of Ritualised Conquests in the Expansion of Ancient Rome* (Uppsala, 2000).

J. P. Hallett, *Fathers and Daughters in Roman Society: Women and the Elite Family* (Princeton, 1984).

E. G. Hardy, "The Provincial Concilia from Augustus to Diocletian," *English Historical Review,* vol. 5, no. 18 (1890), 221–254.

H. Hauben, "Some Observations on the Early Roman Calendar," *Ancient Society* 11–12 (1980–1981), 241–255.

F. Heichelheim, "Matres," *RE* (1930), 2213–2250.

H. Herter, "Die Ursprünge des Aphroditenkultes," in: *Éléments orientaux dans la religion grecque ancienne* (Paris, 1960).

J. Heurgon, "Influences grecques sur la religion étrusque," *REL* 35 (1957), 106–121.

———, "The Inscriptions of Pyrgi," *JRS* 56 (1966), 1–15.

H. Hommel, "Vesta und die frührömische Religion," in: *Aufstieg und Niedergang der römischen Welt,* ed. H. Temporini (Berlin, 1972), 397–420.

M. Ihm, "Der Mütter- oder Matronenkultus und seine Denkmäler," *Bonner Jahrbücher* 83 (1887), 1–200.

R. A. Kaster, "Varro," *OCD* (Oxford, 1996), 1582.

E. Kenney, ed. *The Cambridge History of Classical Literature,* vol. 2 (Cambridge, 1982).

E. Klebs, "Atinius," *RE* 2 (Stuttgart, 1896), 2105–2106.

D. E. E. Kleiner and S. Matheson, *I Claudia: Women in Ancient Rome. Exhibition Catalog* (Austin, TX, 1996).

D. A. Lam and J. A. Miron, "Seasonality of Births in Human Populations," *Social Biology* 38.1-2 (1991), 51–78.

E. Laroche, "Koubaba, déesse anatolienne, et le problème des origins de Cybèle," in: *Élements orientaux dans la religion grecque ancienne,* ed. O. Eissfeldt (Paris, 1960), 113–128.

J. Larson, *Greek Nymphs: Myth, Cult, Lore* (Oxford, 2001).

K. Latte, *Römische Religionsgeschichte* (Munich, 1960).

K. Lembke, *Das Iseum Campense in Rom: Studie über den Isiskult unter Domitian* (Heidelberg, 1994).

J. Linderski, "Roman Religion in Livy," in: *Livius: Aspekte seines Werkes,* ed. W. Schuller (Konstanz, 1993), 53–70.

———, ed. *Imperium sine Fine* (Stuttgart, 1996).

W. M. Lindsay, ed. *Festus: De Significatione Verborum* (Leipzig, 1913).

A. Lintott, *The Constitution of the Roman Republic* (Oxford, 1999).

K. Lorenz, *On Aggression,* trans. M. Latzke (London, 1996).

R. MacMullen, "Women in Public in the Roman Empire," *Historia* 29.2 (1980), 208–218.

D. Magie, *Roman Rule in Asia Minor,* 2 vols. (Princeton, 1950).

B. McCarthy, "Warrior Values: A Socio-Historical Survey," in: *Male Violence,* ed. J. Archer (London, 1994), 105–120.

B. C. McGing, *The Foreign Policy of Mithridates VI Eupator, King of Pontus* (Leiden, 1986).

L. Mehl-Madrona, "Complementary Medicine Treatment of Uterine Fibroids: A Pilot Study," *Alternative Therapies in Health and Medicine* 8.2 (2002), 34–46.

B. Meier, *Dictionary of Celtic Religion and Culture,* trans. C. Edmunds (Rochester, 1997).

A. K. Michels, "The Topography and Interpretation of the Lupercalia," *TAPA* 84 (1953), 35–59.

———, *The Calendar of the Roman Republic* (Princeton, 1967).

R. E. Mitchell, "The Definition of *patres* and *plebs:* An End to the Struggle of the Orders," in: *Social Struggles in Archaic Rome,* ed. K. A. Raaflaub (Berkeley, CA, 1986), 130–174.

L. A. Moritz, "Milch," *Der Kleine Pauly* (Stuttgart, 1979), 1294.

F. Münzer, "Cerrinius," *RE* 6 (Stuttgart, 1899), 1985–1986.

———, "Die römischen Vestalinnen bis zur Kaiserzeit," *Philologus* 92 (1937), 47–67, 199–222.

———, *Römische Adelsparteien und Adelsfamilien,* trans. T. Ridley (Baltimore, 1999).

K. Mustakallio, "The *"crimen incesti"* of the Vestal Virgins and the Prodigious Pestilence," in: *Crudelitas: The Politics of Cruelty in the Ancient and Medieval World,* eds. T. Viljamaa, A. Timonen, and C. Krötzl (Krems, 1992), 56–62.

B. Nagy, "The Argei Puzzle," *AJAH* 10 (1985), 1–27.

G. Nagy, "Six Studies of Sacral Vocabulary to the Fireplace," *HSCP* 78 (1974), 71–106.

R. F. Newbold, "Social Tension at Rome in the Early Years of Tiberius' Reign," *Athenaeum* (1974), 110–143.

C. E. Newlands, *Playing with Time: Ovid and the Fasti* (Ithaca, NY, 1995).

B. Nicholas, *An Introduction to Roman Law* (Oxford, 1987).

J. Nicols, "Patrona Civitatis," in: *Studies in Latin Literature and Roman History* 5, *Collection Latomus* 206 (Brussels, 1989), 117–142.

M. H. Ninck, *Die Bedentung des Wassers im Kult und Leben der Alten: Eine symbolgeschichtliche Untersuchung* (Darmstadt, 1960).

J. North, "Religion and Politics, from Republic to Empire," *JRS* 76 (1986), 251–258.

R. M. Ogilvie, *A Commentary on Livy, Books 1–5* (Oxford, 1965).

E. M. Orlin, *Temples, Religion and Politics in the Roman Republic* (Leiden, 1997).

J. M. Pailler, *Bacchanalia: Le répression de 186 avant J.-C. à Rome et en Italie, Bibliothèque des Écoles française d'Athènes et de Rome,* vol. 270 (Rome, 1988).

———, *Bacchus: Figures et Pouvoirs* (Paris, 1995).

S. Panzram, *Stadtbild und Elite: Tarraco, Corduba und Augusta Emerita zwischen Republik und Spätantike, Historia Einzelschriften* 161 (Stuttgart, 2003).

H. W. Parke, *Sibyls and Sibylline Prophecy in Classical Antiquity* (London, 1988).

H. Parker, "Why Were the Vestals Virgins? Or the Chastity of Women and the Safety of the Roman State," *AJP* 125.4 (2004) 563–601.

R. Parker, *Miasma: Pollution and Purification in Early Greek Religions* (Oxford, 1983).

J. Pokorny, *Indogermanisches Etymologisches Wörterbuch* (Bern, 1989, 2nd ed.).

N. Purcell, "Livia and the Womanhood of Rome," *PCPS,* n.s. 32 (1986), 78–105.

———, "Forum Romanum," *LTUR,* vol. 2 (1995), 313–342.

K. Raaflaub, *Social Struggles in Archaic Rome: New Perspectives on the Conflict of the Orders* (Malden, MA, 2005, 2nd ed.).

G. Radke, "Vesta," *Der Kleine Pauly* 5 (Stuttgart, 1975), 1227–1229.

———, "Gibt es Antworten auf die 'Argeerfrage'?," *Latomus* 49 (1980), 5–19.

———, "Die *dei penates* und Vesta in Rom," in: *Aufstieg und Niedergang der römischen Welt,* eds. H. Temporini and W. Haase (Berlin, 1981), 343–373.

———, "Römische Feste im Monat März," *Tyche* 8 (1993), 129–142.

E. Rawson, "Religion and Politics in the Late Second Century BC at Rome," *Phoenix* 28 (1974), 193–212.

S. Reinach, *Cultes, mythes et religions,* vol. 3 (Paris, 1908).

J. C. Richard, "Patricians and Plebeians: The Origin of a Social Dichotomy," in: *Social Struggles in Archaic Rome,* ed. K. A. Raaflaub (Berkeley, CA, 1986), 105–129.

L. Richardson, *A New Topographical Dictionary of Ancient Rome* (Baltimore, 1992).

A. Richlin, "The Ethnographer's Dilemma and the Dream of a Lost Golden Age," in: *Feminist Theory and the Classics,* eds. N. Sorkin-Rabinowitz and A. Richlin (New York, 1993), 272–303.

———, "Carrying Water in a Sieve: Class and the Body in Roman Women's Religion," ed. K. King, *Women and Goddess Traditions* (Minneapolis, 1997), 330–374.

M. Ridley, *The Origins of Virtue* (New York, 1997).

O. F. Robinson, *Ancient Rome: City Planning and Administration* (London, 1992).

J. Rüpke, *Kalender und Öffentlichkeit: Die Geschichte der Repräsentation und religiösen Qualifikation von Zeit in Rom, RVV* 40 (Berlin, 1995).

M. R. Salzman, *On Roman Time: The Codex-Calendar of 354 and the Rhythms of Urban Life in Late Antiquity* (Berkeley, CA, 1990).

A. E. Samuel, *Greek and Roman Chronology: Calendars and Years in Classical Antiquity, Handbuch der Altertumswissenschaft* 1.7 (Munich, 1972).

G. Sanders, "Kybele und Attis," in: *Die orientalischen Religionen im Römerreich,* ed. M. J. Vermaseren, *Études préliminaires aux religions orientales dans l'Empire romain* 93 (Leiden, 1981), 264–297.

J. Scheid, "The Religious Role of Roman Women," in: *A History of Women,* vol. 1, ed. P. Schmitt Pantel (Cambridge, MA, 1992), 377–408.

———, "*Graeco ritu:* A Typical Roman Way of Honoring Gods," *HSCP* 97 (1995), 15–31.

F. Schwenn, "Kybele," *RE* 11.2 (Stuttgart, 1922), 2250–2298.

H. H. Scullard, *Festivals and Ceremonies of the Roman Republic* (Ithaca, NY, 1981).

L. Ladijmi Sebaï, "A propos du flaminat féminin dans les provinces africianes," *MEFRA* 102 (1990), 651–686.

E. L. Shields, *Juno: A Study in Early Roman Religion* (Northampton, MA, 1926).

M. Siebourg, "Der Matronenkult beim Bonner Münster," *Bonner Jahrbücher* 138 (1933), 103–123.

A. Staples, *From Good Goddess to Vestal Virgins* (London, 1998).

A. Stein and L. Petersen, eds. *Prosopographia Imperii Romani,* vol. 4 (Berlin, 1952–1966, 2nd ed.).

E. M. Steinby, *Lexicon Topographicum Urbis Romae,* 4 vols. (Rome, 1999).

R. Syme, *The Augustan Aristocracy* (Oxford, 1986).

E. A. Syndeham, *Roman Republican Coinage* (Spink, 1952).

S. A. Takács, *Isis and Sarapis in the Roman World: Religions in the Graeco-Roman World* 124 (Leiden, 1995).

———, "Magna Deum Mater Idaea, Cybele, and Catullus' Attis," in: *Cybele, Attis, and Related Cults: Studies in the Memory of M. J. Vermaseren, Religions in the Graeco-Roman World* 131, ed. E. Lane (Leiden, 1996), 367–386.

———, "Isis," *Der Neue Pauly* 5 (1998), 1126–1132.

———, "Kybele," *Der Neue Pauly* 6 (1999a), 950–956.

———, "Mater Magna," *Der Neue Pauly* 7 (1999b), 998–1000.

———, "Politics and Religion in the Bacchanalian Affair of 186 B.C.E.," *HSCP* 100 (2000), 301–310.

———, "Forging a Past: The Sibylline Books and the Making of Rome," in: *Cultures of Forgery: Making Nations, Making Selves,* eds. J. Ryan and A. Thomas (New York, 2003), 15–27.

———, "Isis," *Encyclopedia of Religion* 7, ed. L. Jones (Detroit, 2005).

———, "Cleopatra, Isis, and the Formation of Augustan Rome," in: *Cleopatra: A Sphinx Revisited,* ed. M. M. Miles (Berkeley, CA, 2007).

W. Tatum, *The Patrician Tribune Publius Clodius Pulcher* (Chapel Hill, NC, 1999).

S. Treggiari, *Roman Marriage: Iusti Coniuges from the Time of Cicero to the Time of Ulpian* (Oxford, 1991).

J. H. Vanggaard, *The Flamen: A Study in the History and Sociology of Roman Religion* (Copenhagen, 1988).

H. S. Versnel, *Triumphus: An Inquiry into the Origin, Development and Meaning of the Roman Triumph* (Leiden, 1970).

———, "The Roman Festival for Bona Dea and the Greek Thesmophoria," in: *Inconsistencies in Greek and Roman Religion* (Leiden, 1993), vol. 2, 228–288.

B. Virgilio, *Il "tempo stato" di Pessinunte fra Perganmo e Roma nel II-I saeclo A.C., Bibliotheca di Studi Antichi* 25 (Pisa, 1981).

W. Warde Fowler, "*Confarreatio:* A Study in Patrician Usage," *JRS* 6 (1916), 185–195.

K. Welch, "Subura," *LTUR,* vol. 4, ed. E. M. Steinby (Rome, 1999) 379–383.

S. West, "Notes on the Text of Lycophron," *CQ,* n.s. 33.1 (1983), 114–135.

E. Will, "La grande Mère en Grèce," in: *Élements orientaux dans la religion grecque ancienne,* ed. O. Eissfeldt (Paris, 1960), 95–111.

T. P. Wiseman, *Remus: A Roman Myth* (Cambridge, 1995).

G. Wissowa, *Religion und Kultus der Römer* (Munich, 1902).

K. Wolf, "Pollenius," *RE* 42 (Stuttgart, 1952), 1408–1409.

S. E. Wood, *Imperial Women: A Study in Imperial Images, 40 B.C.–A.D. 68* (Leiden, 1999).

E. Zerubavel, *The Seven Day Circle: The History and Meaning of the Week* (Chicago, 1989).

INDEX